Regulatory quality in Europe

MANCHESTER
1824

Manchester University Press

European Policy Research Unit Series

Series Editors: *Simon Bulmer, Peter Humphreys* and *Mick Moran*

The European Policy Research Unit Series aims to provide advanced text-books and thematic studies of key public policy issues in Europe. They concentrate, in particular, on comparing patterns of national policy content, but pay due attention to the European Union dimension. The thematic studies are guided by the character of the policy issue under examination.

The European Policy Research Unit (EPRU) was set up in 1989 within the University of Manchester's Department of Government to promote research on European politics and public policy. The series is part of EPRU's effort to facilitate intellectual exchange and substantive debate on the key policy issues confronting the European states and the European Union.

Regulatory quality in Europe

Concepts, measures and policy processes

Claudio M. Radaelli and Fabrizio De Francesco

Manchester University Press

Manchester and New York

distributed exclusively in the USA by Palgrave

Published by Manchester University Press
Oxford Road, Manchester M13 9NR, UK
and Room 400, 175 Fifth Avenue, New York, NY 10010, USA
www.manchesteruniversitypress.co.uk

Distributed in the United States exclusively by
Palgrave Macmillan, 175 Fifth Avenue,
New York, NY 10010, USA

Distributed in Canada exclusively by
UBC Press, University of British Columbia, 2029 West Mall,
Vancouver, BC, Canada V6T 1Z2

British Library Cataloguing-in-Publication Data is available

Library of Congress Cataloging-in-Publication Data is available

ISBN 978 0 7190 8670 0 paperback

First published by Manchester University Press in hardback 2007

This paperback edition first published 2011

Printed by Lightning Source

This book is dedicated to our families

Contents

Tables, boxes and figures

Tables

Boxes

Figures

Acknowledgements

We have been working together on better regulation since 2000, but we gratefully acknowledge the support of the European Commission, DG Enterprise, for having funded our research project on indicators of regulatory quality in 2004 (tender ENTR/03/053) at the University of Bradford. Our greatest personal and professional debt is to Robertus Scharrenborg, an economist (with interests in political science as well) from DG Enterprise of the Commission, who chaired the project's steering group. Robertus went beyond the call of duty and standard contractual relations to provide generous guidance and support.

We conducted the project with our colleagues in economics Sam Cameron and Hossein Jalilian, who sent us detailed comments on what is now chapter 3 of the book and helped us to design the questionnaire presented in appendix 1 and discussed in chapter 5. The project team included two advisors, Bruno Dente and Scott Jacobs, who provided perceptive insights at all stages of the project. We wish to acknowledge the quality of the research environment provided by the Centre for European Studies at the University of Bradford, now led by Roberto Espindola. Roberto and the Marie Curie fellows of the Bradford training centre on Europeanisation (especially Ulrike Kraemer and Delphine Tatot) were always keen on providing help, suggestions and, most pleasant of all, discussions over lunch. There was a period in which we had a very lively 'indicators of regulatory quality table' at the University's refectory.

We were fortunate to have an enthusiastic and creative steering group, comprising Peter Ladegaard (at that time at the Organisation for Economic Co-operation and Development, OECD) and, from the Commission, Massimo Angelino, Peter Curran, Lars Holm Nielsen, Ulrik Mogensen, Eric Philippart and Manuel Santiago dos Santos. Together with DG Enterprise, the Secretariat-General of the Commission provided access to work under way in Brussels and engaged in the scientific and policy debate on our findings.

The OECD provided access to its database on indicators of regulatory quality and agreed to meet with us in Brussels and Paris to discuss our work. In addition to Peter Ladegaard, we wish to thank Rolf Alter, Joseph Konvitz and Stephane Jacobzone for their perceptive comments and for having invited us to present the report in Paris at a meeting on regulatory reform with OECD delegates.

The project for DG Enterprise was supported by a network of policy-makers active in better regulation programmes across Europe. Thanks to this support network, our project became a unique experience for us in terms of exchanges and discussions with a very special group of people. Not only did the members of the support network kindly agree to answer our questionnaire but they also provided insights on how the tools of better regulation are implemented, interacted with us by email and telephone, and animated the interim and final project meetings. We wish to thank the members of the support network who joined us from Austria, Belgium, the Czech Republic, Denmark, Estonia, Finland, France, Germany, Greece, Hungary, Ireland, Italy, Latvia, Luxembourg, the Netherlands, Poland, Spain, Sweden, the UK, and, outside the EU, Bulgaria, Norway and Romania. The support network also included business organisations such as the Board of Swedish Industry and Commerce for Better Regulation, Eurochambers (the Association of European Chambers of Commerce and Industry) and Small Business Europe. Officials from Australia and Canada who were not formally included in the support network kindly agreed to answer questions and to give us access to their work on the measurement of regulatory performance.

We benefited from discussions with the Better Regulation Executive and the National Audit Office in London. Mark Courtney of the Better Regulation Executive kindly invited us to address the 'directors of better regulation' at a meeting in London in March 2005. Claudio Radaelli was asked to join the experts panel of the National Audit Office on regulatory reform – an experience that has increased the sophistication of our arguments and the motivation for turning the initial project for DG Enterprise into a book.

A large number of researchers and policy-makers in Europe and the United States provided helpful suggestions on the draft chapters of the book. They include Robert Baldwin, Dominik Böllhoff, Simon Bulmer, Alessia Damonte, Bruce Doern, Robert Hahn, Adrienne Heritier, Ed Humpherson, Oliver James, Jacint Jordana, Yannis Karagiannis, David Levi-Faur, Mick Moran, Susan Owens, Mark Pollack, Carol Weiss and Nikos Zahariadis.

The transition from project to book took one year. It was undertaken at the Centre for Regulatory Governance of the Department of Politics, University of Exeter. We thank the Department for having supported Fabrizio De Francesco with a scholarship in spring and summer 2005. At Exeter we have the privilege of working with a strong public policy team. We wish to thank our colleagues for their support, inspiration and healthy, challenging conversations throughout the year 2005. The series editor at

Manchester University Press, Professor Peter Humphreys, sent us a detailed report on the manuscript in December 2005. Finally, it was a great pleasure to work with Anthony Mason at Manchester University Press and Ralph Footring, freelance production editor.

Abbreviations

ACTAL	Dutch Advisory Board on Administrative Burdens
ASA	Agence pour la Simplification Administrative (Belgium)
DBR	Directors of Better Regulation (EU)
DG	Directorate-General (European Commission)
EBTP	European Business Test Panel
ERI	Effective Regulation Index
EU	European Union
GAO	General Accounting Office (US)
GDP	gross domestic product
GNP	gross national product
IA	impact assessment
ICT	information and communications technology
IMAC	Internal Market Advisory Committee (EU)
NAO	National Audit Office (UK)
NNR	Board of Swedish Industry and Commerce for Better Regulation
OECD	Organisation for Economic Co-operation and Development
OIRA	Office of Information and Regulatory Affairs (US)
OMB	Office of Management and Budget (US)
PART	Program Assessment Rating Tool
RIA	regulatory impact assessment
SCM	standard cost model
SMEs	small and medium-sized enterprises

Introduction

Since the early days of the single market in the European Economic Community and the first wave of privatisations in the 1980s, rules have played an important role in European politics. Mutual recognition, minimum harmonisation and delegation to standardisation bodies were introduced with the aim of completing the single market without the need to create a huge body of legislation and political fatigue over comprehensive harmonisation (Egan, 2001). Some scholars looked at Europe as an example of regulatory cooperation in an interdependent world (Majone, 1994). Independent regulatory agencies emerged as a response to the problem of credibility of political regulatory institutions. The scenario for smooth regulatory reform was set. Reality took a different direction, however. Today, concerns about the quality of European rules and the role of independent regulators in the market are diffuse. So much so that regulatory quality has become one of the priorities of the competitiveness strategies of the Member States and institutions of the European Union (EU).

In this book, we critically discuss the concept of regulatory quality, approach regulatory reform by taking the institutional context and the policy process into consideration, and use indicators to measure the quality of policies designed to enhance the ability of governments and EU institutions to deliver high-quality regulation. We design regulatory indicators by considering four classic tools: impact assessment; consultation; simplification; and access and regulatory transparency.

Regulatory reform and better regulation policy

Regulation provides a fascinating perspective on how politics is changing. Regulatory reform has transformed the nature of the state, opened new domestic and international arenas of power, and created new institutional architectures. The tide of regulatory reform originated in the Anglo-Saxon world. In North America, the rise of the regulatory state preceded the welfare state and, in the USA at least, it was seen as a partial substitute for it. Unsurprisingly then, the demand for smart regulation, sometimes complemented by social scientists' eagerness to test their ideas for new policy instruments, has increased as an obvious response to regulatory explosion.

International organisations have amplified the impact of the regulatory reform movement. The Organisation for Economic Co-operation and Development (OECD) and the World Bank have prioritised regulation in their programmes for 'good governance' and have advocated comprehensive regulatory changes linking regulatory reforms to economic growth and more inclusive and transparent modes of governance. By doing so, the OECD and the World Bank have acknowledged the potential of regulatory reform in terms of governance, participation of stakeholders and more balanced state–society relations (Kaufmann *et al.*, 2003, 2005; OECD, 2002). What started as a movement to open up economic sectors to competition has now become a debate about modes and models of governance, accountability and the role of the public interest in international and domestic regulatory choices. This explains why civil society organisations are nowadays an important stakeholder in the 'regulatory state' and in business regulation at the international level (Braithwaite and Drahos, 2000; European Policy Forum, 2003, 2005).

In Europe, the EU has rapidly emerged as a crucial arena where regulatory policies are defined, especially since the Single European Act in 1986 set the ambitious plan (in some areas still far from being implemented) to complete the single market. With the Lisbon agenda to make the EU the most competitive knowledge-based society,[1] regulatory reform has become a priority for the Member States and the EU institutions. The Mandelkern (2001) report, prepared for the Laeken summit of the European Council, was an important turning point.[2] For the first time, all Member States agreed on the need to introduce principles of regulatory quality in their policies and to implement specific tools in 'key areas'. The principles highlighted by the Mandelkern report are: necessity, proportionality, subsidiarity, transparency, accountability, accessibility and simplicity. Turning to the key areas, the report flagged up the systematic use of several options to solve policy problems – the idea being that regulation should not be the default solution to any problem. These options were: the assessment of proposed EU and national legislation, consultation, simplification, access to regulation, implementation of EU legislation, and the design of specific institutions in charge of these tasks. Most of the ideas aired in the Mandelkern report had already been advocated by the OECD (1997a, 1997b, 2002). But the importance of the Mandelkern report is political: with the report, a political agenda for the Member States and the EU institutions was set. Since then, there has been a flurry of initiatives in Europe.

In 2002, the Commission adopted a system of integrated impact assessment to measure a wide range of costs and benefits of proposed legislation, in the context of the goal of sustainable development. In 2003, the Council, the European Parliament and the Commission signed an 'inter-institutional agreement on better regulation', thus making this issue a joint priority of the three institutions. In January 2004, the finance ministers of Ireland, the Netherlands, Luxembourg and the UK – the Member States in charge of the four EU Presidencies over the course of 2004 and 2005 – proposed to coordinate and intensify action on regulatory reform, following the template set by the Mandelkern report. The finance ministers asked the Commission to monitor the process by using 'indicators to measure progress with regulatory quality and reform at European and Member State level for activation through the open method of coordination and for application in impact assessment'. In December 2004, the Irish, Dutch, Luxembourg, UK, Austrian and Finnish Presidencies of the EU linked progress with the Lisbon agenda to regulatory reform.[3] Specifically, the six Presidencies highlighted the issues of tackling the administrative costs of regulation and the need to test the impact of proposed legislation on European competitiveness; they also (one more time) asked the Commission to develop, in consultation with the Council, 'indicators to measure progress with regulatory quality and reform at EU and Member State level'. The Competitiveness Council of 24 September 2004 called on the Commission and the Member States to evaluate 'the cumulative impact of existing legislation on the competitiveness of industry and of specific industry sectors' and to develop 'a method for measuring administrative burden on business' (Council of the European Union, 2004a: 3). In June 2005, the Council issued a recommendation for a 'new start' for the Lisbon strategy, to include a specific 'broad economic policy guideline' on 'better regulation'. The Council (2005a: 23) argued that:

> the cumulative impact of regulations may impose substantial economic costs. It is therefore essential that regulations are well-designed and proportionate. The quality of the European and national regulatory environment is a matter of joint commitment and shared responsibility at both the EU and Member State level.

In a few years, the EU and its Member States have moved from a discussion of principles of regulatory reform to a debate on indicators of regulatory quality, targets and processes of facilitated coordination to achieve their goals.

In short, regulatory reforms have emerged in the political agenda of the EU, its Member States and international organisations. The demise of Keynesian demand management has shifted priorities from 'command and control' modes of governance to other modes. In this context, regulation provides its own set of unique challenges. While the instruments to govern taxes and public expenditure are now well known across the OECD countries, the debate on how to govern regulation is more speculative and uncertain. Contrast the progress made with policy techniques such as budgeting, anti-inflationary monetary policies and tax policy with the difficulties experienced in measuring cumulative regulatory costs (SQW, 2005) and the complexity underlying the definition and implementation of regulatory budgets (McGarity and Ruttenberg, 2002; Thompson and Weidenbaum, 1998).

Looking at the development of regulatory reform, three aspects stand out. They can be described as: the shift from sector-oriented reform to horizontal, cross-sectoral reform; the priority given to regulatory management; and, most importantly for this book, the emergence of 'better regulation'. The first aspect is the evolution from sectoral reform (think of environmental regulation, health and safety, telecommunications, broadcasting and energy) to the identification of institutional models and specific tools that are applicable across sectors. This is evidenced by the diffusion of independent regulatory authorities, the pivotal role assigned to 'regulation for competition', the commitment to use market-friendly alternatives to 'command and control' regulation, the introduction of mandatory consultation in the preparation of new legislation and the use of cost–benefit analysis to support the introduction or revision of rules.

The second aspect is the attempt to move beyond individual reforms and specific regulatory tools and to create the preconditions for regulatory management. Following the OECD (1997a: 204), regulatory management 'can be seen as a logical evolution of the regulatory state'. It designates the coordination of regulatory policy across the entire life-cycle of regulation by dint of central management institutions situated in the core executive and by managing the aggregate regulatory effects, such as total costs on a sector. Regulatory management sets goals in terms of the government's delivery of high-quality regulation; it is neutral, though, as to the size and scope of government, focuses on regulatory transparency and accountability, and creates 'the longer-term cultural change inside the administration' (OECD, 1997a: 203).

The transition from deregulation to regulatory reform and, more recently, to management is still under way and the results are variable (OECD, 2002; SQW, 2005, on the UK). There is an area, however, where the effort to coordinate regulatory activities and manage them has gone further. This is the area that, broadly speaking, is known in the EU and OECD Member States as 'better regulation' – the third aspect we wish to discuss throughout this volume. This term can be elusive and misleading. Policy-makers use it in a normative sense, to indicate specific reforms that have to be undertaken in order to create the capacity, at the level of governments and EU institutions, to deliver high-quality regulations. As social scientists, we do not assign any normative value to this concept. We use 'better regulation' to designate a set of principles and tools that discipline the regulatory policy process. Put differently, what policy-makers call 'better regulation' is essentially meta-regulation (Morgan, 2003; Parker, 2002; Scott, 2003). In turn, meta-regulation can be successful or fail. The fact that policy-makers call it 'better regulation' does not mean that the quality of the regulations that we observe empirically is high. Although the results achieved by the EU and its Member

States vary markedly, at least at the conceptual level 'better regulation' can be considered a public policy.

This is an innovative aspect of this book. We approach 'better regulation' in the same way we would approach other public policies, such as housing policy or environmental policy. In consequence, we examine this new policy in terms of its actors, problems, resources, rules of interaction, decision-making structures and outcomes. We insist on the fact that we do not assign any normative value to the notion of 'better regulation' – but we will not carry on with the quotation marks to indicate this, hence they will be dropped hereafter.

Why is better regulation relevant to political scientists interested in the transformations of governance? To begin with, it is based on explicit principles and thereby defines what citizens can legitimately expect from public regulation. Advocates of better regulation want both to change the way regulatory institutions think and to provide a new social contract between government, regulatory authorities, citizens and interests. The emphasis on regulatory transparency, accountability, access to legislation and consultation is grounded in a model of governance. Accordingly, better regulation has inspired proposals for governance that go well beyond individual policy domains. The transformations we are talking about involve much more than tinkering with policies. They imply wider changes in the arenas and the nature of power. Hence the current debate in scholarly journals and in policy-making circles makes reference not just to regulation but to the state as well.

Another reason behind our interest is the pervasiveness of this new policy. Better regulation seeks to streamline the whole life-cycle of regulation, from the preparation of new rules to their implementation and enforcement. Accordingly, its tools target the stage of policy formulation (with the introduction of systematic impact assessment of new regulatory proposals), the stage of policy implementation and evaluation (with initiatives for better implementation and enforcement, simplification, and ex-post analysis of regulatory costs and burdens) and in some instances both stages (via consultation standards, rules on policy advice, and broad programmes for access to legislation and regulatory transparency). Better regulation covers the process of formulation both of rules affecting the citizen and the economy, and of rules affecting the public sector, thus covering the broad area of 'regulation inside government' described by Hood *et al.* (1999).

More importantly still, better regulation is a set of principles and instruments for the management of the regulatory process. Impact assessment, consultation standards, simplification procedures and rules for the use of experts and advisors in policy formulation are essentially standards applicable to the regulatory process. This is why we consider better regulation a paradigmatic case of meta-regulation. Let us pause for a moment to reflect on this concept.

Parker and Scott use the concept of meta-regulation to designate rules and standards by which governments control the self-regulatory regimes of corporations (Parker, 2002) or public sector organisations (Scott, 2003). Instead, we follow Morgan's notion of meta-regulation. According to Morgan (2003: 490):

> [meta-regulation] encompasses any set of institutions and processes that embed regulatory review mechanisms on a systematic basis into the every-day routines of governmental policymaking, such that a particular form of economic rationality becomes part of the taken-for-granted ways of policymaking.

As such, meta-regulation brings reflexivity into the design of regulatory policies (see also McGarity, 1991). Morgan mentions the example of the institutionalisation of cost–benefit tests applied consistently to the formulation of public policy as an example of meta-regulation. She goes on to add that:

> This principle is institutionalised as a *general mechanism of governance*, not confined to one-off efforts to reform particular policy sectors, but instantiating generally applicable, sector-neutral and continuously applied techniques of regulatory reform. (Morgan, 2003: 490, emphasis in original)

Further, a key objective of meta-regulation is to control the regulators (Froud *et al.*, 1998; Posner, 2001).

Some caution, however, is in order here. Firstly, as mentioned, we do not assign any normative load to the concept of better regulation policy. When we use this term, what we have in mind is comprehensive, horizontal programmes for the management of regulation. We do not claim that better regulation policy produces better, more efficient, growth-oriented rules. This is an empirical question. We do not claim that better regulation policy is the only way to improve regulation; indeed, there may be better ways to produce smart regulation (Baldwin, 2005; Gunningham and Grabosky, 1998: ch. 6; Sparrow, 2000). We are aware of the limitations and criticisms of meta-regulation (Morgan, 2003). Morgan, reflecting on the Australian experience, argues that meta-regulation makes the regulators think about aspects of social welfare, previously couched in the language of values, need or harm but now couched in the language of economics. We can discuss the implications of the 'economisation of regulatory politics' (Morgan, 2003: 509), although we would observe that, no matter what the values, need, and harm are, policies still have costs and benefits. Economic analysis and other types of evidence can provide a useful point of reference for political argumentation and debate (Majone, 1989), as shown by the use of economic analysis by environmental organisations (Melnick, 1990: 48).[4] Other limitations of better regulation relate to its obsession with slogans and principles rather than with the substance of politics. It may well be true that – as Wegrich (2005: 4) perceptively observes – better regulation is silent 'about how the adoption of tools and formal procedures could influence interest constellations and belief systems in policy networks'.

The resiliency of policy networks is indeed a serious hurdle for meta-regulation. Indeed, in another context (i.e., the analysis of regulatory reform in the USA), Noll has noted that the switch from deregulation to the regulation of the policy process is changing the coordinates of interest group politics and may slow down the whole process of regulatory reform. According to Noll (1999: 25), interest groups that supported deregulation in the past can become 'wary of fiddling with the process'. He illustrates the point with the case of mandatory cost–benefit analysis, a cornerstone, at least in America, of meta-regulation:

> If neither citizens nor elected officials have the skills, let alone the time, to evaluate the quality of economic policy analysis, a decision to give analysts greater policy influence raises quite rational fears that the policies favoured by policy analysts will reflect the values and preferences of the analysts rather than a comprehensive, objective assessment of the issue. (Noll, 1999: 26)

When analysts engage in advocacy instead of trying to produce sound economics and to reconcile the different arguments, 'delegation to economists may cause unreliable and unpredictable decisions that depend on who is assigned the job of analysing a particular regulatory proposal' (Noll, 1999: 27). Thus, the turn to meta-regulation may create uncertainty and 'a rational fear of antidemocratic delegation of policy influence to experts' (Noll, 1999: 27). For these reasons, the key actors in the regulatory reform process may become hesitant, unless an office outside the regulatory agencies insists on systematic peer review of economic analysis of proposed regulations and on the retrospective review and update of major rules (Noll, 1999: 35). Without these conditions, better regulation policy may deliver confusion and uncertainty rather than regulatory quality. The question, therefore, is not whether economic analysis is a good or a bad thing *per se*, but how it is linked to argumentation and political decisions, the ways in which it is reviewed and the embeddedness of economic analysis in processes of reconciliation of different positions. This point leads directly to some of the indicators of regulatory quality we explore in this book.

All things considered, we should not confuse regulatory quality with better regulation policy or the presence of mandatory cost–benefit analysis. In the remainder of the book, we consider better regulation policy as our dependent variable. We introduce indicators that enable us to assess this particular policy. Our indicators measure how better regulation policy is being implemented in the EU and across the Member States. They are not contingent on any assumption about the efficiency and effectiveness of better regulation *policy*. Quality is a variable: it can be low or high. Thus, policies for better regulation can be measured on a continuum from low to high quality.

Another important caveat is that we do not make the assumption that there is a better regulation policy in every country. The EU is a good example of a political system in which some Member States have this policy and others do not. For us, the key step is at the conceptual level. By approaching better regulation as public policy, we can examine it like other policies. Thus, we can describe the different stages of this policy, such as agenda-setting, decision-making, implementation and evaluation. This book falls in the 'evaluation' stage of the analysis. Our aims are to approach better regulation as public policy, to discuss the conceptual coordinates of regulatory quality and to design measures (i.e., indicators) that can assist in the evaluation of this policy. In the EU context, however, this is not a simple issue of measurement. It also involves processes of coordination and definition of common goals and objectives. Hence, another important aim in the work presented here is to link concepts, indicators and processes in which measures can be first agreed upon and then used for political purposes, such as greater competitiveness of the EU, growth and sustainable development.

We design indicators, discuss their quality and explain how data can be gathered – and in doing so we show that data are already available for several indicators. But we do not calculate indicators. Neither do we aggregate them. This is because the selection, adoption and aggregation of indicators should be a component of the political process of coordination at the EU level. They belong to the demand side, not to the supply. Hence, instead of calculating indicators, we provide the coordinates for the design of the processes in which selection, adoption and aggregation should take place. Finally, we show the connection between indicators of regulatory quality and comprehensive policy evaluation.

There are several limitations to the empirical scope of this book. Firstly, it does not discuss sector-specific indicators or policy processes. Secondly, there is no explicit treatment of independent regulatory authorities, although some of the analysis of regulatory quality tools can be applied to them. Thirdly, we mention but do not examine quality in relation to implementation and enforcement because this deserves a stand-alone project. Fourthly, the book does not discuss the notion of quality in relation to the judicial system and the issue of adversarial legalism, although the literature shows that this is a critical factor in the success of regulatory policies (Kagan, 2001; Kagan and Axelrad, 2000; Kelemen and Sibbitt, 2004; Levy and Spiller, 1994; Majone, 1996). Finally, we are concerned with one specific stage of better regulation policy, that is, evaluation. True, we examine learning loops that connect evaluation and policy reformulation and describe the whole better regulation policy-making process at the EU level. We are also aware of the limitations to the stage model of the policy process (Sabatier, 1999). However, it is fair to say that we do not explain the emergence of better regulation or why specific tools such as impact assessment have become so important in the Member States and, more recently, in the EU (see Baldwin, 2005).

The structure of the book

Turning to the structure of the book, we situate better regulation policy in the context of the debate on the regulatory state and regulatory governance and present the key arguments in chapter 1.

Chapter 2 explains better regulation as public policy. We show the theoretical implications of this approach and how better regulation can be analysed in a comprehensive framework that includes actors, principles, tools and measures. We also explain how contextual elements make a difference in the diffusion of better regulation policies. Our aim is not to show *that* context matters (the point has been made persuasively by historical institutional analysis in political science) but *how* it matters. This enables us critically to appraise the current discourse in OECD and EU circles – a discourse that sometimes runs the risk of being based on decontextualised definitions of quality and on simplistic approaches to measures. We show that the benchmark for the appraisal of meta-regulation is a concept of quality that covers both the process through which rules are produced and the economic efficiency of rules. This focus enables us to bring the participatory and democratic quality of governance back into the analytic framework. High-quality regulation does not necessarily mean low levels of regulation. We outline the specific take on regulatory quality selected in this book. The discussion on regulatory quality proceeds along three dimensions (i.e., design of the process, activities and output, and real-world outcome). We expose some of the analytical uncertainties arising out of the notion of 'real-world outcome' and show how these problems can be overcome.

The second part of chapter 2 decomposes the complexity of regulatory quality. 'Quality' is not a monolithic term. Different perspectives, preferences and goals shape the concept. This leads to the assertion that regulatory quality is not an abstract notion. It is contingent on the main assumptions about the behaviour of stakeholders; most importantly, it is contingent on the specific goals of better regulation policies, different stages of the development of regulatory reforms and different institutional contexts. We conclude the chapter with a discussion of the implications of complexity.

Chapter 3 provides a critical analysis of the most important measures used to assess the quality of regulation. The chapter reviews indicators produced by academics, the World Bank and the OECD. We link indicators to policy processes by showing how and when they can be used, in relation to what set of principles of better regulation and by what type of policy-makers. Consequently, we prioritise the policy implications of measures over the technical discussion.

We start with economic studies that rely on statistical analysis and propose systems to aggregate indicators of regulatory quality into an overall index. For each of these studies, we provide a short summary – explaining the general context and background, the methodology and the main findings and conclusions – and an assessment of their advantages and limitations. Within this broad approach to composite measures, a distinction is made between studies based on subjective indicators and those based on objective measures.

Then we turn to simple measures to assess the quality of regulation. Simple measures do not involve any statistical sophistication, even if, in some cases at least, to get a precise number to explain a phenomenon is an extremely heavy and complex task. However, the advantage of simple measures is related to the direct link between a phenomenon and a number. This intense scholarly activity on both composite and single measures has resulted in the production of indicators and – in some cases – rankings of countries. We show that the distinction between objective and subjective indicators of regulatory governance is not clear-cut. We present a more sophisticated matrix for the analysis of measures. We conclude by looking at the implications of different indicators for regulatory policy processes and discuss to what extent measures represent 'usable knowledge'.

Chapter 4 is dedicated to the cross-national experience of the measurement of better regulation policies. The focus is on countries with experience in the development and management of tools aimed at assessing regulatory quality. We examine three non-EU countries, namely the USA, Canada and Australia. These are countries with a relatively long history of attempts to forge a quality assurance culture in regulation. We then move on to examine Belgium, Denmark, the Netherlands, Sweden and the UK. Our data and information were collected in spring 2004 via desk research, correspondence and meetings with the project's support network. While several countries have introduced formal mechanisms to oversee and monitor the quality of better regulation tools, the experience with indicators is still limited. Australia, Canada, the UK and the USA have a robust network of quality assurance actors and also look at impact assessment beyond the issue of red tape. By contrast, Belgium, Denmark and the Netherlands focus on administrative burdens and are characterised by a simpler system of monitoring.

The profile of better regulation varies across the Member States of the EU (chapter 5). The emphasis on different principles and tools is not the same in all EU countries. Chapter 5 draws on the results of our questionnaire sent to the directors of better regulation policy in May 2004. The questionnaire was designed by the authors of the book with input from two professional economists, Professor Sam Cameron and Dr Hossein Jalilian, and two advisors, Professor Bruno Dente and Mr Scott Jacobs.

The main purpose of the discussion of the questionnaire results is to ascertain whether the Member States are converging in terms of the definition of better regulation principles, use of tools and measures. We try to map out the specific details of better regulation policies and what progress has been made in terms of measures. Evidence from the questionnaire helps us to identify, in addition to the two clusters of countries reviewed in chapter 4, a third cluster of countries, with no systematic experience of quality indicators, limited investment in quality assurance and a basic approach to impact assessment.

Chapter 6 turns to the better regulation policy of the EU. The main thrust is to look at and assess the tools, current quality assurance practice in the Commission and other EU institutions, projects under way and pilot projects on measurement undertaken by academics and stakeholders. We show how quality assurance processes, mechanisms and measurements provide either conceptual foundations or information that can be used in the design of a system of indicators. Another aim is to provide a clear picture of the EU institutions' own standards of regulatory quality, exploring how EU institutions approach the issue of quality. Indicators – we argue – can be derived from this analysis.

Chapter 7 presents our indicators of regulatory quality. At the outset, we present some technical properties of indicators. We draw on the previous discussion of the notion of quality, the role of different stakeholders, the suggestions arising out of the literature, the new initiatives of Member States and the EU in terms of measurement, and the questionnaire dataset. We first discuss the definition, purpose, limitations and types of indicators, and then illustrate how indicators of regulatory quality can be used in the EU – with reference to the open method of coordination (defined by the Lisbon Council in the context of the so-called EU agenda for competitiveness). Finally, we develop indicators.

We flesh out the basic elements of a possible open method of coordination applied to indicators of regulatory quality. There are several mechanisms of governance in the EU – as shown by Bulmer and Padgett (2005) – but, given the aims and treaty limitations of EU better regulation policy, we argue that the only feasible way to make progress with quality measures is via facilitated coordination. We discuss the overall approach we use to design indicators and why we do not argue for benchmarking and aggregation – two controversial points in the current debate at the Commission and in the Competitiveness Council. Our analysis of policy processes leads us to the design of three systems of indicators. For each system we discuss how it can be used and by whom, how indicators should be interpreted and data collection issues.

In chapter 8, the concluding chapter, we assess better regulation policies in Europe by looking at the evolution of concepts, the role of new regulatory quality tools in processes of policy formulation and the question of measurement of quality. Our conclusion is that measurement should not proceed by way of decontextualised scorecards, league tables and traffic light systems. The institutionalisation of better regulation policy is still low and the variance across the EU too high. We discuss how indicators can contribute to the process of institutionalisation and 'learning by monitoring' (drawing on Sabel, 1994). Finally, we relate better regulation to contrasting images of regulatory governance (Moran, 2003) and conclude that this policy has evolved from a set of technical tools. It has entered the territory of politics. As such, it will become even more prominent in the agenda of the EU and its Member States, but also more contested. The crucial challenge for better regulation is not the efficiency of its tools, but the overall legitimacy of policy.

Notes

1 On the EU's Lisbon strategy, see the 'Presidency conclusions' of the European Council in Lisbon on 23–24 March 2000 at http://consilium.europa.eu/ueDocs/cms_Data/docs/pressData/en/ec/00100-r1.en0.htm, and for the present implementation see http://ec.europa.eu/growthandjobs/index_en.htm.
2 The Mandelkern Group on Better Regulation was formed by a resolution of the ministers of public administration at Strasbourg, which gave it the 'mandate to develop a coherent approach to this topic and to submit proposals to the Ministers, including the definition of a common method of evaluating the quality of regulation'.
3 See, respectively, Irish, Dutch, Luxembourg and UK Presidencies of the European Union (2004) and Irish, Dutch, Luxembourg, UK, Austrian and Finnish Presidencies of the European Union (2005).
4 Examples of such economic analyses by environmental organisations appear at www.carbonneutral.com and www.climatecare.org.

1

Appraising regulatory policy

Introduction

This chapter introduces our approach to the measurement of better regulation policy, in the context of the wider discussion of regulatory quality appraisal. It can also be read as a summary of the main arguments developed throughout the book. The notion of policy appraisal (Owens *et al.*, 2004) covers a broad set of approaches and techniques. Ultimately, however, appraisal hinges on the idea of answering the question of whether a policy is successful or not. The concepts of 'good regulatory governance' and 'high-quality regulation' raise some of the thorniest questions in political science. Quality for whom? In relation to what? And for what purposes?

To clarify how we handle these questions, we chart the development of regulatory reform and regulatory governance in Europe and limit our analysis to better regulation. We then deal with the issue of how to measure the performance of better regulation policy. Having established that better regulation is a public policy, it can be appraised with the same conceptual and methodological tools used for other public policies. Indicators are a component of policy appraisal.

The crucial step – we argue – is to link measures to conceptual analysis and policy processes. Conceptual analysis is a fundamental step in research design (Brady and Collier, 2004). It does not make sense to design indicators without specifying how quality and better regulation policy are defined. More importantly still, indicators should be linked to the processes in which they can be used. All too often, the debate on indicators of governance and institutional quality tends to discuss the technical properties without considering the political processes in which measures will be handled. Technical properties such as validity and reliability are fundamental (although basic) elements of the design of indicators. But measures should be also designed in relation to their potential use, their link with variables that can be controlled by policy officers and their impact on learning processes. This leads us to our triad of concepts, indicators and policy processes – the cornerstone of our analytical framework.

The regulatory state and regulatory governance

Regulatory reform has changed the nature of the state. The notion of the regulatory state (often used in the specialised literature – see Eberlein and Grande, 2005; Jordana and Levi-Faur, 2004; Levi-Faur and Gilad, 2004; Majone, 1996, 1999a; Moran, 2002, 2003) evokes an association between regulation and the transformations of the arenas and nature of power. But if the notion alludes to transformations, it does not necessarily explain them. In this section, we examine the scholarly debate on the regulatory state. We conclude that the academic discussion provides several important insights for the identification and measurement of regulatory quality in the EU. However, on balance we think that we do not need a state-centred concept in a context of multi-level governance, networks of regulators and increasing attention to the openness of policy-making processes.

The notion of the regulatory state comes from Seidman and Gilmour (1986), with reference to the US federal government (see also Majone, 1996: 54–6). They make a distinction between the positive state and the regulatory state. The former provides services directly, by engaging in the functions of the market alongside private actors, while the latter delivers public policies by regulating markets. Regulation is a mode of governance characterised by the use of rules as a main instrument.[1] By contrast, the positive state relies on the classic Musgravian functions of macroeconomic stabilisation, redistribution and resource allocation. The regulatory state is not a monolith: countries still exhibit different regulatory styles, and regulatory governance can be embedded in (or co-evolve with) other modes (Jordana and Levi-Faur, 2004). But one striking feature is its international diffusion. US-style regulation has influenced the process of European integration. 'American regulatory philosophy and practice' inspired 'policy developments in Europe during the phase of privatisation and deregulation in the 1980s' (Majone, 1996: 53). Nowadays, the USA and the EU show similarities in that they have not developed a large 'federal' welfare state. However, they have specialised in the 'production' of economic, social and environmental regulation, so much so that the concept of the regulatory state has been used to describe both the US federal government and the EU.

In the USA, both interest group politics (Noll, 1999) and the emergence of new policy ideas (Derthick and Quirk, 1985) have contributed to the major changes of the regulatory state since the 1970s. The diffusion of the regulatory state among the EU Member States is partly the result of the integration process and partly an endogenous political switch from the Keynesian welfare state to supply-side policy, independent regulators and varieties of monetarism.

The OECD is more normative in its reference to the regulatory state. The term is contrasted with the 'interventionist' or 'Keynesian' state (OECD, 2002). The reference to interventionism is misleading. All regulatory policies 'intervene' in the economy, society or the public sector, although 'command and control' regulation is the supreme form of 'interventionism'. What the

OECD means is that market-friendly and smart modes of regulation can be efficient and respectful of the preferences of market operators. Drawing on Moran (2003), this can be called the image of the regulatory state as the 'smart state'.

One point made by the literature on the regulatory state is that regulatory reform has become a priority in the political agenda because of the complexity raised by the growth of regulation. It is indispensable, however, to be clear about the nature of the complexity. Is regulation a political problem because of its quantitative growth? If this were the case, all policies of better regulation should be eminently concerned with deregulation and a reduction of regulatory burdens.

True, regulation is constantly growing, partly because citizens and policy-makers want to control more areas of social and physical risk than in the past, partly because of the multi-layered nature of several types of regulation in which different levels of governance impose rules on the same stakeholders, and partly because of the failure of previous regulatory regimes and the need to create new rules to overcome the limitations of previous rules. As Levi-Faur and Gilad (2004: 106) observe:

> This development is altogether puzzling since, amidst the rise of neoliberalism, the prominence of the American deregulation movement, and the teleology of privatisation, a retreat of the state and a relaxation of rules and regulation might have been expected. Yet … liberalisation and managerial reforms that were supposed to hollow out the state were intimately coupled with the rise of multi-layered regulatory institutions and formalisation of codes of behaviour at the corporate, state, and international levels.

However, the political focus on regulation is not simply a matter of quantity. Put differently, the notion of the regulatory state is not limited to the observation that the cross-national processes of privatisation and deregulation have ended up in re-regulation. There are also qualitative aspects to consider. As mentioned in the Introduction, one important element of qualitative change is the emergence of a new type of regulation, that is, meta-regulation. Another qualitative aspect is the interest in principles and standards of good regulation.

The literature has not reached uncontroversial answers. Contemporary regulation can be seen as originating from the market-protecting and efficiency-driven rationale of the smart state (Gunningham and Grabosky, 1998; Majone, 1996; OECD, 2002) or as being spawned by hyper-modernistic syndromes (Moran, 2003), the obsession for regulation inside government (Hood *et al.*, 1999), technocratic meta-regulation (Morgan, 2003) and rituals of verification looking at form over substance (Power, 1999), with high potential for regulatory pathologies and policy fiascos. The differing perceptions of the probability and severity of market failures (and, conversely, of government failures) explain why opinions diverge.

The differences in the academic camp should not be exaggerated, though. Majone (1996) argues that the *justification* of regulation is efficiency and the protection of competitive markets, but this does not mean that *real-world regulation* is necessarily 'good', efficient or 'better' than other policies. If we step outside the academic territory, however, the gulf is wider. Contrast the optimistic and normative tone of the OECD publications on regulatory reform (1997a, 2002) with the more sceptical conclusions of Moran and Morgan. This difference makes the elaboration of measures of quality an exciting task. But one cannot jump into measurement without having carefully analysed the concept of quality in relation to specific institutional settings and the whole range of actors involved in the politics of regulation. This is one of the key tasks in this volume. We do not make any *a priori* assumption about the quality of the regulatory state. Instead, we propose an approach to performance measurement that enables us to transform the 'big' question about the quality of the regulatory state into a more manageable set of questions about how better regulation policies are being implemented in the EU and across the Member States. The cost of this choice is that our study does not provide any bold conclusion on the overall success or failure of the regulatory state.

One limitation of the concept of the regulatory state is that, by drawing attention to the state, it seems to suggest that all the main arenas of power are still domestic. We would therefore much prefer to use the expression 'regulatory governance'. The latter designates a broad set of objectives, principles, institutions, mechanisms and tools to manage regulatory processes and regulation. This set is not confined to the political perimeter of the nation-state. Regulatory governance puts emphasis on the multi-level nature of the politics of regulation and on the role of governance mechanisms within political institutions and in society. As one of the challenges in this area of enquiry is to connect the regulatory state to the regulatory society (Levi-Faur and Gilad, 2004), we argue that 'regulatory governance' is a more useful and comprehensive concept than 'regulatory state' or 'regulatory capitalism' (Levi-Faur and Jordana, 2005).

Explaining the emergence of regulatory governance

Having established that the growth of regulation is both quantitative and qualitative and that regulatory arenas go beyond governments (without excluding them, of course), what are the explanations of regulatory governance? The diffusion of regulatory governance is not easily explained by rational delegation. One typical explanation is based on principal-agent models of delegation of regulatory power to independent regulatory authorities. Credible regulatory commitments cannot be taken by governments sensitive to the electoral cycle. Regulatory power is therefore delegated to independent authorities and, when there is a problem over the international credibility of policy commitments (Majone, 1996), to supranational bodies like the European Commission. The explanation works both at the horizontal domestic level, where new independent regulatory authorities have been created in several regulatory domains and in monetary policy, and at the vertical supranational level, where the most important phenomenon is the creation of the European single market regulated by the Commission (Gilardi, 2002; Majone, 1996).

Although this approach has the merit of avoiding *ad hoc* mechanisms based on the supposedly unique nature of European integration, the evidence shows that delegation to the EU level is limited and far from covering a wide range of policies (Eberlein and Grande, 2005). Additionally, recent work suggests that historical trends in variables such as trust can also play a role. One argument aired in the literature (Jordana and Levi-Faur, 2004; Levi-Faur and Gilad, 2004; Moran, 2002; Power, 1999) is that the historical decline of social trust and the increased relational distance between regulator and affected parties (see Hood *et al.*, 1999) have led to an increase in regulation. The idea is that markets can be governed either by club-like mechanisms based on trust and wider social reciprocity rules, or, in the absence of these mechanisms, formal regulation produced and enforced by political authorities. In the context of the critique of rationalistic explanations, a diffusion perspective has emerged in the literature.

A focus on diffusion can provide a convenient lens for the analysis of the different worlds of regulation. Explanations of diffusion relax the assumption that there is an efficient logic to the rise of regulatory governance (Holzinger and Knill, 2005; Levi-Faur, 2002; Radaelli, 2005). While Majone (1996) provides a rationale for the adoption of new regulatory tools and institutions based on credibility and the need to deliver efficient markets, diffusion studies explain the growing popularity of new regulatory tools and institutions such as independent regulatory authorities by using a wider set of variables, including coercion, normative pressure and mimetism (Pollitt *et al.*, 2000; Radaelli, 2000). The adoption of a diffusion angle shows that efficiency is not the only logic at work. Governments may decide to adopt new institutions to increase their legitimacy. If more than one logic is at work in regulatory governance, it becomes easier to account for different results. An important implication for the arguments aired in this volume is that the diffusion perspective does not assume that regulatory governance is necessarily and functionally associated with the efficiency of regulation. By doing so, it stimulates an open-minded approach to the notion of quality of regulation and to the overall exercise of appraising regulatory policies and their tools.

However, both functionalist and diffusion models are somewhat silent on history, context and politics. For the former approach, regulatory governance is the result of rational delegation. For the latter, emulation, herding and 'epidemiological' diffusion go a long way in explaining the pervasiveness of the phenomenon. The presence of historical contingencies in the

European integration process, the unique institutional architecture of the EU and above all the tense political conflicts over the attribution of regulatory power to independent regulators and the European Commission cannot be easily accounted for in rational delegation analysis and diffusion studies.

A comparative approach can be used to explain and assess regulatory governance in the EU. The questions are nevertheless daunting. What is the nature of EU regulatory governance? Is it a case of transfer of regulatory powers to the supranational level? Or do national regulatory institutions still provide the most important political context for economic and social regulation? Eberlein and Grande (2005) describe the hypothesis of comprehensive transfer as 'Europeanisation' (and associate it with the work of Majone, 1996) and the alternative, of resilient domestic regulatory regimes, as 'nationalisation' (broadly speaking, following Scharpf, 1999).

Let us follow Eberlein and Grande for a moment. On 'Europeanisation', they observe that the growth of EU-level regulatory powers is far from being complete and wide-ranging. Turning to 'nationalisation', the evidence is that national independent regulatory authorities are embedded in wider regulatory regimes that go beyond authorities and beyond the national domain. The evidence shows the emergence of differentiated regulatory regimes, in which the domestic and EU levels of regulatory power are intertwined. The notion of regulatory regimes helps us to go beyond the focus on regulatory authorities to include the full range of actors, operating at different levels and with variable degrees of formal institutionalisation. Even when there is a functional need for full delegation of regulatory power to the EU, the constellation of different interests among Member States hinders the development of Community-wide economic regulation. This regulatory lacuna – Eberlein and Grande argue – can be filled by informal regulatory networks that bring together EU institutions and domestic institutional actors and non-institutional actors, such as large firms operating in the markets for utilities.

Turning to the implications for the issues covered by our study, the presence of multi-level regulatory governance and informal governance in regulatory policies makes the assessment of quality problematic. Quality cannot be measured by looking at the EU-level policies in isolation from the domestic context. Further, the presence of informal governance shows that quality assurance systems targeting formal institutions may not capture the very substance of regulatory policy, especially when the latter is developed by informal regulatory networks. Our analysis, however, is limited to four specific tools used in better regulation policy, namely regulatory impact assessment (RIA), consultation, simplification, and regulatory access and transparency (see chapter 2). We do not cover the quality of policies produced by regulatory fora and informal governance networks, and therefore do not have to deal with this type of complexity. All the same, our indicators can be used for a broad set of regulatory policies, including some regulatory standards produced by informal networks.

Obviously, the multi-layered nature of the EU regulatory system is an element of complexity for measurement. Indicators of better regulation policy cannot be limited to EU-level regulatory activities: the better regulation policies of the Member States have to be considered too. We follow this argument through our design of indicators and make suggestions for how they can be used both at the EU level and by the Member States (in chapter 7).

Multi-level regulatory systems are not just sources of analytical complexity. They can also produce political assets for the diffusion of quality measures. Reflecting on the conditions that encourage the use of policy research, Weiss (1999: 480) argued that 'with more centres (or "de-centres") of power, there are more ears to listen and eyes to read, and thus more possibilities of access for the results of evaluation'. The non-centralised or decentralised nature of the EU policy-making system (Richardson, 1996) presents some interesting preconditions to a joint commitment, on the part of the EU institutions and the Member States, to the measurement of regulatory quality; such a joint commitment will have to be made in the context of 'facilitated coordination'. We explore this issue in chapter 7.

Measuring quality via indicators

There are several ways to appraise the quality of public policy. All forms of appraisal are contingent on methodological frameworks and purposes. Let us take the framework first. The benchmark for the methodological choice can be the efficient allocation of resources, the achievement of targets, support for learning and self-correction mechanisms, participation, and cause–effect explanation (Tavistock Institute, 2003). Briefly, there are many ways in which a policy can be 'successful'. Turning to purposes, in multi-layered institutional settings like the EU, the analysis can be informed by the idea of strengthening institutional capabilities, delivering accountability, improving implementation, supporting planning and assisting knowledge production.

As noted in a comprehensive guide to policy evaluation in the EU produced by the Tavistock Institute (2003), purposes and methodological frameworks can be combined in pairs. For example, explanation is usually matched with knowledge production. Our choice is to deconstruct the notions of success and quality by referring them to the different actors involved in policies for better regulation (chapter 2) and to make proposals for the design and selection of indicators that maximise opportunities for learning among actors at the EU level and in the network of Member State actors in charge of these policies at the domestic level. We draw on the concept of 'learning by monitoring' (Sabel, 1994) and on existing processes of facilitated coordination to make our points in chapter 7.

We approach the thorny issue of measuring the quality of better regulation policies by designing indicators. It is important to clarify that indicators are one of the tools available for the evaluation of policies. In the end, we argue that better regulation policies should be informed both by indicators and by wider structures and methods of policy evaluation.[2] Indicators can be a useful component of the broader attempt to evaluate policies. Comprehensive evaluation of better regulation policy, in turn, can be used to assess the quality of the indicators themselves, whether they are making an impact on actors or not, and whether they should be changed, aggregated in different ways, or revised.

But what do we mean by 'indicator'? The Joint Research Centre of the European Commission (2002: 1) suggests the following definition:

> Indicators are pieces of information that summarise the characteristics of a system or highlight what is happening in a system.

A more precise definition is the one used in the context of policy evaluation:

> An indicator can be defined as the measurement of an objective to be met, a resource mobilised, an effect obtained, a gauge of quality or a context variable. An indicator produces quantified information with a view to helping actors concerned with public interventions to communicate, negotiate or make decisions. (Tavistock Institute, 2003: 127)

In this book an indicator is a gauge of quality. Specifically, indicators are used in the first place to operationalise and measure the quality of better regulation policy. In turn, quality of policy is a necessary condition for the improvement of actual regulations. We use indicators to discuss this link, with all the caveats needed in this type of exercise. Finally, regulatory policies contribute to economic outcomes, although there is yet another set of caveats and limitations to consider. Our indicators are not limited to the measurement of the quality of a specific policy, in our case better regulation. They also provide empirical information on regulations and their economic impact by looking into real-world outcomes.

Linking measures to concepts and processes

Before one attends to the construction of indicators, one has to answer the following question: are indicators useful, dangerous, or simply irrelevant? The question is blunt, but not trivial. We address it by setting scope conditions, that is, conditions under which indicators pay off. But first let us look at the critiques.

One critique arises out of the use of indicators as targets. The Lisbon strategy of the EU is based on targets, and so are several processes of open coordination generated by this strategy. The Competitiveness Council of the EU has endorsed indicators in the context of better regulation on more than one occasion. In areas such as social inclusion and (to mention a case that pre-dates Lisbon) employment policy, indicators define targets for the

Member States. Alesina and Perotti (2004: 35) have described the 'insistence on setting numerical targets' as 'a practice reminiscent of the discredited industrial plans of the Sixties'. They are particularly concerned about the undifferentiated (among EU Member States) use of targets. Although they do not mention the word 'indicator' in their paper, they are worried about the 'dirigiste and regulatory approach to the economy, with a heavy emphasis on coordination, intervention and quantitative targets' (Alesina and Perotti, 2004: 34). They go on to note that:

> this emphasis on 'coordination' and 'plans', has had (so far!) a relatively limited impact because the powers of EU institutions in many policy areas are indeed limited yet. But precisely because the scope for actual intervention is constrained, the result ... is often inaction and a pompous rhetoric. (Alesina and Perotti, 2004: 34)

The conclusion is that those who believe in 'social engineering, coordination, public goals, market regulation' have more say in the EU than those who want 'to let markets take their undisturbed course' (Alesina and Perotti, 2004: 34). One can read similar criticisms in the newspapers as well. Whiteley (2005) argued, with reference to New Labour's enthusiasm for indicators in the context of 'command and control' governance methods, that 'the multi-level nature of government makes such methods, and the targets and indicators culture that accompanies them, increasingly ineffective'. Indicators can bring us back to hierarchical notions of governance.

Another cluster of critiques arises out of the technical complexity of measurement in regulatory policy. Regulation is an incomplete contract between the regulator and the regulatee. The costs of regulation depend on how regulation is implemented and enforced, and on the nature of regulator–regulatee interactions (Coen, 2005). Better regulation policies assume that costs can be usefully estimated ex-ante, and a typical batch of indicators on the quality of ex-ante RIA would include information on the procedures used to prepare the estimates. But this can miss the whole point of regulation being an incomplete contract and give the false sense of certainty that regulatory costs can be defined at the stage of policy formulation. Black (2005) elaborates on this point by arguing that the rational-managerial style of meta-regulation may infuse public organisations with procedures, rules and ultimately an erroneous sense of certainty that are inadequate when governments have to manage unpredictable and rapidly changing regulatory domains.

Finally, there is political complexity. Experience with indicators for EU policies such as social inclusion shows that the design and adoption of indicators, and the move from indicators to targets, are political processes (Atkinson *et al.*, 2004; Radaelli, 2003). Indicators can be designed only after having made a choice on the purpose and the method for the appraisal of policy. They point towards one purpose instead of another; they imply one notion of success but not another. As Member States differ greatly in terms of their progress with regulatory reforms, any set of indicators generates winners (those whose policy models are reflected in the definition of success implied by the indicators) and losers. Targets put differential pressure on Member States – in terms of the amount of change needed to achieve a target. We can expect the discussion on indicators to be highly political and the type of learning taking place in processes of coordination at the EU level to be more similar to political learning than to a truth-seeking exercise (Radaelli, 2003).

How do we handle these criticisms? We respond to the points made by Alesina and Perotti by ignoring their own rhetoric (about markets taking 'their undisturbed course') and focusing on the substance. We agree that systems of regulatory indicators should not be undifferentiated among the Member States. To avoid old-fashioned planning syndromes, the major step of adopting indicators should be situated in a broader policy of regulatory reform, one that takes on board the specific institutional context in which better regulation operates. We suggest that coordination can be useful at the EU level, but that EU-wide targets may be less important than measuring progress in Member States and fostering learning dynamics. In chapter 7, we propose three systems of indicators. Member States and EU institutions should adopt a common set of indicators drawing on a range of baseline indicators (what we call 'system 1'). Baseline indicators measure the quality of better regulation tools ex-ante. We present a broad range from which the Member States and the EU institutions can derive a smaller common set of baseline indicators via a process of facilitated coordination. This process would enable (and push) the participants to make explicit choices about selection. The common set of baseline indicators can be used to map progress. Sophisticated indicators (covered by system 2) reveal the preferences of Member States. Given that the institutionalisation of better regulation policy in the EU is on average low, and that there is a lot of variance around the average, we do not envisage 'one size fits all', decontextualised indicators of activity and real-world outcome. The third system of indicators should be used to link measurement with the comprehensive evolution of better regulation policy.

At the EU level, coordination should be based first and foremost on discussing the reasons behind any change of a given Member State's indicators, promoting a thicker debate on the priorities of regulatory reform, and encouraging comprehensive evaluations of better regulation. By 'telling their stories' about changes in indicators, Member States would be in a position to learn and to provide useful information to the other participants. Drawing on Sabel's seminal work on how to reconcile monitoring and learning (Sabel, 1994), the issue is how to combine the need to monitor common progress via shared standards and routines with the unpredictability of genuine learning. In our case, the problem is compounded by the fact that Member States have different preferences on better regulation policies. This difference in preferences has to be factored into the design of policy processes. Hence one should avoid the dirigiste approach of targeting and monitoring compliance with targets. In Sabel's words, a learning-oriented discussion is a process through which a 'common understanding of the world' emerges (Sabel, 1994). Indeed, a common understanding of what the EU 'wants' from better regulation is precisely the most important result to achieve – and of course also the most ambitious.

On technical complexity, our answer is to focus on a limited range of tools, here namely RIA, consultation, simplification, and regulatory access and transparency. These are well known tools (see chapter 2 for details). Technical problems exist and are discussed in the remainder of this volume, but so does knowledge about how to cope with them. Black's point about the false sense of certainty induced by meta-regulation leads us to design indicators that do not confuse the presence of procedures with the more complex notion of good regulation. Procedures should be there to help regulators to ask the right questions and to make institutions think, not to provide simplistic answers.

The real issue is political complexity. After having looked at the international experience (chapter 4), our own data (chapter 5) and the economics literature (chapter 3), we take the drastic approach of acknowledging the role of politics up front, rather than ducking under pseudo-technical solutions. We very much agree with the argument made by Carol Weiss when she spoke to the European Evaluation Society annual conference and said: 'Evaluators will never supersede policy makers nor take the politics out of policy making' (Wess, 1999: 483). Thus, we discuss concepts, indicators and policy processes *together*.

Regarding concepts, we problematise the definition of better regulation policy and regulatory quality. We relate quality to the different stakeholders and to institutional contexts. This enables us to contextualise indicators and to show how they should be used. Further, by drawing on regulatory governance we distinguish our indicators from the traditional indicators of product market regulation. The switch from 'markets' to 'governance' as a conceptual centre of gravity is important. It provides a different focus on indicators. Conceptual analysis leads us to the decision not to aggregate indicators and to suggest that Member States perform this task in the context of a process of 'facilitated coordination'. In terms of EU modes of governance (Bulmer and Padgett, 2005; Bulmer and Radaelli, 2005), facilitated coordination is the most efficient way to start a process of learning and mutual progress in the context of diversity. Other modes, such as formal harmonisation, presuppose a degree of convergence that is not there.

Weiss noted some years ago that the link between policy analysis and policy processes is often problematic and lamented the absence of mechanisms for linking analysis to policy-making. Thinking specifically of policy evaluation, she observed that 'governments do not usually have institution-alised channels and procedures to connect evaluation findings to the arenas in which decisions are being reached' (Weiss, 1999: 479). This is where our contribution to the normative analysis of processes lies – that is, how processes should be designed.

As is often the case, positive analysis provides the basis for the suggestions and the normative analysis presented in this volume. Some of the techniques of meta-regulation, for example cost–benefit analysis, originated within the technical-rational or 'rational-synoptic' model. In this model, policy analysis provides the decision-maker with the information needed to make efficient choices. These techniques are not supposed to substitute for political decision-making, but the assumption is made that politics can be bracketed with or, to paraphrase Weiss, taken out of policy analysis. Other important assumptions are that there is one decision-maker, and that the policy process revolves around making a choice – that is, whether a proposed rule should be adopted or not. Essentially, at time t_0 the decision-maker has an informa-tion gap, at time t_1 information is made available by the rational analysis of policy and at time t_2 a decision is taken. All decision-makers face the same information problems – there may be differences of degree, of course. This makes the elaboration of decontextualised indicators a viable option. Owens *et al.* (2004: 1947) summarise a consistent body of literature on the limitations of this model by arguing that:

> it is inadequate in three (interrelated) ways. It fails to provide a convincing account of observed relationships between analysis and policy (theoretical inadequacy); it can disguise important ethical and political judgments as technical ones (political inadequacy); and exposure of these shortcomings may result in loss of legitimacy for appraisal techniques and policies; in effect, appraisal based on this model may cease to function (practical inadequacy).

Indeed, the model breaks down when there are multiple actors, with different preferences and diverse ideas about regulatory quality. Actors have multiple sources of information, and policy analysis, indicators and evaluations of regulation are only one type of information. Although the technical-rational model stresses the information needs of the decision-maker, the reality is that 'almost never does the choice of policy hinge on the absence of information' (Weiss, 1999: 471). The social sciences do not provide definitive answers to complex policy problems and, perhaps, they do not even try to answer some important policy questions (Lindblom, 1990). When policy analysis is used, it is employed more often in the context of political argumentation than in the form of raw data or neutral information (Radaelli, 1995; Weiss, 1999).

Add to this that making policy cannot be reduced to a single decision taking place at one point in time. For one thing, policies are long courses of action (and/or inaction) in which individual decisions are only com-ponents of broader and more complex developments. For another, people in government working on regulation may not even realise they are producing 'decisions' – typically there will be several committees and teams probing different aspects of policy formulation. Data, indicators and policy studies have therefore more than one function: they may well contribute to a decision, but they may also help organisations to develop interpretations of events and, in the long run, provide the discourse for policy arenas. Weiss (1999) refers to the latter function as 'policy enlightenment'. She argues that rarely does policy analysis contribute to one specific policy choice, but in the long term there may be a percolation of ideas – originating from policy research and data – that seep into the arenas in which policy develops. Policy analysis thereby contributes to the definition of issues and to the framing of alternatives. This enlightenment role is an important function of indicators. Over time, well designed indicators can contribute to the quality of discussion and to more informed processes of policy coordination in the EU, without necessarily thinking that data will automatically lead to specific decisions in the short term.

Indicators and their use (or misuse, and even lack of use) are contingent on the presence or absence of conflicting policy frames. In policy controversies where actors conflict over problem definition and filter the same evidence but through radically different cognitive 'frames', empirical evidence produced via indicators will not solve the classic problem of 'talking past each other'. Neither, however, should we jump to the opposite conclusion and argue that only participation and processes of deliberation (rather than data and policy analysis) can solve policy controversies. Open participation may simply make the different actors more grounded in their beliefs and more prone to conflict (Owens *et al.*, 2004), for example on the issue of whether environmental problems require a radical change of modes of production and lifestyle or more limited end-of-pipe solutions. The starting point should be another, namely, to accept that policy analysis (and therefore policy analysts) is endogenous to the policy process (Radaelli, 1995) and see how this resource can modify the system of interaction in which actors develop better regulation policies.

Following Radaelli and Dente (1996), the two dimensions of the policy process that have to be considered in the debate on indicators and their use are the degree of conflict (low or high) and the degree of innovation (low or high) of the policies that are being measured. When innovation is high (i.e., change is radical rather than incremental) and conflict is low (or, in the EU context, the spread of national preferences on policy is limited), the dominant logic in the policy process is one of discovery, that is, how to learn under conditions of radical and genuine uncertainty. Quantitative information can assist processes of discovery and policy experimentation by revealing interesting patterns and by showing how unexpected phenomena may occur (say, better regulation policy producing particularly 'bad' rules). Under conditions of low innovation and low conflict, indicators can effectively support monitoring processes and a rather incremental logic of learning. When conflict and policy innovation are high, the main problem is conflict management under conditions of high uncertainty. Participation and deliberation are more important than indicators. But the point is not about black and white solutions (either quantitative information or participation): it is about the intelligent use of indicators in different logics of learning (Owens *et al.*, 2004; Radaelli and Dente, 1996). Finally, when conflict is high but policy innovation is limited, there is more political conflict than radical uncertainty. Here, indicators can perform an enlightenment function rather than an instrumental one (Radaelli and Dente, 1996: 63). Over time, they may support iterative games and processes of socialisation among better regulation policy-makers, which can be valuable in fostering cooperation, thus unclogging the arteries of the policy process.

To sum up, the integrated analysis of concepts, indicators and policy processes is a valuable strategy. It enables us to understand the role of policy analysis in the process, to create contextualised indicators, to link measures to multidimensional notions of quality and to make proposals for regulatory governance (as opposed to the narrow notion of product market regulation). In consequence, 'quality' is not limited to the technical properties of indicators. It also includes properties such as how indicators can be understood and managed by the actors of better regulation networks at the EU and domestic levels. The emphasis on governance is particularly useful in devising linkage mechanisms between indicators and policy-making processes – the thorny issue of knowledge utilisation (Weiss, 1979, 1999).

Put differently, we pursue a strategy that connects demand and supply of indicators (and more generally policy analysis). Most of the current debate on indicators of regulatory quality is confined to a technical discussion of the supply, specifically technical properties, the econometric links between regulation and final economic outcomes, and the possibility of using indicators for large-scale comparisons (chapter 3). We add that the providers of indicators (i.e., the supply) should make explicit the theories of the policy processes embedded in them. Turning to demand, we start from the question 'Why would the actors involved in better regulation policies want to make use of indicators?' and explain how different actors perceive quality. We then use a theory of the policy process in which there are multiple actors involved in the formulation and implementation of public policy. We relax the assumption that research and data are used simply to fill an information gap of the (unitary) decision-maker. Alongside the function of supporting decisions, we explore two other functions of indicators, namely understanding and making sense of change in better regulation policies and 'policy enlightenment'.

Notes

1   There are three main meanings of 'regulation': as a mode of governance based on rules; as political steering of the economy; and as a range of mechanisms for social control (Jordana and Levi-Faur, 2004). Following Baldwin *et al.* (1998: 3) we use a classic definition of regulation as 'promulgation of an authoritative set of rules, accompanied by some mechanisms … for monitoring and promoting compliance with these rules'. We do not restrict our understanding of regulation as a mode of governance to independent regulatory authorities because we are interested in broader regulatory regimes (drawing on Eberlein and Grande, 2005).
2   There are several types of policy evaluation, including ex-ante, formative and ex-post evaluation. In this book we refer to ex-post evaluation when we mention 'policy evaluation'.

2

Defining quality

Introduction

The emergence of better regulation on the agenda of governments, parliaments and organisations like the European Commission has been fast, to the extent that, at least conceptually, we can examine better regulation as a public policy, for the reasons illustrated in chapter 1. If better regulation is a priority for the EU and its Member States, what is the core concept around which it has evolved? At the cost of oversimplification, we can say that the cognitive anchor of better regulation policy is quality. Yet it is difficult to pin down precisely what this concept means. Here are a few questions to be considered carefully:

- What is regulatory quality?
- How do governments, international organisations and academics approach this concept?
- What are the advantages and limitations of an approach focused on quality?
- How does the institutional context affect quality?

This chapter tackles these questions. As mentioned in chapter 1, our analysis is confined to the policy known as better regulation, that is, a set of initiatives to improve the capacity of governments and the EU to deliver high-quality regulation. Better regulation policy is essentially a type of meta-regulation. Its aim is to set rules that discipline the regulatory process, from formulation to enforcement, compliance and ex-post review of regulations. There are other components of regulatory reform that fall outside better regulation. The quality of regulatory institutions and regulations is determined by a vast array of factors.

There is an interesting connection, though. In this volume, we look at three dimensions of better regulation policies, that is, design, activity and real-world outcome. Definitions and measures of design and activity refer to the process of rule-making. When we consider real-world outcome, instead, we are interested in the quality of the regulations produced via the policy process. This is an area where the policy we examine in this book (i.e., better regulation) intersects with the wider notion of 'quality of regulation'.

A few words are necessary on the dimensions selected for our study. They have been chosen following the solid experience of the OECD country reviews of regulatory reform. They are also the analytical backbone of the OECD recommendations on governments' capacity to deliver high-quality regulation. Further, the literature on policy evaluation has consistently highlighted that policy appraisal should tackle both activities and outcomes (Shadish *et al.*, 1991). Activities refer to what a programme being evaluated has done (e.g., money spent, resources employed, training). Outcomes refer to the impact of activities on society or the economy (e.g., whether a programme has improved the business environment or not).

We add institutional design to activity and outcome for three reasons. Firstly, the experience of regulatory reform has shown that getting institutions right is fundamental. Issues of institutional design dominate the political science literature on regulatory governance. As Majone (1999b: 309–10) put it:

> the new research no longer focuses exclusively on industry performance and first-order policy instruments, as much of the older literature did, but pays careful attention to institutional factors that affect both industry performance and the choice of policy tools.

Secondly, design is considered a key dimension by all OECD and EU reports on better regulation, as will be shown by the discussion below of their principles and vision. Thirdly, quality is sensitive to how operational and strategic management have been designed: who does what and when, what are the resources allocated to different tasks, and so on (Metcalfe, 2003).

Dimensions must be measurable to allow for their empirical analysis. In box 2.1 we link the dimensions to their measures, to show how indicators can be designed.

Turning to tools, better regulation policies contain several. In this book, we focus on the following four tools (see box 2.2):

- RIA;
- consultation;
- simplification;
- regulatory access and transparency.

Of course, there are other important tools, such as the systematic use of regulatory alternatives, tools to strengthen compliance and enforcement, and the mechanisms of administrative justice. We selected tools that are common in the experience of the OECD and the EU Member States.

This chapter next gives an overview of the policy discussion around principles of better regulation. These principles raise important questions

**Box 2.1 Dimensions of better regulation:
indicators of design, activity and outcome**

Design

This dimension shows how the institutions for better regulation policy have
been designed. Indicators of this dimension measure inputs into the regulatory decision rather than the quality of the final regulations. However, good
processes are highly correlated with good decisions. They identify variables
that governments can control and are more easily measured than outcome
indicators.

Activities and outputs

This dimension measures the level of effort made by governments to regulate
and improve regulatory quality. Some indicators of this dimension – the
number of pages of laws, for example – have been discredited as indicators
of regulatory quality, on the grounds that they are unreliable. Other performance indicators of administrative regulatory processes, such as the number of
consultations, investment in RIA and use of alternative instruments, can be
more useful in gauging the investment in quality control mechanisms.

Real-world outcomes

This is the dimension where better regulation and the concept of quality of
regulations intersect. It is difficult, but not impossible, to tap this dimension
via indicators. Real-world indicators need information on actual regulatory
impacts and most governments have scant information on these. Perceptions
of the regulated community can be useful in determining costs, but must be
handled very cautiously. Perceptions are relative to implicit benchmarks that
are not always clear. For example, perceptions of burdens usually become
worse when the government launches initiatives to reduce red tape, even if
the actual situation is improving, because the problem is higher profile and
easier for businesses to identify. Measures of compliance rates are rarely done
openly by governments because of the fear of political backlash if compliance is low. Measurement of the actual market effects of regulatory regimes
merits considerable thought: the innovativeness of the economy, the speed of
introducing new technologies, the level of investment in emerging sectors and
so forth could be useful in combination with other indicators.

about the nature of governance and therefore provide information on how
policy-makers think about regulatory governance. The following succinct
analysis of the academic debate – the detailed examination of indicators
being the topic of the next chapter – is useful to raise the question of
whether regulatory quality is a good point of departure, or, alternatively,
whether one should use the classic concept of efficiency. Our answer is that,
on balance, quality has more mileage than efficiency (with some limitations
and caveats).

Box 2.2 Tools of better regulation policy

Regulatory impact assessment (RIA)
RIA is a systematic process of identification of problems addressed and the objectives pursued. It identifies the main options for achieving the objective and analyses their likely impacts. It can be based on benefit–cost analysis, cost-effectiveness analysis, business impact analysis and other techniques.

Consultation
Consultation is the process of ascertaining the views and opinions of relevant experts, parties that would be affected by regulation and stakeholders. In RIA, it is also a means to ascertain the need for regulatory intervention and the likely costs and benefits arising out of different regulatory options.

Simplification
Administrative measures
These are measures that reduce administrative burdens (paperwork and informational requirements) imposed by governments on enterprises, citizens and the public sector. They include diverse instruments such as drafting in plain language, physical one-stop shops, simplification of licensing procedures, time limits established for decision-making, and the use of information technology to simplify dealings with administrations, such as e-government initiatives and web portals.

Non-administrative measures
These measures include, for example, review and improvement of the substance or legislative approach of existing regulation with the aim of reducing any regulatory burden imposed by governments on enterprises, citizens and the public sector. The reviews can be generalised, covering the entire body of the regulation, or more specific, concentrating on a type of regulation or sector.

Access and transparency
Access can be improved by practical arrangements (especially using information and communication technology). Transparency can involve programmes aimed at improving the understanding and use of European and national regulation. This leads to coherence and clarity of regulations.

Having established this, we take issue with the notion, prevailing in policy-makers' circles (examined in detail by Radaelli, 2004), that the quality of better regulation policy can be defined unequivocally and measured via decontextualised indicators. The convergence on principles of better regulation – we argue – has led to the false impression that quality is a one-size-fits-all entity. This obfuscates important differences between regulatory regimes and styles of regulation.[1] Institutional design, the capacity to deal with distributional problems, heterogeneity in multi-level governance systems, policy styles and the 'weights' given to the preferences of different actors explain how the institutional context shapes the different pathways to quality pursued by governments and international organisations.

Principles of regulatory quality: governments and international organisations

Quality is defined by principles. Several OECD countries and the EU are committed to sets of principles contained in their main policy documents on regulatory reform. Interestingly, more often than not the principles of better regulation are considered principles of regulatory quality *tout court*. At the conceptual level, this is a neglect of the difference between meta-regulation and the other dimensions of regulatory governance. At the political level, however, this is the clearest manifestation of how better regulation has become pivotal in the agenda of regulatory reform.

In Australia, the Productivity Commission (Argy and Johnson, 2003) defines high-quality regulation as effective and efficient. Effective means that regulation achieves a range of objectives without creating unnecessary burdens on business and citizens. Efficient means that regulation provides the greatest net benefit to the community. It follows that high-quality regulation should be:

- the minimum necessary to achieve objectives, with minimum compliance burden;
- not unduly prescriptive;
- integrated and consistent with other regulations;
- accessible;
- transparent;
- accountable;
- enforceable;
- communicated effectively.

In Canada, the guide *Assessing Regulatory Alternatives* (Government of Canada, 1994) makes a distinction between different types of principles, such as practical principles and more strategic principles. The 'best regulatory system' is – according to the Canadian government (see Treasury Board of Canada, 1996) – one that:

- respects legal and constitutional requirements;
- gives the most regulatory protection at the least cost to both the private sector and the government;
- promotes a culture of openness and accountability;

- enacts regulations based on input from stakeholders;
- is user friendly, accessible and understandable;
- is continuously updated and improved.

Turning to Europe, the UK has defined principles of better regulation. The Better Regulation Task Force (2003), the champion of better regulation operating at arm's length from the executive, but with the full support of the prime minister (see chapter 4), has adopted the following principles:

- proportionality;
- accountability;
- consistency;
- transparency;
- targeting.

When regulation is proportionate, the government intervenes only when necessary and with measures which are appropriate to the risk. Accountability goes beyond the idea of providing justification for action: it also includes a commitment to public scrutiny. Consistent regulation provides a set of rules and standards that are joined up and implemented fairly. Transparency is a principle of openness. It covers both the process by which regulations are produced (e.g., systematic consultation, regulatory agendas, formulation of transparent standards for the use of scientific advice in the policy-making process) and the quality of regulations (opaque regulations that are difficult to find produce high compliance costs). Finally, targeting refers to regulations that are focused on the problem and – as the Better Regulation Task Force explains – 'minimise side effects'.

This short description of the principles used in the UK is indicative of how principles inform the choice of tools and affect measurement. To illustrate, transparency and targeting suggest minimum standards for consultation, guidelines for the use of scientific advice and RIA. In terms of measurement, they lead to indicators on effective consultation and the consideration of adverse effects in the formulation of RIA.

In some countries, such as Canada and New Zealand, the commitment to principles of better regulation is strengthened by the systematic implementation of the ISO 9000 approach. ISO 9000 is a set of quality assurance standards created in order to facilitate international trade (Johnson, 2000: 6). Through accurate guidelines, ISO 9000 addresses every stage related to the process that creates products and services: from implementing auditing techniques to developing quality manuals. In Canada, departments follow self-assessment checklists based on ISO 9000. The checklists require the department to report on the analysis of regulatory proposals. The regulatory process is also monitored by the Privy Council Office. In New Zealand, ISO 9000 has informed the policy-makers' thinking about the 'sound regulatory process'. The process is broken down into five stages: strategy, tactical steps, operations, legislation, and implementation and review. Each stage is covered by a dedicated 'quality assurance' checklist.

'Quality management is both a technical subject and a behavioural subject' (Hoyle, 2000: 31): every organisation is created by people. Their behaviour shapes the culture within the organisation itself. Organisational culture is 'shaped by the core values expressed by the management'. In consequence, 'quality results not only from using the right tools, the right processes etc. but also approaching the task with the right attitude' (Hoyle, 2000: 31). The implication for the measurement of regulatory performance is straightforward. When looking at real-world outcomes, one should focus both on classic economic outcomes, such as the growth of gross domestic product (GDP), and, most importantly perhaps, on the change in the behaviour of policy-makers. Indeed, one of the main goals of better regulation is to change the culture of regulators.

Turning to international organisations, the OECD defined better regulation in 1997 on the basis of the following principles: regulations should be necessary, efficient, effective, transparent and geared towards the public interest (OECD, 1997a: 193). The 1997 OECD study on regulation (OECD, 1997a) is innovative in two major ways. On the one hand, it extends the checklist approach to the identification of specific characteristics of the regulatory process (such as legitimacy and openness). The link thus becomes the following:

Good practice → Standards → Checklists → Characteristics of the
                                              regulatory process

On the other hand, the OECD evolution from the generic idea of reforming regulation to 'regulatory governance' has been accompanied by an increasing attention to measurable standards and indicators. The implication is that measures of quality should refer explicitly to the wider objectives of good governance. The OECD draws attention to new quality issues such as bringing principles of regulation across levels of governance, the institutional interplay between governments and parliaments, and the need to bring together the economic and legal approaches to regulation.

The OECD's 2005 recommendations for regulatory quality and performance define the substance of better regulation policy and get very close to identifying quality with the presence of well functioning better regulation policies. Specifically, the OECD recommends the following (quoted from OECD, 2005: 3–8):

1 Adopt at the political level broad programmes of regulatory reform that establish clear objectives and frameworks for implementation.
2 Assess impacts and review regulations systematically to ensure that they meet their intended objectives efficiently and effectively in a changing and complex economic and social environment.

3 Ensure that regulations, regulatory institutions charged with implementation, and regulatory processes are transparent and non-discriminatory.
4 Review and strengthen where necessary the scope, effectiveness and enforcement of competition policy.
5 Design economic regulations in all sectors to stimulate competition and efficiency, and eliminate them except where clear evidence demonstrates that they are the best way to serve broad public interests.
6 Eliminate unnecessary regulatory barriers to trade and investment through continued liberalisation and enhance the consideration and better integration of market openness throughout the regulatory process, thus strengthening economic efficiency and competitiveness.
7 Identify important linkages with other policy objectives and develop policies to achieve those objectives in ways that support reform.

The World Bank is another international organisation which has been very active in the debate. In its *Doing Business in 2004 – Understanding Regulation*, the World Bank defines the principles of good regulation. According to the World Bank (2004a: 92), governments should regulate:

• 'only when private ordering or litigation are not sufficient to induce good conduct';
• 'only if there is capacity to enforce'.

Similar to the OECD vision, the approach of the World Bank insists on the link between high-quality regulation and wider principles of good governance. Another element of convergence is about the systematic use of indicators, although the indicators produced by these two organisations differ in some important respects, as will be shown in chapter 3.

In the EU, the better regulation vision is contained in the following documents: the white paper on governance (European Commission, 2001a); the Mandelkern (2001) report prepared for the Laeken summit of the European Council; the better regulation action plan of the Commission (European Commission, 2002a); and a report for the Hellenic Presidency of the Council of the EU (2003), which provided information on the implementation of the Mandelkern principles of better regulation. The Mandelkern report presents seven of these principles:

1 necessity;
2 proportionality;
3 subsidiarity;
4 transparency;
5 accountability;
6 accessibility;
7 simplicity.

The better regulation action plan of the Commission and the Mandelkern report make an explicit connection between the principles and tools of regulatory quality. The main tools are alternatives to regulation, RIA, consultation, simplification and access to regulation.

In the EU context, better regulation policy is not the exclusive task of one institution (such as the Commission) but involves institutions at different levels of governance. Since the early 1990s, the Commission has identified better regulation as a crucial policy for the single market and the EU goals for good governance (Radaelli, 1999). The white paper on governance (European Commission, 2001a) makes several references to the links between regulatory quality and good governance. In addition to principles such as efficiency, effectiveness, coherence, simplicity and clarity, 'good regulation' should also respect the standards for the revitalisation of the *acquis*, the guidelines for the democratic use of expertise and the minimum standards for consultation. In 2002 the Commission redesigned its major tool, that is, RIA. The new approach to RIA is unique in that it stresses the need to balance economic growth, employment and environmental protection. This is an ambitious goal, especially if one considers that the experience of several Member States is still confined to the analysis of administrative burdens (DBR, 2004; Radaelli, 2001; and chapters 4 and 5 in this volume).

The vision of the Commission is contained in its action plan for better regulation (European Commission, 2002a). The action plan lists the initiatives to be taken by the Commission and the initiatives suggested to Member States and other EU institutions – yet another example of the need to bring better regulation across levels of governance.

The academic debate: efficiency, quantity or quality of regulation?

Regulatory analysis is an interdisciplinary field, where economists, political scientists and lawyers contribute from various angles and with different methodological perspectives. At the cost of oversimplifying a rich debate, one can argue that economists would look at the efficiency of regulation rather than using the language of quality. Or, alternatively, they would claim that either regulatory quality boils down to efficiency or it is not a useful concept. In the economic analysis of regulation, efficiency has a broad meaning. Indeed, the benchmark for regulatory efficiency is the maximisation of economic welfare. It follows that regulatory quality is all about the economic impact of regulation. However, efficiency is only one component of regulatory governance. The other component is the quality of the process of rule formation and implementation. The notion of quality that we use covers both the efficiency of regulations and the quality of the *process* by which regulations are produced and enforced. Thus, fundamental elements of good regulatory governance (and therefore quality of better regulation) such as consultation and the democratic use of science are somewhat neglected in an approach limited to efficiency. In turn, this leads to the three dimensions of institutional design, activity and outcome.

It is not entirely clear whether economists are really interested in quality or quantity. Some of the classic studies on the efficiency of regulation, such as that by Koedijk and Kremers (1996), are based on the assumption that 'less regulation' is better than 'more regulation' in terms of its economic impact. This is a classic statement grounded in quantity, not quality. The concept of regulatory quality does not proceed from the assumption that regulated markets are bound to fail. Instead, it is grounded in the belief that quality regulation strengthens the business environment and the legitimacy of governmental action.

The point about legitimacy brings us to the discussion of quality provided by lawyers and political scientists. Baldwin and Cave (1999) make two important observations. Firstly, they note that the efficiency benchmark used by economists in their approach to quality should also be sensitive to distributional impacts. To illustrate: very rarely do real-world regulatory decisions provide an improvement in terms of Pareto efficiency. Usually, one person will gain and another will lose from regulation. Instruments such as RIA tend to become more political (as opposed to technical) when distributional issues are important. Hence the regulators cannot look at quality from the exclusive point of view of Pareto efficiency.

Secondly, Baldwin and Cave argue that quality should in any case be understood in terms of legitimacy. Efficiency is of course one possible legitimacy claim. But policy-makers use other legitimacy claims, such as respect of the legislative mandate and accountability. Their argument is that regulatory policy should be assessed by making claims about the value of five different possible sources of legitimacy: efficiency, the legislative mandate, accountability, due process, and how expertise is used in regulatory choices.

The five legitimacy claims bring the notion of regulatory quality closer to the principles of better regulation reviewed in the first part of this chapter. The conclusion is that one should not confuse quality with efficiency, nor should one confine legitimacy to efficiency. A proper legitimacy test of the quality of regulation would include items that cannot be captured by efficiency. And, indeed, the principles previously reviewed place great emphasis on fair consultation, openness of the regulatory process, transparency and accountability. These principles are not captured by efficiency. Thus, the upshot of this discussion reinforces the argument that quality concerns both the real-world impact of regulation and the quality of the process through which regulations are produced, assessed and implemented.

Finally, the academic discussion has raised questions about the relationship between quality and the general principles of better regulation. So far we have assumed that principles lead to quality. This is conceptually correct, but, looking at real-world regulation instead of concepts, do the principles adopted by governments really produce better regulation? In a provocative article, Baldwin *et al.* (2000) make the argument that principles may not help much. They show that even regulations that are unanimously considered of low quality could have passed the test of the principles set by the Better Regulation Task Force (2003) in the UK. They argue that it is more important to evaluate systematically the results achieved by regulation and to steer effective implementation than to rely on keywords and principles. For the purposes of this volume, the message is that principles define the meaning of quality, but process, robust networks of stakeholders and, for the reasons we will explain in chapter 7, indicators are indispensable.

So, does the notion of quality of better regulation have some mileage? Regulatory quality is a complex notion. As shown in the previous chapter, it is conceptually and historically distinct from the 'liberalisation plus deregulation' agenda. It is focused on regulatory management rather than regulatory reform. Regulatory quality as a new policy agenda stands in stark contrast to the poor achievements of the regulatory state, such as hyper-regulatory trends and colonisation of civil society in the UK (Moran, 2003). Thus, it is not complacent with regard to the status quo.

In the context of better regulation policies, quality is neutral to the scope and size of public intervention (OECD, 1997a: 193). High-quality regulation does not mean 'low levels of regulation' but rather regulation that is proportionate, targeted, efficient, accessible and transparent. This locates the agenda of regulatory reform in a context that is compatible with different political agendas. The question is not one of 'small' versus 'big' government.

There are also limitations to the concept of regulatory quality. Firstly, the notion is a bit fuzzy and sometimes it seems that regulatory quality is nothing but a set of principles and tools – no matter what the institutional and historical contexts are. The difference between better regulation policy and regulatory quality is often neglected. Further, it is not clear what the normative emphasis on *better* regulation leads to. This is why the OECD has often opted for the more neutral phrase 'policies that increase the capability of governments to produce high quality regulation' – with the complication that then one has to be specific about what 'high quality regulation' means. Another problem is that the rise of better regulation may have crowded out other possible and perhaps more effective options for reform. Is the better regulation policy a Procrustean bed, in that policy instruments that fall outside the range of typical better regulation tools are neglected? There may be a danger that the tools of better regulation gather too much importance and occupy an excessive space in the agenda of governments. By contrast, fundamental issues of quality of governance, such as deliberation and participatory governance (Grote and Gbikpi, 2002), may not be captured adequately in the rigid list of principles and tools currently fashionable in the EU and the OECD.

Principles are useful to get rid of the fuzziness, and perform the important function of signalling political commitment, but they do not explain how to achieve quality. The lesson provided by international experience is that, in order to achieve quality, one has to place principles in the context of the history and dynamics of regulatory reforms in different countries. Context matters to a large extent in programmes for better regulation. Similar principles may obfuscate the basic fact that two countries may pursue regulatory reform as a solution to very different problems (as shown by Radaelli, 2004).

Entering complexity

Although the current debate shows some convergence around concepts, definitions and tools, it is useful to acknowledge the complexity of quality up front. To acknowledge complexity has important implications for measurement and the construction of indicators. Quality is not a monolithic term – we argue. Different actors or 'stakeholders'[2] 'see' quality through the lens of their own particular preferences. Further, quality is sensitive to the institutional context. Institutional analysis of various types (Hall and Taylor, 1996; Weaver and Rockman, 1993) has persuasively demonstrated that political context matters – especially in the historical-institutionalist version (Steinmo *et al.*, 1992). Drawing on 'new institutionalism' in political science, one can reason that institutions play a role with respect to how better regulation is embedded in policy processes, the approach to meta-regulation, which actors are in a pivotal position in policy formulation, and the concepts of regulatory legitimacy that dominate in each country. Specifically:

- Institutional theories (Hall and Taylor, 1996; Weaver and Rockman, 1993) predict that institutions shape the behaviour of actors and the use of policy tools. The key variables are the bureaucratic context and government's capacity to deal with distributional conflict.
- In the original approach (see the historical overview provided by the OECD, 1997a, 1997b), the tools of better regulation were supposed to work in a rational, orderly policy process where problems are defined, alternative solutions are probed and decisions are finally taken by unitary actors. However, theories of the policy process (Sabatier, 1999) provide a continuum from rational-synoptic models to 'garbage cans', where solutions, actors and problems are somewhat independent and constantly modified. Between these two extremes, one can find cases of limited structuration of the policy process – as shown by Lindblom's partisan mutual adjustment (Lindblom, 1959; Lindblom and Woodhouse, 1993), Sabatier's advocacy coalitions framework (Sabatier, 1999: ch. 6) and Kingdon's multiple streams model (Kingdon, 1984; Zahariadis, 1999).
- Politico-economic models and pressure group theory (Bernauer and Caduff, 2004) suggest that different actors will try to use better regulation for their own goals. For the politician, tools such as consultation and RIA have to deliver in terms of consensus and political rents. For bureaucrats, 'high quality' means respecting formal procedures that

define the legitimate activities of the civil service. For the citizen, the test of better regulation is its real-world outcome (whether it produces regulation that delivers a high level of protection and enables the citizen to carry on with socio-economic activities without dissipating the economic and environmental resources of the community). For the firm, different approaches stipulate that companies will try to secure either regulation that protects them from new entrants and guarantees rents, or regulation fostering a better business environment.

• Finally, the literature on regulatory legitimacy (Majone, 1996: ch. 13) suggests that the Achilles' heel of better regulation policies is legitimacy. When policy tools lack credibility, they become at best bureaucratic tick-the-box routines, and at worst they are highly contested. The legitimacy of better regulation policies may also be connected to risk cultures. In some countries, the legitimacy of science and rationality makes cost–benefit analysis more acceptable than in countries where the culture of risk regulation is not grounded in evidence-based policy.

The official rhetoric about better regulation and the 'celebration' of its major tool, that is, RIA, may give the false impression that better regulation has now become a fairly common policy with relatively standardised properties across countries. True, there has been diffusion. But the process is one of diffusion more than convergence. In political science, it is common to distinguish between 'policy diffusion' (in which the analytical focus is on the process of international diffusion of policy ideas and the dependent variable is the pattern of adoption of the same policy across countries) and 'policy convergence' (focused on the effects of diffusion and with similarity or lack of it as the dependent variable). The polemical target of our analysis is the 'one size fits all', decontextualised approach to better regulation policy. Our approach is critical of the dominant discourse in policy-maker circles that better regulation policy can be designed (and its quality measured) in a decontextualised manner by using checklists and benchmarking tools. Our main theoretical underpinning is neo-institutional analysis. Let us then look at how political context matters by breaking it down into different dimensions, well known to neo-institutional analysis. We present below the following dimensions: the bureaucratic context, the capacity of governments to handle conflict and the structure of the policy process. We then go back to the preferences of actors and how they play a role in institutional contexts.

Bureaucracies and better regulation

In its original institutional context – that is, the USA (see Hahn and Litan, 2004) – better regulation tools are managed by independent regulatory agencies monitored by the Office of Management and Budget via the Office of Information and Regulatory Affairs (OIRA). This is a regulatory context characterised by delegation of regulatory powers to non-majoritarian institutions. The institutional context is based on sector-level, specialised policy-making. Tools such as RIA and consultation are instruments for a discussion at the level of sectoral policy networks (environment, health and safety, food regulation, etc.). The legitimacy of the regulatory process is not based on parliamentary control of government but on the credibility of executive agencies. The bureaucratic context is one in which agencies and the OIRA are well staffed in terms of professional economists. The dominant criterion is efficiency and the main logic is technical. Negotiation and standard operating procedures are not absent, but they are not overwhelming. Indeed, when negotiation among agencies, regulated firms and committees in Congress has historically become the dominant logic, this has been seen as a pathology of the system – and referred to as 'agency capture'.

In the EU's Member States, the bureaucratic contexts are quite different. Better regulation tools are still used for technical discussions at the level of sectoral policy networks but, most importantly, they are also used for communication purposes – between the government and the parliament, and between the government and affected interests. The 'regulator' performing simplification, RIA, consultation and so on is generally not an independent agency but a minister reporting to the executive or the prime minister. Most independent regulators in Europe have not even been requested to perform RIA. Only very recently did countries like the UK introduce RIA as a duty of independent economic regulators.

The bureaucratic context of the Member States varies. But in several cases it is a context characterised by generalist civil servants or bureaucrats trained in public law. Efficiency still comes second to formal respect of legitimate procedures in the list of criteria used by bureaucracies in countries like Austria, France, Germany and Italy. Almost invariably, the civil servants 'read' RIA and other tools in terms of formal (as opposed to substantial) legal logic and conformity to other rules and processes. Not only does the logic of negotiation dominate the behaviour of ministers engaged in RIA but it also characterises the interactions between public administration and pressure groups, and between civil servants and politicians (with the minister, for example, and her or his cabinets).

The capacity of governments

The capacity of institutions to handle conflict is also decisive. The more distributional problems play an important role, the more regulatory choice becomes political because it goes beyond Pareto optimisation. True, distributional weights can be used to address these problems in a transparent manner. But the political problem simply shifts to the issue of who sets the weights and how, and why the process should be considered legitimate by all stakeholders.

EU Member States have different capacities to deal with distributional problems, depending on whether they are majoritarian or consensual political systems (Lijphart, 1984) or, to use Schmidt's typology, simple or compound democracies (Schmidt, 2002). In majoritarian democracies like the UK, better regulation policy is used by the core executive to coordinate policy. As such, it becomes a component of the discourse within the executive. Schmidt has shown that this discourse is relatively 'thin' in terms of actors and negotiations – hence there are not many distributional problems. The minister draws on RIA to show that the policy choice is being made in the common interest and that the benefits justify the costs. Distributional conflicts kick in when better regulation is 'used' outside the executive, in the context of the overall broad argumentation used by the government to persuade the parliament, the affected interests and the public.

In consensus democracies like Denmark, policy formulation is multi-actor and 'thick'. Accordingly, socio-economic and governmental elites draw on better regulation tools to define the content of policy. Consultation is part of the wider coordinative discourse, that is, the set of interactions through which elites assign a shared meaning to what they are doing. Distributional problems are addressed directly at the stage of policy formulation. It is at this stage that the various checklists and partial estimates of costs and benefits are used (by civil servants, ministers, economic elites and unions) to articulate a discourse leading to the formulation of regulatory proposals. This is where most of the conflicts arising out of the distributional impact of regulation are settled. Accordingly, RIA provides different partial estimates that are available to the stakeholders for the coordination of discourse and negotiation before proposed rules are adopted by the government. There is not much evidence of large debates on better regulation and its distributional effects at the level of public opinion.

The policy processes

Institutions provide the riverbeds for policy processes.[3] What are the assumptions behind the process that is being subject to meta-regulation? One way of looking at meta-regulation is to assume that there is a policy process with unitary actors and limited information gaps – a model close to the pole of rational-synoptic policy-making mentioned above. In this model, policy decisions are based on the systematic use of empirical evidence. Quality is measured in terms of sound, unbiased economic analysis of regulation. Some of the early ideas about RIA in countries like the USA were informed by this implicit notion of the policy process. Consequently, all meta-regulation was supposed to do was to provide information to the decision-makers and support more efficient decision-making. The disillusionment with this model has been great (Owens *et al.*, 2004).

The rational-synoptic model breaks down under conditions of bounded rationality and policy controversies where actors conflict over problem definition and filter the same evidence through radically different cognitive 'frames'. Additionally, it is almost impossible to draw systematically on empirical evidence in 'garbage can' policy processes, where problems are constantly reformulated by different political actors, solutions are changed frequently and the competences of different departments are reshuffled or unclear.

Let us illustrate some examples from the EU's Member States, focusing on RIA. In countries like Germany and Italy, the regulatory process is highly fragmented, with multiple points of contact between politics and administration, and between different logics and criteria. The Italians have formally adopted RIA, including specific rules on how and when it should be performed, but cannot use it in the ordinary formulation of policy. The problem is the clash between a rather chaotic process of formulation of new legislation (different ministers respond to their political parties more than to the prime minister and often table proposals for new legislation that are not contemplated in the coalition agreement) and an idealistic rational-synoptic process portrayed in the official written guidance on RIA.

In France, the nature of the policy process matters in a different manner. In comparison with Italy, there is more coordination at the level of the executive and consequently more coherence at the level of policy formulation. But coordination and coherence are achieved politically. Once political agreement has been achieved, RIA is undertaken (in a few cases and not systematically) in haste and superficially, to legitimise choices that have already been taken. Therefore RIA plays a post-decisional role, rather than informing the decision-making process.

In the UK, the annual reports of the National Audit Office (NAO) show that RIA is associated with different policy processes. The 2005 NAO report shows various 'types' of RIA in the British political system. In some regulatory processes, when the political pressure to reach one specific decision is high, RIA is used in a post-decisional mode to justify a political choice. The fact that RIA was produced according to high or low standards of economic analysis does not affect the final choice made by the government.

In other cases in the UK, RIA starts early, when more than one option is still available politically, collects evidence from a variety of sources, including the stakeholders, and engages those who will take the final decision. Put differently, the timing of assessment and political decisions are well integrated. This is a rather exceptional circumstance. Not only may politicians be tempted to decide quickly to respond to public opinion but they may also have already agreed to introduce policy rules in their electoral manifesto, or they may have already instructed commissions of enquiry and produced white papers which backdate the start of a given RIA. Finally, the NAO (2005) notes that there are still cases of a bureaucratic 'tick the box' attitude to RIA, in which the main goal is to fill in the forms rather than to learn from evidence and explore alternatives to traditional regulation.

These findings show that not only does policy formulation vary across nations but that even within a single country one can find different types of RIA. The more general implication is that the results achieved with better regulation tools are contingent on the type of policy process in which they operate. There are cases in which the process described in the official guides is rational-synoptic and entirely evidence-based but where decisions are in fact taken in a 'garbage can' fashion or on political grounds. The clash leads to the non-use of RIA or to its post-decisional use. Even when the description provided by the official guide to RIA is not too different from the reality of decision-making, the NAO report shows that there may be obstacles to the proper use of RIA, depending on regulatory sectors, departments in charge of policy and the vicissitudes of policy formulation.

Better regulation for whom?

Institutions provide differential empowerment of actors. As the logic, preferences and criteria used by the actors involved in policy formulation are not the same, different institutional contexts explain the variability in terms of who is 'in charge' of RIA across countries and how the notion of regulatory quality is approached.

Drawing on a classic study of decision-making in international politics – Allison's *Essence of Decision* (1971) – Farrow and Copeland (2003) argue that better regulation can be interpreted in three different (yet not mutually exclusive) ways. They argue that there are at least three 'stakeholders' (as mentioned, political scientists would prefer to stick to 'actors'), namely the 'expert', the 'civil servant' and the 'politician'. It is useful to add a fourth important 'stakeholder', the 'citizen'. And, finally, we enter the 'corporation' (more precisely, the firm at the micro level and business organisations at a more aggregate level).

Different actors bring into better regulation policy diverse logics, criteria and quality assurance mechanisms. More fundamentally, better regulation policies across the EU 'weigh' actors' preferences differently. This is the result of institutional settings and more specific characteristics of the adoption process. Let us first examine the different actors in terms of criteria, logic and definition of 'successful' meta-regulation, and then move on to illustrate divergence and how institutions and the adoption process explain it.

To begin with, one may legitimately question whether meta-regulation in a given country is based on the assumption that politicians are rent-seeking (and if so, should better regulation target this problem and empower Weberian civil servants?). Or does better regulation policy make the implicit assumption that policy-makers regulate in the public interest, for example because they want to be re-elected and good-quality regulation may increase their popularity? To what extent do the preferences of independent agencies differ from the preferences of elected officials and with what impact on the efficiency and credibility of RIA?

The literature on the political economy of regulation is vast. One finding is that although elected regulators respond to pressure groups and re-election incentives, they are also driven by their own ideological preferences (Kalt and Zupan, 1984). Turning to agencies, in an analysis of decisions made by the US Environmental Protection Agency, Cropper *et al.* (1992) show that regulators take into account both private interests and diffuse interests (such as the general welfare of the community) when they set environmental standards.

These results come with several qualifications. But in any case, without a model that specifies the preferences of policy-makers (be they politicians or civil servants) it is impossible to say what meta-regulation should do. A 'good design' means different things depending on whether one makes the assumption that civil servants have a preference for regulatory expansion, or are captured by powerful pressure groups, or regulate in the public interest.

Other questions arise from models of the firm in regulatory policy. What do corporate actors want from regulation? Do they seek efficiency or protection? Indeed, the literature suggests very different approaches to the preferences of firms:

- In the public interest theory of regulation, regulators provide rules for the common good and therefore firms should not be necessarily hostile to regulation. One may expect that regulators acting for the common good care about quality.
- In positive political economy, however, firms seek regulation as a shelter from competition and new entrants. They try to capture regulators and secure protection. The implication is that dominant companies in a sector would prefer 'low quality', inefficient regulation. A classic paper by Buchanan and Tullock (1975) shows that companies prefer inefficient direct regulation to cost-effective instruments such as environmental taxes because quotas that restrict entry to a market originate scarcity rents.
- In some modern forms of regulatory theories, high levels of environmental and health and safety protection can be a comparative advantage in open markets. Firms may form coalitions with green groups and press for high levels of protection (Vogel, 1995). Using different arguments, Porter (1990) suggests that regulation can stimulate innovation and produce competitiveness. One should therefore expect that competitive firms support this type of regulation, whereas marginal firms object to it.
- Finally, another strand of regulatory analysis, this time more focused on empirical studies, has reached the conclusion that the locational choices of companies are not systematically influenced by the presence or absence of high labour and environmental standards (Jaffe *et al.*, 1995). This

conclusion has been attacked by those who claim that 'good regulatory governance matters' in terms of productivity, better regulatory environment and ultimately growth (Kaufmann *et al.*, 2003, 2005).

The problem is compounded by the fact that firms differ in size, sector and exposure to international trade. Recent models of the firm in regulatory policy break down the notion of the corporate sector as a unitary actor and show how different companies join different coalitions in the regulatory game (Bernauer and Caduff, 2004).

The result is that one has to clarify the issue 'better regulation for whom' before one can design meta-regulation and measure its quality with indicators and benchmarking tools. Moreover, the criteria used to evaluate success differ markedly between actors (table 2.1). Let us illustrate this with a simple five-actor approach. Imagine that one can settle the issue of the models of actors by deciding that experts are neutral and rational actors, bureaucrats are all Weberian civil servants, politicians are best described by public choice theory, citizens are attentive and want to participate, and the firm's utility function does not deviate too much from the neo-classical model (this means that profit maximisation is the overriding goal, but we do not say whether firms want to reach it via protectionist regulation or via a reduction of red tape). Consequently, one can reason that:

- The economist (the classic 'expert') is concerned about efficiency.
- The civil servant approaches better regulation policy by following proper and legitimate procedures in the regulatory process. This actor will use conformity to rules as the main criterion.
- For the politician, better regulation policy may well mean responsiveness to pressure groups, or the median voter, or even responsiveness to external pressure created by the EU, the International Monetary Fund and so on. Let us assume that for the politician quality is evaluated in terms of the outcome of negotiations.
- The firm perceives the opportunities of meta-regulation (especially in tools like simplification and RIA) in terms of minimisation of costs and defines success of better regulation policies in terms of the firm's bottom line, that is, profit.
- The citizens use yet another criterion, effective protection from risk.

The criteria used to establish whether meta-regulation is good or bad vary considerably. They are not necessarily mutually exclusive, though. While proper and legitimate procedures may result in efficient and fair regulation, one cannot establish a mechanical equivalence of every criterion used by different stakeholders. The idea that better regulation should be approached and evaluated only in terms of the quality of its economic analysis is based on institutions and policy processes that give a weight of 100 per cent to one actor, that is, the expert. This looks more like a technocratic dystopia than

Table 2.1 How different stakeholders look at better regulation

	Expert	Civil servant	Politician	Firm	Citizen
Criteria used to evaluate policy	Efficiency	Conformity to rules	Consensus	Cost minimisation	Cost-effective protection from risk
Meaning of quality	Achieving goals in terms of real-world impact	Following legitimate procedures	Outcome of negotiation	Profit	Enabling regulation
Logic of action	Social sciences	Standard operating procedures	Negotiation	Logic of influence	Participation

a realistic description of how actors' preferences are weighted by real-world better regulation programmes.

The logic of action is also different. The civil servant follows the logic of standard operating procedures, the politician uses negotiation and the expert draws on the logic of the social sciences. The citizen's behaviour, instead, is informed by the logic of participation. Finally, the firm draws on the logic of influence. Interestingly, a survey on the 'ideal regulatory system' conducted with different group of experts in the USA has shown variability in what this concept is taken to mean, including 'adaptive', 'democratic', 'efficient', 'equitable', 'scientifically sound' – with an obvious preference, considering the sample, for the last item (Brown *et al.*, 2004).

Institutions provide an opportunity structure which empowers actors differently. Depending on the constellation of logics and criteria, and on the stakeholders in charge of the policy process, better regulation policies pursue different goals. In a context where the logic of formal respect of procedures predominates, a tool like RIA is performed by governmental departments to show how the various steps in policy formulation were handled. If the context is also one of administrative cooperation, RIA is additionally shaped by inter-administrative cooperation. It is a tool that enables different departments to manage cooperation (this is to some extent the case in Denmark and the Netherlands). Contrast this with the Westminster model of the UK, where the Cabinet Office is in charge of RIA and communicates directly with departments about the content. In this case the logic is more 'vertical' than 'horizontal'.

Beyond public administration, the real issue is the institutional effects on policy styles and their persistence (Unger and van Waarden, 1995). A prevailing corporatist style has shaped the Danish approach, where RIA is used by policy-makers in a governance mode that is more 'negotiation' than 'technical analysis of options'. In Italy, where unions and employers' federations were involved in the formulation of policy for most of the 1990s, the initial steps towards the adoption of RIA were marked by an emphasis on consultation and participation of the affected interests.

However, institutional variables (consensus versus majoritarian models) do not tell the entire story. Different governments in the same country try to steer RIA in one political direction or another. Consequently, the constellation of dominant actors in better regulation changes over time. The early approach of the UK (a programme for compliance cost assessment introduced by the Conservative governments in the 1980s) was based on the assumptions that regulatory reform is the solution to the problem of excessive bureaucratic power, that firms are too often excluded from the regulatory process and do not seek protectionist rules, and that policy-makers do not regulate in the public interest but seek bureaucratic expansion. The adoption of new regulatory tools was therefore a component of a political effort to rebalance power in policy-making processes and provide more political opportunities to the business community. With the first Blair government, the opportunity structure for actors involved in RIA changed, with no privileged position granted to corporate actors and an emphasis on a balanced approach to the assessment of a wide spectrum of costs and benefits. Recent changes in the UK, with the emphasis on administrative burdens, seem to be swinging the pendulum back towards the business community.

In the 1990s, the adoption of better regulation tools in the Netherlands was the solution to the problem of a regulatory process dominated by 'corporatist triangles' (of policy-makers, employers' organisations and unions). The assumptions were that the regulatory process was not open enough to diffuse interests, that policy-makers tended to coalesce with powerful pressure groups to the detriment of the public interest, and that without a deliberate effort to open up the process (via consultation and RIA) the formulation of regulations would become an opaque, unaccountable process. Hence better regulation was used by the government to alter the opportunity structure and to provide more power to diffuse interests.

Conclusions

Policy elites may well speak the same language of better regulation, but the content of policy still differs where the institutional context is different. The regulatory systems of the EU have not yet converged, and better regulation policy is no exception to the trend. Therefore, the quality of better regulation policy cannot be measured in a decontextualised manner. We need first to go back to why a government is pursuing better regulation policy, and then ask questions about who is going to be empowered and how. Although there is convergence on the need to prioritise quality and on the tools to achieve it, context, different constellations of actors and diverse assumptions about what stakeholders want steer better regulation in more than one direction. The implication for measurement and the use of indicators is straightforward. Systems of indicators should not be designed according to one abstract notion of quality. One should account for the specific context. It should also be clear whether they measure the quality of better regulation policy or the quality of regulations produced via better regulation processes, and indicate where the two interact.

We mentioned but did not explore issues of credibility and legitimacy. Accurate economic analysis will obviously offer credibility to better regulation, but it should present the decision-makers with some important issues *they* have to address. The discourse in policy circles has emphasised the importance of good economic analysis. But regulatory quality is achieved only when better regulation tools are embedded in the wider regulatory policy process. Better regulation tools may be said to be 'embedded' when they change the way regulators think about public policy and inform ministerial decisions; they are embedded when they change the way stakeholders – organised interests, firms and citizens – engage in the policy-making process, and when they understand and consider legitimate the regulatory framework. We operationalise our definition by using indicators, presented in chapter 7. Before we analyse our own indicators, we need to discuss the literature on this topic, the experience of governments and the EU, and our own findings on quality measures in Europe. These are the topics of the next chapters.

Notes

1 See Vogel (1986) on the concept of regulatory style.
2 Although we prefer the concept of 'actor' (as defined in economics and political science) to the fuzzier notion of 'stakeholder', the literature on better regulation makes extensive use of the term 'stakeholders' to include those who may not participate in the formulation of regulation but who should nevertheless be considered because they are affected by rules. Occasionally, we will use 'stakeholders' to refer both to both policy-makers and policy-takers of regulatory policy. In this case, however, we need to clarify that information about how stakeholders behave is provided by models of 'actors' in the classic sense of political science and political economy, that is, ideal types (individual or collective) with a common, specific set of preferences.
3 The metaphor of institutions as riverbeds appears in Mucciaroni (1992: 466).

3

How indicators perform:
a review of the literature

Introduction

One of the characteristic features of better regulation policies is the pivotal role assigned to institutions. Indeed, as mentioned in chapter 2, the whole intellectual agenda of regulatory analysis in law, economics and political science has moved from a focus on economic variables to institutional analysis (Majone, 1999b: 309–10). The institutional turn is reflected in the attention paid by international organisations such as the World Bank to the institutional factors behind development and economic growth. Property rights, contracts, the rule of law and the design of institutions in charge of the regulatory process have become prominent in the World Bank's own understanding of how development works.

International organisations have linked regulatory quality to the broader concept of governance (Conway *et al.*, 2005; Kaufmann *et al.*, 2003, 2005; Nicoletti *et al.*, 2000; World Bank, 2004a, 2005). The Index of Economic Freedom (IEF) computed on an annual basis by the US Heritage Foundation[1] is yet another attempt to link regulation to other dimensions of governance. 'Good governance matters' is not only a slogan used successfully by international organisations – it is also a manifestation of the interest in how institutional design, governance mechanisms and the quality of the regulatory process affect economic outcomes.

In this context, the institutional turn has fed back into economic analysis, by spawning new research on the relationship between quality of governance, regulatory policies and economic growth. This is a complex relationship, both theoretically and empirically. One way to reduce this complexity is to rely on sets of indicators. The World Bank has done much of the pioneering work in this area. The first generation of World Bank indicators were related either to political instability, usually measured by variables such as the number of revolutions, coups and assassinations within a given period, or the efficiency of property rights and contract enforcement. More recently, measures of the quality of governance have become an important aspect of the indicators used by the World Bank to decide on lending allocations and by the OECD to assess the capacity of governments to deliver high-quality regulation. This chapter looks at the state of the art in the area of indicators of regulatory quality. As mentioned, regulatory quality is just one of the dimensions of governance, and it is important to distinguish a part from the whole. However, the importance of regulatory quality indicators has increased. The EU institutions and several Member States have made public statements on the role of indicators in their better regulation policies – thus creating momentum for indicators of regulatory quality in Europe. In the academic camp, there is a relative long tradition of measures of quality of regulation. We review here both the progress made by international organisations and the work of academics, with the caveat that there are several connections between the two.

We start with economic studies that rely on statistical analysis and propose systems to aggregate indicators of regulatory quality into an overall index. For each of these studies, we provide a short summary – explaining the general context and background, the methodology, the main findings and conclusions – and an assessment of their advantages and limitations, bearing in mind the main purpose of this book: to design both indicators and a process in which they can be used. Consequently, we make remarks on how indicators are used or can be used by policy-makers and for what purposes.

A final remark before we start: as explained in chapter 2, regulatory quality is not limited to better regulation policy. In consequence, in this chapter we chart the debate on indicators of regulatory quality – a debate that includes better regulation policy but often goes beyond that. This is useful because it enables us to show the connections between the specific policy we deal with in the rest of the book and other important dimensions of regulation.

Capturing regulatory complexity via composite measures

Composite measures are based on the aggregation of individual variables. For example, the quality of labour market regulation can be measured by a broad set of variables, such as flexibility and employability. A composite measure would capture the overall quality of labour market regulation in one index.

Measures can be classified according to two dimensions: the source of the data and the type of use. The first dimension is related to the characteristics of the primary data on which studies rely. Their source can be either objective (such as an analysis or observation of facts) or subjective (such as a survey of citizens and businesses on the perception of regulatory quality). Typically, subjective measures are constructed by elaborating the responses to questionnaires. The most popular form of questionnaire for subjective measures is the survey of business views and perceptions of regulation. The Business Environment and Enterprise Performance Survey, developed jointly by the World Bank and the European Bank for Reconstruction and Development, is a survey of over 4,000 firms in twenty-two transition countries conducted in 1999–2000. Indicators based on the perceptions of experts are common. An example is the Economic Freedom of the World index, published by the Canadian Fraser Institute, which aggregates the results of polls of experts. Very rarely have studies covered citizens' views; one exception is the International Social Survey Programme and the Beliefs in Government study (Kaase and Newton, 1998), which measured citizens' opinions and beliefs on the role of government in economic regulation.

The second dimension looks at the use of the primary data. Basically, the difference is between a neutral approach to data and a more subjective approach. Some studies rely on aggregation techniques and methods of data analysis that may be considered 'neutral', where personal judgements do not feature. Others contain weights and methods of data analysis that reflect personal judgement of the importance of a particular aspect of regulatory quality, for example aggregation conducted through weighted averages. Table 3.1 illustrates the main studies according to these dimensions (and table 3.5, at the end of the chapter, provides a summary of the studies discussed below).

Table 3.1 Classification of the main studies with composite measures

	Source of data	
	Subjective	*Objective*
Use of data		
Subjective	Pryor (2002a, 2002b)	Koedijk and Kremers (1996) Conway *et al.* (2005) on OECD data
Objective	Kaufmann *et al.* (2003, 2005) on World Bank data	Knack and Kugler (2002) Goff (1996) Djankov *et al.* (2001) Botero *et al.* (2003)

Quality measures based on subjective sources of data
As mentioned, most composite measures and indexes of regulatory quality produced by economists use perceptions of stakeholders, especially (but not exclusively) business. Pryor (2002a, 2002b) and Kaufmann *et al.* (2003, 2005) have conducted the most important research in this context. Whereas Pryor works on indicators of firms' perceptions, Kaufmann and his associates cover perceptions of a wide spectrum of regulatory stakeholders, including firms, experts and citizens. In doing so, they address the issue of multiple views of regulatory quality introduced in chapter 2. Both Pryor and Kaufmann draw on the most extensive questionnaires and databases

produced in recent years by international organisations, non-governmental organisations and think tanks.

The focus of Pryor's analysis is American competitiveness (Pryor, 2002a). His main tool is an index of laissez faire, derived from surveys of business on their perception of different aspects of regulatory quality. The index enabled him to rank countries and thus to compare their perceived overall regulatory quality. As mentioned in chapter 2, there are three main dimensions of quality: design of the process, activities and output, and real-world outcome. Pryor's index of laissez faire is a real-world outcome indicator.

Pryor decomposes the complexity of regulatory quality into three types of regulations, which are easier to handle conceptually: legal framework regulations, such as property rights; industry-specific regulations; and general economic regulations, which work across sectors. By drawing on two large-scale surveys of business executives' perceptions of the 'international competitiveness' of various nations,[2] and by using indicators on a scale from 1 (highly regulated) to 10 (no regulation), Pryor combines business executives' assessments 'for 32 different areas into six broad categories of general economic regulation, which, in turn, are merged into one overall index' (Pryor, 2002a: 293). These six broad weighted categories are as follows: foreign sector (which measures trade barriers, control of capital flows and investment and rules affecting cross-border business – weight 20 per cent); labour market (weight 20 per cent); product market (weight 20 per cent); finance (weight 15 per cent); environment (weight 5 per cent); and general economic/administrative rules (weight 20 per cent). Each category is assigned a weight in order to aggregate them in an overall index. The weights are given according to the author's personal judgement about the relative importance of such measures on the economy as a whole. As such, they are subjective (Pryor, 2002b: 705). The index of laissez faire covers only general economic regulations. Thus, it does not inform on sector-based regulation but has the advantage of covering the impact of rules that operate 'across the board', so to speak.

Although there was no 'statistically significant relationship between the measure of laissez faire and the average annual per capita GDP growth between 1985 and 1995' (Pryor, 2002a: 300), there was a statistically significant relationship between the index of regulatory laissez faire and governmental effectiveness. The strongest conclusion is that 'governments govern the economy best when they govern least; or, less tendentiously, that it is easier for governments to fulfil a few goals than many' (Pryor, 2002a: 300).

One must be aware of the fact that these statistical results are influenced by the perception, ideology and political culture of the respondents to the surveys. Firstly, the respondents' assessment of the extent of regulation is affected by the perception of general governmental effectiveness. Secondly, the surveys are conducted by interviewing exclusively business executives, 'who may be ideologically predisposed to believe that governmental ineffectiveness and the extent of regulation are directly related' (Pryor, 2002a: 300–1). Finally, executives from highly regulated countries may be inclined to believe that regulation is ineffective.

With these limitations, surveys of firms capture the impact of regulations issued by all levels of government – supranational, national, regional and even local government (Pryor, 2002a: 296). Thus Pryor's index can be used by governments using regulatory tools to create a better regulatory environment for business. This is a focused but narrow approach. The basis of the index of laissez faire is the firm, as the only stakeholder in regulatory policy. Pryor is very careful to address the limitations of his approach, and indeed the major merit of his work is that it produces a clear definition of quality for *one specific* stakeholder. It should not be stretched to the point of considering it a universal definition of quality.

Another limitation of this approach is the confusion between quality and quantity. The whole approach boils down to the narrow economic precept that governments should do less. As such, the policy implications are not neutral with respect to the size of government intervention – and therefore violate the assumptions about quality mentioned in chapter 2 (OECD, 1997a: 193). Although Pryor is the first to acknowledge possible biases of the respondents, this is an intrinsic limitation of his index.

Let us turn to a study that attempts to overcome some of the limitations of Pryor's approach and looks at a larger pool of stakeholders. In a study commissioned by the World Bank, Kaufmann *et al.* (2003, 2005) start from governance and situate regulatory policy therein. In particular, they identify six dimensions of governance: voice and accountability, policy stability, government effectiveness, rule of law, control of corruption, and regulatory quality. For each of these dimensions an overall index has been developed in order to rank, over five time periods (the years 1996, 1998, 2000, 2002 and 2004), 209 countries according to the performance of their governance system. The regulatory quality index is hence a real-world outcome indicator. It can be useful to policy-makers willing to connect regulatory reform to other reform programmes.

The main aim of Kaufmann and associates' study is to develop a system of indicators, named 'best measure of quality of governance worldwide', able to carry out cross-country comparisons. Turning to regulatory quality, this dimension of governance 'includes measures of the incidence of market-unfriendly policies such as price control or inadequate bank supervision, as well as perception of the burdens imposed by excessive regulation in areas such as foreign trade and business development' (Kaufmann *et al.*, 2003: 3). Regulatory quality variables are aggregated into an overall index that varies between –2.5 and 2.5. High scores mean better governance outcomes. Variations of the index show how countries change their relative position over time.

Kaufmann *et al.* (2003: 39) acknowledge that their system of subjective indicators contains substantial margins of error, which should be carefully taken into account in comparing countries. However, they argue that the same margin of error exists in objective measures as well when they are used to portray broader concepts, such as regulatory quality or the efficiency of governance (Kaufmann *et al.*, 2003: 28). Their system of indicators makes explicit (and takes into account) this margin of error. In addition, ideological biases in the perceptions of experts have been addressed, investigated and mostly discounted by Kaufmann *et al.* as irrelevant. On balance, this approach provides countries with a tool for comparison and benchmarking.

Quality measures based on objective sources of data
In this section we discuss composite measures based on objective variables. Typically, objective variables are based on factual statements such as 'Does the government control prices in sector X?' or national economic statistics. However, as we have already mentioned, the statistical methodology used to handle primary data can rely on some personal biases.

Let us start with studies characterised by objective methodology. An objective methodology for the design of indicators of governance has been suggested by Knack and Kugler (2002). They observe that 'different indicators of good governance are appropriate for different purposes' (Knack and Kugler, 2002: 1). This is consistent with our analysis in chapter 2. According to these authors, there are two main dimensions that motivate different indicators. One is pretty conventional in this literature and refers to the degree of aggregation. Indeed, most of the literature on indicators of governance or regulatory quality deals with different approaches to aggregation, with the implicit (but often flawed) notion that the more one aggregates, the better is the measure of quality. Knack and Kugler warn that the choice of indicators should account for the trade-off between the precision of measurement (of a phenomenon) and the robustness of more highly aggregated indicators. The other dimension used by Knack and Kugler is more innovative and refers to the degree of transparency and the extent to which indicators are replicable. Given the importance that Knack and Kugler (2002: 1) assign to transparency and 'replicable' indicators, their main goals are to describe 'a methodology for constructing an index of objective indicators of good governance' and to discuss how to create an index in relation to explicit purposes.

The design of indicators of regulatory quality should be based on the following three principles. Firstly, the number of indicators should be small, in order to ensure that the measures are 'easy to understand'. Secondly, and in partial contradiction to the first principle, since objective indicators focus on specific aspects of an institution or governance system, it is necessary to draw on a large number of them to map out complex phenomena. Thirdly, in order to strike a balance between accuracy and measures that are 'easy to understand', indicators have to be aggregated 'into a smaller number of indexes' (Knack and Kugler, 2002: 1).

Accordingly, Knack and Kugler aggregate the following nine objective indicators into an index of good governance:

1 regulation of entry (the number of procedures to start a new business);
2 contract enforcement (the number of formal independent procedures to collect a debt);
3 contract-intensive money (the proportion of the money supply that is not held in the form of currency, which is an indicator of the trust in government and in the financial sector);
4 international trade revenue;
5 revenue source volatility;
6 budgetary volatility;
7 waiting times for telephone line set-up;
8 telephone faults;
9 percentage of firm revenues paid as bribes (as reported in surveys of business firms).

The index measures the strength of governance in countries.

The selection of indicators to aggregate in the overall index has been based on the fact that all the variables included correlate well with each other. This correlation has been tested through a sophisticated statistical analysis. All thirty-six of the inter-item correlations among the nine variables are in the expected direction, with the majority of these relations being statistically significant at the 0.05 level. Moreover, 'all 9 of the objective indicators are significantly correlated with each of the 6 [Kaufmann *et al.*] indexes' (Knack and Kugler, 2002: 4), based on subjective indicators. We return to the issue of convergence between subjective and objective measures in the conclusion to this chapter.

To conclude, this approach has some interesting methodological properties. Different purposes and governance goals generate different systems of indicators. Therefore, one has to be explicit about the model of governance before one designs indicators. The second methodological finding is that measures should not be assessed only on the basis on the degree of aggregation and statistical sophistication. Transparency and the possibility to replicate indicators are also important. Although Knack and Kugler do not elaborate much, this property is fundamental in terms of how indicators can and should be used by policy-makers. It is also important for the overall legitimacy of regulatory policy based on indicators. The limitation of this approach is that it does not contribute much to our understanding of specific indicators of regulatory quality, as it is focused on governance.

Goff (1996) is another scholar who has relied on sophisticated statistical analysis to develop an indirect measure of regulatory impact on macroeconomic performance. As a result, the measurement of regulatory quality ideated by Goff belongs to the real-world outcome dimension. He focuses on four aspects of regulation:

- the macroeconomic influence of regulatory policy;
- the influence of regulation on other policies (government spending, taxation, monetary policy);
- an estimation of the intensity of regulatory policy and its economy-wide effects, developing an 'index of effective regulation';
- an explanation of the regulatory trend (increasing or decreasing in the production of regulation), using the above-mentioned index.

The major issue, of course, is how to get a measure of 'macroeconomic influence'. A solution is to look at the microeconomic effects and then consider how these influences could build into 'economy-wide disturbances' (Goff, 1996: 16). This concept of microeconomic effects leads to an original classification of regulations. Indeed, it is possible to classify regulation according to a supply/demand framework:

- *Supply-altering regulation.* This is the type of regulation that can alter the productivity and the profit of firms. It can be classified as *direct-effect regulation* when regulation has a direct impact on productivity, provoking a change (higher or lower) in the cost of production and consequently in prices; or as *indirect-effect regulation* when regulation produces effects on the innovation and rate of economies of scale and indirectly causes variations in productivity.
- *Demand-altering regulation.* This type of regulation alters the determinants of market demand – income, product quality and preferences.

Goff (1996: 85) notes that there is a 'lack of estimates across all regulation across all sectors of the economy'. Given the impossibility of measuring regulatory costs and benefits directly, he argues for the need to use indirect measurements of the regulatory impact on macroeconomic performance. Factor analysis – he argues – is the solution to 'the major problems of inconsistency, obsolescence, and inattention to regulatory intensity' (Goff, 1996: 85). Consequently, he builds an Effective Regulation Index (ERI) by applying factor analysis to selected variables. Arbitrariness was avoided in the selection of variables, as 'data were collected on a wide range of variables that might have some link to observable characteristics of effective regulation' (Goff, 1996: 92). Goff's further selection of variables was based on two guides: a preference for variables for which data were continuously available; and a preliminary factor analysis on the number of pages in the Federal Register.[3] The latter variable is the most relevant for defining the quantity aspects of regulatory effectiveness. As a conclusion of this process of selection, the six variables included in Goff's index are the following:

1 the number of pages in the Federal Register;

2 the number of people employed by the Environmental Protection Agency;
3 lawyers as a percentage of the population;
4 civil cases as a percentage of total federal district court cases;
5 non-education-related state government employment;
6 number of people employed by the Department of Agriculture as a percentage of total farm employment.

In order to assess whether the ERI is an important determinant of macroeconomic performance, this index can be related to percentage growth of gross national product (GNP), the unemployment rate, the employment–population ratio, Standard and Poor's 500 index and output per hours worked (i.e., average productivity):

> The evidence shows ERI increases are correlated with diminished macroeconomic performance, the correlation is relevant from a technical, statistical standpoint, and the correlation exists even after taking account of some other influences. (Goff, 1996: 108–9)

An average increase of 7.5 per cent in ERI over a forty-year period is associated with:

- a 1.4 per cent decline in the GNP growth rate;
- a 0.5 per cent increase in the unemployment rate;
- a 0.3 per cent reduction of the employment–population ratio;
- a 7.5 per cent reduction in the real Standard and Poor's 500 index;
- a 0.6 per cent decline in productivity growth.

The ERI is an aggregation of crude measures (see above). It cannot be related to a specific a regulatory quality tool. Nevertheless, according to Goff it is an index that can be used to measure the impact of the extent of regulation on macroeconomic performance, and thus it can be considered an indicator of real-world outcome. Even assuming that this indicator is reliable, it is difficult to think that through this indicator policy-makers and regulators can evaluate the quality of better regulation policy. In conclusion, this indicator does not look promising. However, in the debate on EU simplification an argument has often been made that the EU's plans for better regulation should include a reduction in the number of pages of the *acquis communautaire*.

Let us turn to two studies that rely on less sophisticated statistical treatment of data. Djankov *et al.* (2001) draw on a dataset on the regulation of entry of start-up firms in eighty-five countries. The aim of this study, conducted in association with the World Bank, was to rank countries according to the number of procedures, time and costs necessary to establish a standard firm. The study tested which economic theory of regulation was consistent with its main findings.

To begin with, all procedures required of an entrepreneur to obtain the necessary permits to set a new firm up were recorded. The accuracy of data collected through government publications and on-line information was tested by contacting government agencies. Additionally, reports on entry regulation were commissioned from independent and local law firms. In case of disagreement on regulatory requirements with government officials, the law firms reached an agreement on the number of procedures needed to set up a new firm. The procedures were classified according to their function: health and safety, labour, taxes, environment, and a residual category, aimed at selecting entrepreneurs appropriately in relation to their skills (Djankov *et al.*, 2001: 11–14).

The next step was the computation of the time (expressed in business days) and costs (the identifiable official expenses, such as fees, costs of procedures and forms, photocopies, fiscal stamps, legal and notary charges) necessary for the completion of each procedure. The calculations were based on a typical firm, one which performs general industrial or commercial activities, operates in the largest city, is exempt from industry-specific requirements and is a domestically owned limited liability company (Djankov *et al.*, 2001: 7).

Time and official cost were aggregated into a summary 'full cost' measure, 'which adds up the official expenses and an estimate of the value of the entrepreneur's time, valuing his time at the country's per capita income per working day' (Djankov *et al.*, 2001: 11). The number of procedures was highly correlated with both the time and cost variables.

An interesting finding was that stricter regulation of entry was not associated with higher-quality products, better environment, or better health and safety performance. This supports the public choice theory, in which 'politicians use regulation both to create rents and to extract them through campaign contributions, votes, and bribes' (Djankov *et al.*, 2001: 2).

This methodology was based on objective measures able to quantify the total and monetary cost of setting a firm up. As a result, the 'full cost' indicator is precise and comprehensive, even if the total cost was not assessed through the 'opportunity cost of the entrepreneur's time and the foregone profits associated with bureaucratic delay' (Djankov *et al.*, 2001: 11). The 'full cost' indicator can be easily related to simplification programmes dealing with the regulation of entry. As a result, it is a precise measure of the quality of simplification, performed in a specific regulatory sector: regulation of entry. This is also a limitation, since regulation of entry is just one element of the regulatory environment. To overcome this limitation, the World Bank has already developed indicators on other regulatory sectors, namely employment protection law, bankruptcy laws, as well as regulation on access to credit, property registration, protection of investors and contract enforcement (World Bank, 2004a, 2004b).

Another study conducted in collaboration with the World Bank (and this one also with Yale University) and presented in the World Bank publication

Doing Business deals with regulation of the labour market (Botero *et al.*, 2003). The analysis covered three areas of regulation – employment, collective bargaining and social security laws – in eighty-five countries. Each of these three areas was divided into more specific fields. For example, the employment laws category was split into the following three regulatory areas: alternative employment contracts; conditions of employment; and job security (legal protection against dismissal).

The aggregation methodology was multi-staged. Firstly, all variables of a regulatory area were codified. Variables were assigned a value of one when regulation constrained the negotiation between employer and employee, and zero otherwise. For example, fixed-term contracts are allowed in Venezuela only for temporary tasks, while in Vietnam they are allowed for any task. On this component of the employment law index, Venezuela scores 1, Vietnam 0. Similar procedures were followed for the industrial relations and social security laws. Secondly, the variables comprising a regulatory area were aggregated into sub-indexes. Finally, the three overall measures, namely employment law, collective bargaining and social security law indexes, were derived from an arithmetic sum of the sub-indexes.

The aim of this approach, as in the previous study, was to rank countries. The authors found a correlation between the measures of regulation of labour and measures of entry. Countries that tend to regulate labour markets strictly also tend to regulate procedures for setting a new firm up and judicial proceedings relatively more heavily than other countries (Botero *et al.*, 2003: 26–9).

This study relied on indirect sources to describe the legal protection of workers. As a result, the regulatory provisions database is constructed on information gathered through other studies of the regulation of labour markets, which in turn have made assumptions regarding a 'standard' worker (Botero *et al.*, 2003: 9). Assumptions are also made regarding the 'standard' employer (Botero *et al.*, 2003: 10).

These studies by Botero and Djankov and the World Bank's *Doing Business* publications provide templates or models. Specifically, Djankov's approach provides a template of data-gathering methods. Botero's study is an interesting model of how complex measures of quality of regulation of labour should be designed. The methodology used to construct the indicators of labour market regulation is quite easy to replicate, even if updating the dataset of regulatory variables is a heavy task.

The last two studies presented in this section lean on more subjective methods of data analysis. Koedijk and Kremers (1996) – in one of the most often cited papers – set out to examine the impact of regulation on economic performance. They argue that 'regulation needs to be assessed on a case-by-case basis' in order to measure, for example, the ex-post effects of liberalisation or deregulation of a specific sector on economic performance and growth (Koedijk and Kremers, 1996: 448). With this caveat in mind, they conducted a cross-country empirical analysis in order to gauge the macroeconomic impact of regulatory policies. Their aim was to analyse how different regulatory styles in Europe correlate with different growth rates. The study was based on a regression analysis between the determinants of macroeconomic performance (growth, productivity and employment) and indexes of overall market regulation, product market regulation and labour market regulation. It is important to note that this analysis dealt only with regulation and ignored other factors that can enhance the structural growth of an economy. Regression analysis was followed by cluster analysis. The latter identifies different groups of countries, according to their economic performance and regulatory styles.

Regression analysis showed a significant relationship between the degree of regulation and growth rankings. Cluster analysis produced four clusters of countries. Ireland, the UK and Denmark formed the 'Anglo-Saxon' cluster, which was characterised by 'light' overall regulation and the highest growth rate. Given their highly regulated product and labour markets, Italy and Greece formed one single group, dubbed the 'Mediterranean' cluster. The 'Iberian' cluster, composed of Spain and Portugal, ranked high in the quality of product market regulation, but it suffered from rigid regulation of the labour market. Finally, France, Germany, Belgium and the Netherlands had the opposite characteristics of the Iberian cluster: a highly regulated product market but a more flexible labour market. Koedijk and Kremers argue that less regulation and more dynamic markets, especially in the product market, could benefit several continental European countries. Dynamic product markets and a flexible regulatory environment are an essential determinant of economic growth.

Arguably, regulatory reforms and regulatory quality have different goals, depending on whether a country belongs to one particular 'world' of regulation or another. This is a useful antidote to the 'one size fits all' approach to policy recommendations. However, there are several limitations, and on balance they outnumber the advantages. The approach is narrow. The focus is not on regulatory quality, but the quantity of regulation. The quality of statistical analysis, based on crude regressions, is another weak point. To illustrate, the authors make a simple average of the indexes to construct the main composite measures. Although this avoids the problem of arbitrary weights, there is no justification of why all the indexes should weigh the same. Finally, their data are a bit out of date. Regulatory reforms have changed the landscape of regulation in several EU countries.

Authors working on OECD data have made more specific progress on indicators of regulatory governance and statistical analysis. The economic department of the OECD has developed a database on objective indicators of product market regulation, covering both economic and administrative types of regulation. This database is designed to produce an overall indicator that measures the extent of regulation. The aim is to assess the relative friendliness of regulation to market mechanisms across countries and to show the interrelations between certain types of indicators and clusters of countries, covering several regulatory areas (Conway *et al.*, 2005). Specifically, the OECD dataset covers the following areas: state control over business enterprises; barriers to entrepreneurship; and barriers to international trade and investment (Conway *et al.*, 2005: 8). Another important aim in this approach is the explicit orientation towards policy-relevant recommendations. As shown below, the analysis of indicators leads these authors to formulate specific suggestions for policy reform.

The OECD product market indicators cover an important sector of regulation. However, important types of regulation are kept out of the database, such as environmental regulation, health and safety, and the regulation of utilities. Moreover, the meaning of regulatory quality is not extremely broad – as noted in chapter 1, there is a difference between a focus on markets and a focus on governance.

The study by Conway *et al.* is built on previous work conducted by OECD economists. In 1999, Nicoletti and colleagues built the so-called International Regulation Database using a multiple-choice questionnaire (self-assessed by governments) and, in minimal part, on external sources, namely documents (published and unpublished) by the OECD and other organisations (Nicoletti *et al.*, 2000: 9). 'The questionnaire ... asked for information on around 1300 different regulatory provisions concerning economy-wide and industry-specific laws, regulations and administrative procedures' (Nicoletti *et al.*, 2000: 12).[4] The same methodology has been used to update the database (Conway *et al.*, 2005: 5–6).

All regulatory provisions have been grouped according to specific areas. To illustrate, the administrative burdens on start-ups are an indicator based on four regulatory provisions (see table 3.2). Qualitative information has been transformed into a numerical format by creating a scale from 0 (little market regulation) to 6 (a highly regulated market). A subjective weight has been assigned to each variable. The sum of values of each regulatory provision of a specific regulatory area provides the first level of indicators. The system of indicators is designed as 'a pyramid with 16 low-level indicators at the base and one overall indicator of product market regulation at the top' (Conway *et al.*, 2005: 7).

The analysis of product market regulation produces three clusters of countries. The first group includes 'common law' countries (the UK, Australia, the USA, New Zealand and Canada) and Iceland as well as Denmark, which are characterised by a relatively liberal approach to both labour and product markets. The second group of countries includes France, the Czech Republic, Italy, Greece, Hungary, Mexico, Turkey and Poland. These countries have restrictive regulation. The third group comprises several continental European countries: the Slovak Republic, Ireland, Luxembourg, Sweden, Finland, the Netherlands, Germany, Austria, Belgium, Norway, Portugal, Spain and

Table 3.2 An example of the construction of first-level indicators – administrative burdens on start-ups for corporations – in the study by Conway et al. (2005)

Coding (of the responses)	Weight (c_k)	Score assigned						
		0	1	2	3	4	5	6
Number of mandatory procedures required to register a public limited company	¼	≤3	≤5	≤8	≤12	≤16	≤20	>20
Number of public and private bodies to contact to register a public limited company	¼	0	1	2	3	4	5	6
Number of working days required to complete all mandatory procedures for registering a public limited company	¼	≤4	≤8	≤12	≤16	≤20	≤24	>24
Total cost (euros) of registering a public limited company	¼	<500	<1,000	<1,500	<2,500	<5,000	<7,500	≥7,500
Country scores (0–6)	$\sum_k c_k \, answer_k$							

Source: Conway et al. (2005).

Switzerland, as well as Japan and Korea. This cluster of countries is 'in the middle of the distribution of product market regulation indicators' (Conway *et al.*, 2005: 22), since they 'were not statistically distinguishable from these two groups at the 90% level of confidence' (Conway *et al.*, 2005: 12).

It is useful to note that this methodology of data collection involves some subjective judgements, which may cause three kinds of error. Firstly, there may be errors in the design of the scoring procedure used to transform qualitative information into ordinal indicators. The 2005 study, however, improved the aggregation methodology. The product market indicators were not presented as point estimates but rather in confidence intervals. Indeed, Conway *et al.* (2005: 3) relied on a random weights technique to test the sensitivity of summary indicator values to different weighting schemes used in the aggregation. Secondly, 'errors may have been made in replying and interpreting the responses to the OECD questionnaire', which relied on the personal judgement of national civil servants. Finally, 'errors may be due to the personal interpretation of the compilers of the data' (Nicoletti *et al.*, 2000: 16–17).

As observed, the OECD approach is limited to product market regulation. However, it connects indicators to better regulation tools. For example, the indicator 'barriers to entrepreneurship' can lead a country to redesign its policies for simplification. The indicator contains a number of variables that can be easily referred to simplification programmes.

Another limitation of this system is that it is not clear whether it develops subjective or objective measures. Indeed, although the framework seems to be constructed in order to provide objective measures, the collection of data relies on questionnaires that contain a measure of subjective discretion. Other systems focus on objective measures more directly and less ambiguously.

Simple measures

Some measures of regulation require only the recording of a simple number or a yes/no answer to a question. They do not involve any statistical sophistication, even if, in some cases at least, to get a precise number to explain a phenomenon is an extremely complex task. For example, to estimate costs of complying with a specific regulation involves several degrees of uncertainty. Moreover, the nature of the impact of regulation – in term of costs and benefits – on citizens' wealth is a hotly debated subject. So, a certain degree of disagreement over methods adds to the technical complexity of estimation. However, the advantage of simple measures is related to the direct and evident link between a phenomenon and a number.

The development of the literature has been skewed. There is a considerable amount of information on two of our four classic measures, simplification and RIA. In contrast, academic discussion of indicators of access and consultation has been minimal and generally overshadowed by the initiatives of governments. Therefore the discussion of access and consultation will be left for the next chapter.

In this section, we review simple measures that can be used to appraise the quality of two tools of better regulation, that is, RIA and simplification. We start from a basic illustration, discussion and comparison of simple measures, and then turn to the methodologies that can be used to produce simple measures of costs, with emphasis on compliance costs. Costs cannot be considered in isolation, however. Hence, we also show how the quality of cost and benefit measures can be assessed. In doing so, we go slightly beyond the topic of simple measures and look briefly at the overall quality of cost–benefit analysis.

Simplification and regulatory quality
There is a vast array of measures, and some of them will be introduced in chapter 4 (which is dedicated to indicators used by governments). However, the simplest indicators provided in the literature are:

- the number of pages of laws (primary laws, decrees, statutory instruments, other regulations);
- the number of regulatory agencies;
- the number of privatisations (or their value in euros, or the number of sectors liberalised over a number of years);
- the number of acts of devolution (weighted by type of act or by value of resources devolved);
- the number of laws limiting competition (for example, in some EU Member States people cannot enter a profession unless they are recognised by chartered associations; another example is the presence of a fixed maximum number of taxi licences).

The number of laws can be turned into an indicator of simplification. One can look at the number of pages in two or more different periods and calculate the rate at which pages decrease. The number of pages in the US Federal Register has been used as a crude measure of the extent of regulation (Goff, 1996; Viscusi *et al.*, 1995). Dawson and Seater (2004) based their statistical analysis on the number of pages of the Code of Federal Regulations. Gatti (1981) looked at the number of US regulatory agencies in order to measure the proliferation of regulation during the 1970s.

There may be a trade-off between the 'classic' indicators of simplification and the quality of regulatory access and transparency – one of the better regulation tools examined in this volume. Take the example of the number of pages of an official legal journal. A reduction in the number of pages can be negatively correlated with access to legislation if shorter laws are more difficult to understand. This brings us to the argument that simplification is not a quantitative notion but a concept based on quality. It is not enough to cut the average length of a law (yet another measure): it is indispensable that the newly created processes are streamlined and easy to understand. This is where simplification and techniques of drafting meet.

Targeting the estimation of regulatory costs

Simple measures are particularly effective when they target the costs of regulation, particularly the costs of administering regulation and compliance costs. In the USA, for example, economists often look at the expenses incurred by regulators (mainly regulatory agencies) in carrying out their activities. The indicator is the percentage of the public budget dedicated to regulatory agencies, sometimes referred to as the 'regulators' budget' (Dudley and Warren, 2005). To calculate the regulators' budget makes sense in a country such as the USA, where most regulatory programmes are devolved to *ad hoc* agencies. In European countries, however, regulations are mostly issued by government departments and, in a minor part, by parliaments. True, there is a drift towards independent agencies in EU Member States and at the EU level as well, but the majority of regulatory measures are still produced by governments. As a consequence, it is difficult to rely on the share of the budget designated to regulatory activities.

Turning to compliance costs, there is no wide agreement on the definition. Indeed, there are several classifications of compliance costs according to their components and the purpose of the analysis (Chittenden *et al.*, 2002).The total regulatory costs include direct and indirect costs: direct costs are related directly to complying with the regulation; indirect costs are not linked with actual compliance costs but are indirectly related to the purpose of regulation, and include psychological and opportunity costs, as well as any negative impact on productivity, innovation and investment. Direct costs can be further classified as recurring and non-recurring costs: recurring costs can be fixed (those that do not vary with the volume of product or employees) or variable (those that decrease or increase with the number of employees, products or volume of output covered by the regulation). Another classification of direct costs is on the basis of their purpose. Accordingly, it is possible to distinguish between administrative costs, the costs related to the paperwork burden necessary to comply with regulation and operating costs (i.e., the costs incurred in meeting the policy objectives of the regulation).

Another classification of regulatory costs was used in a study for the Directorate-General for Enterprise and Industry (henceforth DG Enterprise) undertaken by the Danish consultancy firm PLS Ramboll (figure 3.1). As figure 3.1 shows, compliance costs are just an element of the overall regulatory burden on firms. The costs to enforce a law and the sanctions costs are another important aspect that can overturn the advantage of a regulation. Kagan and Axelrad (2000) argue that the cost of implementing a policy and resolving a dispute can be in some countries as relevant as the compliance

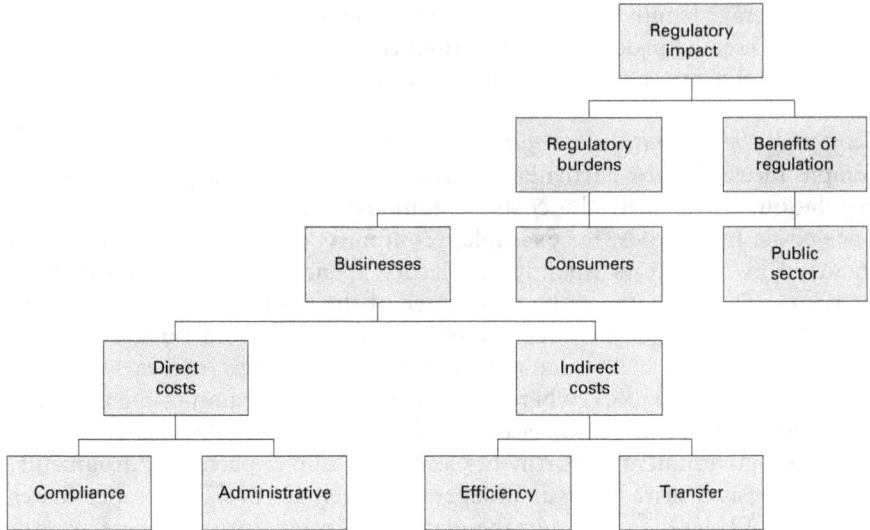

Figure 3.1 A typology of regulatory burdens. Source: PLS Ramboll, 'Ex-Post Evaluation of EC Legislation', final report for DG Enterprise, May 2005, p. 4.

costs. Although these costs are just transfers of money between different agents, the transfers may affect productivity.

Four methodologies for regulatory cost assessment
There are several methodologies for the calculation of compliance costs (Chittenden *et al.*, 2002; Goff, 1996; Hahn and Hird, 1991). Hahn and Hird (1991) identify the following:

- engineering approaches;
- expenditure evaluations;
- econometric studies;
- economy-wide modelling of the impacts of regulation.

Engineering approaches focus on the operating costs of social regulation. Such an approach is used 'to calculate the added cost of installing equipment directly, adjusting for quality change' (Hahn and Hird, 1991: 240). However, these approaches do not take into account the counterfactual analysis: total production costs may not be the sum of the previous total costs and the calculated compliance costs, since firms may reduce the cost of other elements of production.

Another simple method to assess compliance costs relies on the out-of-pocket expenditure incurred by firms to comply with a regulation. This method leads to the so-called expenditure evaluations. Basically, they follow a three-stage methodology (Goff, 1996: 60). The first step is a survey questioning businesses on the expenditures to comply with a regulation. Analysis of balance sheets and other financial data can usefully complement the survey data. Secondly, expenditure estimates are added across a specific industry sector or the whole economy. Thirdly, the final estimate of direct costs produces a measure of the total impact of the regulation on productivity. Denison (quoted in Goff) has found that the growth rate of productivity declined over the period 1969–75 by about 0.15 per cent owing to environmental regulation and 0.07 per cent owing to health and safety regulation.

There are five main limitations to expenditure evaluations (Hahn and Hird, 1991: 233). Firstly, survey respondents may have biases. Secondly, these studies consider just one aspect of regulatory effects, and ignore any benefits of regulation. Thirdly, the analysis is not able to account for indirect regulatory costs – for example on innovation and investments. Fourthly, some adverse effects of regulation on a firm or a product are not taken into account. Firms can be forced out of a market, and products can be prevented from coming to the market or altered in their quality characteristics. Finally, this kind of study does not specify an adequate counterfactual, one which describes what might have happened if a regulatory change had not occurred (Hahn and Hird, 1991: 237).

Turning to econometric studies, they evaluate the effect of a regulation by simulating the demand and supply before and after a regulatory change:

> Some can look at the total amount of output by a firm or industry before or after a regulatory shift. Others examine output per labour hour (productivity) or production costs. (Goff, 1996: 63)

These studies thus measure the direct cost of a regulatory change.

The last methodology discussed here is based on large-scale general equilibrium models that incorporate the inter-market and inter-temporal effects of regulatory activity. Essentially, the analyst simulates with a model how the economy changes when specific regulatory changes are introduced. Thanks to the general equilibrium features of models, it is possible to measure total compliance costs by taking into consideration indirect effects.

Summing up data: compilation studies and RIA-based compilations
Another approach to measuring compliance costs is the 'compilation study'. The latter aggregates all estimates of compliance costs produced by several data sources (see a short description in Goff, 1996). Often these studies aggregate data from RIAs performed by governmental departments or agencies. Otherwise, they simply construct a reasoned compilation of data from different econometric or survey studies. One example of the approach is the study by Hahn and Hird (1991). More recently, Crain and Hopkins (2001) estimated that, to comply with federal regulations, Americans spent $843 billion.

RIA-based compilations have been used by governments (e.g., in the USA by the Office of Management and Budget; OMB, 2000, 2001) and stakeholders (e.g., Ambler *et al.*, 2004, for the British Chamber of Commerce) – as will be shown in the next chapter. Typically, they take the form of annual reports, scorecards and even simple tables showing the sum of the costs revealed by all RIAs performed in one period, usually a year. A deeper analysis looks at the quality of the economic analysis. This approach is associated to the work of Robert Hahn and his associates (Hahn *et al.*, 2000; Hahn and Dudley, 2004).

Table 3.3 illustrates the relation between type of compliance costs and the methods of measurement. American scholars have questioned the accuracy of regulatory costs estimates from RIAs produced by regulators (Goodstein, 1997; Harrington *et al.*, 2000; McGarity and Shapiro, 1996; Office of Technology Assessment, 1995). There are several causes of the overestimation of regulatory costs. It can be due to flaws in the methodology used for risk assessment and economic analysis. Additionally, RIA usually does not take into account the learning curve and dynamic effects. As a result, the analysis does not consider how the regulatory costs will develop in the future, with the evolution of technology.

From costs to the quality of cost–benefit measurement and cost-effectiveness in RIA

In terms of overall regulatory quality, the most solid approach is to extend the analysis of costs to the overall quality of cost–benefit analysis contained in RIA. There are many and sophisticated ways of examining how benefits are measured, but more often than not we found simple measures drawn from either surveys on willingness to pay (subjective measures) or other economic analysis revealing indirectly the willingness to pay (objective measures).

Compilation studies of cost–benefit analysis included in RIA performed by one or several administrations are common in the USA (for a recent study see Hahn *et al.*, 2004). In their sample of forty-five RIAs spanning three US administrations, Hahn *et al.* (2004) found that, although some costs and benefits are regularly monetised, and more than half calculate either net benefits or cost-effectiveness, the majority of RIAs do not calculate both net benefits and cost-effectiveness. This approach is intimately linked to simple measures (however compiled): Hahn and his associates used scorecards that recorded the presence or absence of certain prerequisites for quality – more often than not set by the regulatory quality body (the OIRA). Consequently, this is a yes/no format procedure, thus falling in the category of simple indicators.

The use of scorecards to assess the quality of RIA has been questioned by some US lawyers. Parker (2003: 1381–2) observes that scorecards disregard unquantified costs and benefits, neglect distributive impacts and do not disclose the true level of uncertainty. Additionally, RIA is, in most countries, selective. Governments perform RIA on a selected number of proposed

Table 3.3 Type of regulatory costs and methodologies

	Type of compliance costs analysed	Type of regulation	Type of analysis of regulation		
			Sector-specific	Cross-sector	Type of measures
Engineering approaches	Operating costs	Social regulation	Yes	No	Objective
Expenditure evaluations	Direct costs	Social regulation (including administrative regulations and burden)	Yes	Yes	Subjective
Econometric studies	Direct costs	Economic and social regulation (including administrative regulations and burden)	Yes	No	Objective
Macroeconomic models	Total costs	Social regulation	Yes	No	Subjective
General equilibrium models	Total costs	Social regulation	Yes	No	Objective
Compilation of studies	Direct costs	Economic and social regulation	No	Yes	Objective
Compilation of RIA	Direct (or indirect) costs	Economic and social regulation	Yes	Yes	Objective

Source: Authors' elaboration on Chittenden *et al.* (2002) and Hahn and Hird (1991).

regulations. To infer total costs and benefits introduced by new legislation via an analysis of RIAs is not correct.

A well known objective measure of the quality of an RIA system is the cost-effectiveness of regulatory programmes. For example, Morrall (2003) has computed the cost of saving a life across different health and safety regulatory programmes (table 3.4). Some scholars have found 'ample room for disagreement with the picture of the regulatory system drawn by Morrall' (Heinzerling, 1998: 1984). To begin with, some regulations included in table 3.4 do not exist – and so there are no real costs associated with them. As the table shows, eight proposals were rejected. Additionally, they question the opportunity to discount regulatory benefits (Heinzerling, 1998: 1984). Finally, Heinzerling has taken issue with Morrall's narrow list of regulatory benefits.

Conclusions

This chapter has reviewed different measures of regulatory quality proposed by economists and classified them by degree of complexity (simple versus complex measures), by type (subjective versus objective) and by scope. One element that the indicators produced by international organisations have in common is the emphasis on comparative statistics: indicators are used to compare and benchmark countries. Benchmarking is contingent on the assumption that there is a 'one size fits all' notion of quality – a normative judgement that implicitly assigns to all countries one and only one set of weights to the different actors (the citizen, the politician, the civil servant, the expert – see chapter 2). The normative judgement can be defended empirically in a situation of convergence across countries towards principles, policies and outputs. But the reality is still one of remarkably different regulatory systems, in Europe and elsewhere. In consequence, the benchmarking/comparative statistics approach has some important limitations (see Radaelli, 2004, for details).

Let us now turn to the distinction between different types of measure. All studies that develop indicators with subjective measures draw on a comprehensive concept of regulatory quality. As a matter of fact, Pryor and Kaufmann do not focus on specific aspects of regulation and regulatory effects; rather, they mainly assess the perception of businesses of a broader concept of quality of regulation. However, this comprehensiveness makes it difficult to assess the success of a specific policy tool. Their indexes may not inform policy-makers adequately on the key variables they can actually control. In other words, indexes (and the variables upon which indexes are built) are not directly related to the better regulation tools introduced in chapter 2. Hence, a policy-maker willing to improve on a country's performance by using an index would not obtain a precise message in terms of tools and policies to adopt.

Table 3.4 Cost of risk-reducing US regulations per life saved

Regulation	Year	Status[a]	Number of lives saved annually	Cost per life saved[b]
Steering column protection	1967	F	1,300,000	100
Unvented space heaters	1980	F	63,000	100
Oil and gas well service	1983	P	50,000	100
Cabin fire protection	1985	F	15,000	200
Passive restraints/belts	1984	F	1,850,000	300
Fuel system integrity	1975	F	400,000	300
Trihalomethanes	1979	F	322,000	300
Underground construction	1983	P	8,100	300
Alcohol and drug control	1985	F	4,200	500
Servicing wheel rims	1984	F	2,300	500
Seat cushion flammability	1984	F	37,000	600
Floor emergency lighting	1984	F	5,000	700
Crane-suspended personnel platform	1984	P	5,000	900
Children's sleepware flammability	1973	F	106,000	1,300
Side doors	1970	F	480,000	1,300
Concrete and masonry constructions	1985	P	6,500	1,400
Hazard communication	1983	F	200,000	1,800
Grain dust	1984	P	4,000	2,800
Benzene fugitive emissions	1984	F	310	2,800
Radionuclides/uranium mines	1984	F	1,100	6,900
Asbestos	1972	F	369,000	7,400
Benzene	1985	P	3,800	17,100
Arsenic/glass paint	1986	F	110	19,200
Ethylene oxide	1984	F	2,800	25,600
Arsenic/copper smelter	1986	F	60	26,500
Uranium mill tailings: inactive	1983	F	2,100	27,600
Acrylonitrile	1978	F	6,900	37,600
Uranium mill tailings: active	1983	F	2,100	53,000
Coke ovens	1976	F	31,000	61,800
Asbestos (OSHA)	1986	F	74,700	89,300
Arsenic	1978	F	11,700	92,500
Asbestos (EPA)	1986	P	10,000	104,200
DES (cattle feed)	1979	F	68,000	132,000
Arsenic/glass manufacturing	1986	R	250	142,000
Benzene storage	1984	R	43	202,000
Radionuclides/DOE facilities	1984	R	1	210,000
Radionuclides/elemental phosphorus	1984	R	46	270,000
Acrylonitrile	1978	R	600	308,000
Benzene/ethylbenzenol	1984	R	6	483,000
Arsenic/low-arsenic copper	1986	R	90	764,000
Benzene/maleic anhydride	1984	R	29	820,000
Land disposal	1986	P	2,520	3,500,000
EDB	1983	P	2	15,600,000
Formaldehyde	1985	P	10	72,000,000

[a] Proposed (P), rejected (R) or final (F) rule.
[b] Thousands of dollars at 1984 prices.
Source: Morrall (2003: 23).

Table 3.5 Advantages and disadvantages of different types of measure

Study	Type of measure	Scope	Index	Strengths	Weaknesses	Relation with dimensions	Relation with tools
Pryor (2002a, 2002b)	Composite subjective	Across-the-board rules (general economic regulation)	Laissez faire	The concept of regulatory quality is comprehensive	Quality is related to only one stakeholder, i.e., business. This relationship between regulation and quality is indirect as it is mediated by government effectiveness. The index is not informative for policy-makers	Real-world outcome (businesses' perceptions)	No specific relation to any tool
Kaufmann et al. (2003, 2005)	Composite subjective	Across-the-board rules	Index of regulatory quality as a component of the overall index of 'good governance'	All stakeholders' perceptions are taken into account. Margins of error and ideological biases are taken into account. Possible benchmarking tool. Integration between regulatory quality and wider reforms of governance	The index may not be sufficiently informative for policy-makers. It may not achieve the learning purpose at the level of civil servants	Real-world outcome	No specific relation to any tool
Knack and Kugler (2002)	Composite objective	Regulation of entry, and legal framework regulation (contract enforcement)	Index of good governance, regulation of entry, and contract enforcement	Sound methodological approach	The index does not provide any useful input for understanding regulatory quality	Real-world outcome	Simplification
Goff (1996)	Composite objective	Across-the-board rules	Effective Regulation Index	Indirect measurement of the regulatory impact on macro-economic performance. Variables comprising the index were selected according to the constant availability of data and to the results of a factor analysis	The index is a crude measure that cannot assess the quality of better regulation tools. It does not provide useful recommendations to policy-makers	Real-world outcome	No specific relation to any tool

Source		Objective	Index	Strengths	Weaknesses	Outcome	Relation to tools
Djankov et al. (2001)	Composite objective	Regulation of entry	Index of regulation of entry	Good data-collection methodology; Methodology is easy to replicate; The index is precise and comprehensive; Clear relation to simplification	Wide scope of analysis; Narrow scope of quality (regulation of entry)	Some limited dimensions of real-world outcome; Activity	Simplification
Botero et al. (2003)	Composite objective	Employment legislation	Index of employment legislation	Good data-collection methodology; Statistical methodology is easy to replicate	Wide scope of analysis; Analytical focus on the extent of regulation; Ideological bias ('less regulation is always good regulation')	Real-world outcome	Simplification RIA
Koedijk and Kremers (1996)	Composite objective	Product market and employment regulation	Index of product market, employment, and overall market regulation	Regulatory quality in EU context; Regulatory quality differs by cluster. Hence the indexes are sensitive to context ('worlds of regulation')	The analysis is focused on the extent of regulation, not on quality; Quality of statistical analysis can be questioned; Data out of date	Real-world outcome	Few specific relations to any tool, except the indicators of business establishment and shop-hours, which can be associated with simplification
Conway et al. (2005)	Composite objective	State control over the market, regulation of entry, regulation of trade and international investment, and employment legislation	Overall index of economic regulation, and employment protection legislation	Three-stage methodology leads to evaluation of tools and policy; Flexible system of measurement that can be applied to specific policies (e.g. innovation policy)	Limited coverage of regulatory areas; The indexes do not refer to macroeconomic performance; Presence of subjective discretion	Real-world outcome	Simplification RIA

On the other hand, objective measures are characterised by other limitations and disadvantages. For instance, in some cases the methodology used to handle primary data relies on somewhat personal assessments. Nicoletti and others have worked on OECD data collected via questionnaires sent to governments. True, most of the questions in the OECD questionnaire used by Nicoletti ask for factual information. Yet these 'facts' are reported to the OECD by government officers. Koedijk and Kremers use a simple average of variables to construct their overall index, avoiding the problem of assigning weights to specific sectors of regulation but, as mentioned, they do not explain why all sectors should be assigned the same weighting. Apart from these more detailed observations, the main limitations of objective studies are essentially the following two.

Firstly, this type of study focuses on the extent of regulation. As we have observed, this cannot be considered a direct (albeit crude) measure of quality. Less regulation can mean good regulation for some stakeholders or actors, but not for all.

Secondly, objective measures are developed through a careful analysis that requires a limited field of research. As a result, the studies developing objective measures are confined to specific regulatory sectors. They do not provide information on the overall quality of the regulatory environment. Nevertheless, the OECD and the World Bank are financing other studies and releasing data that overcome this limitation. Alesina and colleagues have produced other studies covering specifically the relationship between regulation and investment (Alesina *et al.*, 2003). The World Bank's *Doing Business in 2006* includes other sectors of regulation affecting the economic performance of a firm (World Bank, 2005). Combining the different studies could offer a means of having a set of indicators of regulatory quality.

The difference between subjective and objective measures is relevant, but it should not be exaggerated. Nicoletti and Pryor (2001) have found that indicators contained in three different studies – conducted by Kaufmann (subjective), Pyror (subjective) and Nicoletti (objective) – converge. This should not be taken as an argument for convergence of every type of subjective or objective measure. However, convergence is still remarkable because it relates to some of the most sophisticated studies ever conducted on regulatory quality.

We have discussed the limitations and advantages of each indicator and index. Table 3.5 summarises our discussion. It would be wrong to look for a single index of regulatory quality – no matter how aggregated or sophisticated it may be. Quality has different dimensions. It is determined by different tools. It is shaped by different priorities of regulatory reform. Accordingly, systems of measures balanced by dimension and tool are preferable.

One major limitation of indexes and composite measures in general is that they may not inform policy-makers of the performance of variables and programmes under their control. Simple measures are easier to communicate and lead to suggestions for policy improvement, but they should be included in systems of indicators rather than being considered alone.

In terms of tools, the literature has not produced much, with the exceptions of Hahn's approach to the quality of RIA (see Hahn *et al.*, 2000; Hahn and Dudley, 2004) and of some ideas about indicators of simplification. The studies considered in this chapter have not much to suggest about measures of quality of consultation and access to regulation.

Notes

1 See www.heritage.org/research/features/index/.
2 The two surveys were carried out by the International Institute of Management Development and the World Economic Forum.
3 In a similar fashion to Goff, Dawson and Seater (2004) correlated economic growth with the number of pages in the Code of Federal Regulations. Whereas the Code is the US government publication that prints all federal regulations in existence during a given year, 'the Federal Register is a daily publication in which proposed regulations appear first in draft form and eventually in final form, if passed into law' (Dawson and Seater, 2004: 2–4).
4 The International Regulation Database also covered employment protection legislation. The employment data were drawn from a specific review of legislation conducted by the OECD in its 1999 *Employment Outlook* (OECD, 1999). In contrast, the new OECD database is limited to product market regulation.

4

Measuring the performance of better regulation policies: the cross-national experience

Introduction

In this chapter we present and discuss how governments (and in some cases stakeholders) go about measuring the performance of better regulation policies. We focus on several countries with experience in the development and management of tools aimed at assessing regulatory quality. At the outset, it is useful to make a distinction between fully fledged systems of indicators and simpler quality assurance mechanisms that routinely check whether better regulation tools conform to the government's principles and requirements. While several countries have introduced formal mechanisms to oversee and monitor the quality of better regulation tools, experience with performance measures is still limited. Another distinction concerns what is measured (either via systems of indicators or through detailed regular reporting and checklists). We use the three dimensions introduced previously in this volume: design, activity and real-world outcome. In the context of better regulation policies, activities (often also referred to as 'outputs') cover two elements:

1 oversight activities carried out by bodies in the executive (cabinet office and/or departments), such as training, drafting guidelines and monitoring departments;
2 'services' produced through a specific better regulation tool.

We also examine the role of governmental bodies in charge of assessing quality. A consolidated structure in charge of the systematic assessment of better regulation tools is in itself a manifestation of a 'quality assurance culture'. The quality assurance system typically involves both bodies within the executive – often a central unit in the prime minister's office – and bodies at an arm's length from the executive – typically, independent auditors reporting to parliament. We consider both.

The following sections illustrate the performance measurement in three non-EU countries, namely the USA, Canada and Australia. These are countries with a relatively long history of attempts to forge a quality assurance culture in regulation. We then discuss the Netherlands, Belgium, Denmark, Sweden and the UK.

The USA

In the USA, the system used for the appraisal of regulatory quality is multi-faceted. It covers essentially RIA and regulatory management. Additionally, regulatory programmes are subjected to 'performance budgeting'. The latter covers 'government-wide initiatives designed to better align spending decisions with expected budgeting' (GAO, 2004a: 1).

For our purposes, it is worth focusing on evaluation activities based on performance indicators. Firstly, we describe the performance measurement approach developed by the Office of Management and Budget (OMB) to evaluate government programmes, including regulation. Secondly, we provide a short description of how the OIRA monitors executive agencies in order to get compliance with the executive order no. 12866, which established the federal regulatory policy. Thirdly, we turn to how the General Accounting Office (GAO), the auditing and investigative arm of Congress, provides measures of quality. The questions we are tackling are whether there is an integrated concept of quality as process and whether auditing is based on measurement or not.

The OMB's predominant mission is to assist the president of the USA in overseeing and coordinating the preparation of the federal budget, the administration's procurement and financial management, and information and regulatory policies. In each of these areas, the OMB has developed performance measurement and coordinating mechanisms in order to assess competing funding demands among agencies and to set funding priorities. The Program Assessment Rating Tool (PART) is 'a diagnostic tool meant to provide a consistent approach to evaluating federal programs as part of the executive budget formulation process' (GAO, 2004b: 2–3). It systematises OMB performance measurement, achieving transparency and accountability in budget formulation.

PART is composed of items (i.e., questions) covering grants, capital assets and service acquisition programmes, credit programmes, regulatory-based programmes, direct federal programmes, and research and development programmes. It targets the following four sections of policy formulation, to each of which a specific weight is given:

1 'Program purpose and design' assesses whether the purpose is clear, and whether the programme design makes sense (weight = 20 per cent).
2 'Strategic planning' checks whether the agency sets valid programmatic annual and long-term goals (weight = 10 per cent).
3 'Program management' rates the administration of the programme, including financial oversight (weight = 20 per cent).

Box 4.1 The fiscal year 2005 PART – regulatory program section

Program purpose and design
- Is the program purpose clear?
- Does the program address a specific and existing problem, interest, or need?
- Is the program designed so that it is not redundant or duplicative of any other federal, state, local or private effort?
- Is the program design free of major flaws that would limit the program's effectiveness or efficiency?
- Is the program effectively targeted, so that resources will reach intended beneficiaries and/or otherwise address the program's purpose directly?

Strategic planning
- Are all regulations issued by the program/agency necessary to meet the stated goals of the program, and do all regulations clearly indicate how the rules contribute to achievement of the goals?
- Does the program have a limited number of annual performance goals that demonstrate progress towards achieving the long-term goals?
- Do all partners (grantees, sub-grantees, contractors, etc.) support program-planning efforts by committing to the annual and/or long-term goals of the program?
- Does the program collaborate and coordinate effectively with related programs that share similar goals and objectives?
- Are independent and quality evaluations of sufficient scope conducted on a regular basis or as needed to fill gaps in performance information to support program improvements and evaluate effectiveness?
- Is the program budget aligned with the program goals in such a way that the impact of funding, policy, and legislative changes on performance is readily known?
- Has the program taken meaningful steps to address its strategic planning deficiencies?

---

4 'Program result' rates performance – basically by reference to annual and long-term goals (weight = 50 per cent).

Box 4.1 presents PART's questions on regulatory programmes monitored by the OMB. The OMB states that:

> the questions are written in a Yes/No format and require the user to provide a brief narrative explanation of the answer, including any relevant evidence to substantiate the answer. Responses should be evidence based and not rely on impressions or generalities. (OMB, 2002: 2)

Program management
- Did the program seek and take into account the views of all affected parties (e.g., consumers; large and small businesses; State, local and tribal governments; beneficiaries; and the general public) when developing significant regulations?
- Did the program prepare adequate regulatory impact analyses if required by executive order no. 12866, regulatory flexibility analyses if required by the Regulatory Flexibility Act and Small Business Regulatory Fairness Act, and cost–benefit analyses if required under the Unfunded Mandates Reform Act; and did those analyses comply with OMB guidelines?
- Does the program systematically review its current regulations to ensure consistency among all regulations in accomplishing the program's goals?
- Are the regulations designed to achieve the program's goals, practicable, by maximizing the net benefits of its regulatory activity?
- Does the program collaborate and coordinate effectively with related programs?
- Does the program use strong financial management practices?
- Has the program taken meaningful steps to address its management deficiencies?

Program results
- Were programmatic goals (and benefits) achieved at the least incremental societal cost and did the program maximize net benefits?
- Does the program (including the program's partners) achieve its annual performance goals?
- Does the program demonstrate improved efficiencies and cost effectiveness in achieving its goals each year?
- Does the performance of this program compare favorably to other programs, including government, private, etc., with similar purposes and goals?
- Do independent evaluations of sufficient scope and quality indicate that the program is effective and achieving results?

Source: Guidance for Completing the Program Assessment Rating Tool (PART), Office of Management and Budget, March 2005.

As a result, these performance indicators are categorical and designed to be objective. They provide 'a consistent approach to rating federal programs' and pay particular attention to the individual programme results (GAO, 2004b: 9). There are five overall ratings, namely: (a) effective; (b) moderately effective; (c) adequate; (d) ineffective; (e) results not demonstrated, in any case where performance and evaluation documents were insufficient or inadequate.

The four sections of the OMB questionnaire target design, activities and outputs, and real-world outcome. Indeed, the principle guiding the rating exercise is that programmes are appropriate and deserve funding when they show a clear link between outputs and real-world outcome. In particular, questions on the maximisation of benefits to society from the regulatory programme, and assessments of the regulatory programme's effectiveness, refer to two measures of real-world outcome.

The main thrust of PART is to achieve a high degree of objectivity in the assessment of performance. However, in a recent analysis, the GAO (2004a: 6) found that any performance assessment tool 'that is sophisticated enough to take into account the complexity of the US government will always require some interpretation and judgment'. The degree of discretion is increased by the presence of subjective terms in the questionnaire's formulation that leave some room for interpretation. Another problematic aspect of the PART questionnaire is that the yes/no format has been judged too restrictive for the assessment of complex programmes with multiple purposes and goals, as acknowledged by the GAO itself (2004b: 6).

Besides PART, the OIRA evaluates departmental compliance with federal regulatory policy. In particular, it reviews all RIAs on proposed regulations to verify full compliance with the requirements of executive order no. 12866. Moreover, the OIRA is required to assess the benefits and costs of existing federal regulatory programmes and to recommend specific regulations for reform or elimination. Congress annually receives a report issued by the OIRA on the results of RIAs alongside the estimate of the total annual regulatory costs and benefits – in aggregate, by agency and programme, and by major rule (i.e., the most important regulations).

The annual report contains an analysis of the impact of federal regulation on state, local, and tribal government, small business, wages and economic growth. In short, the OIRA annual report to Congress is the principal document illustrating the overall result of better regulation policy in the USA. Several indicators are considered. One is the sum of costs and benefits of regulations in a year calculated via RIAs. The report adds up the results for the last ten years to provide an estimate of the total impact of regulations over the decade. Another indicator is the overall impact of regulation on the public sector. There are also indicators of the impact on small business (microeconomic indicators) and on wages and economic growth (macroeconomic indicators). All these are, in our terminology, real-world outcome indicators.

However, this approach does not really resolve the tricky problem of measuring the impact of regulation on economic growth. The OMB indicators are a compilation of several economic analyses of the impact of regulatory proposals. As such, there is the common problem of drawing inferences from different methodologies (see also GAO, 2005). Moreover, the regulatory costs and benefits compiled in the OIRA annual report are estimations performed prospectively. As a result, there is a methodological flaw if estimations are treated as measures of the actual impact of regulations – given the high probability of ex-ante errors in the economic analysis of regulatory impact. As Parker (2003: 1367) argues, confusing ex-ante estimations with the actual regulatory costs and benefits is a mistake similar to confusing a pre-match guess with the actual result of a game (see also McGarity and Ruttenberg, 2002).

The review of regulatory tools' performance by auditing bodies external to the core executive is also a consolidated feature of the US system. The GAO produces several reports on the effectiveness of regulation in the context of the executive's general auditing activity. The GAO has investigated the federal regulatory process in several different ways. Most reports are required by Congress, which asks the GAO to analyse different aspects of the federal regulatory policy. Consequently, the GAO has reviewed regulatory agencies and reported on: any failure to incorporate all of the best practices contained in the OMB's guidance (GAO, 1998); the OIRA and its role in reviewing agencies' draft rules (GAO, 2003), as well as its annual report (GAO, 1999); and the whole regulatory process as designed by executive order no. 12866 (GAO, 2000).

These reports do not quantitatively assess regulatory quality and performance. Nevertheless, some evaluation activities of the GAO are innovative. For example, the GAO (2001) report on information and communications technology (ICT) illustrates how the principles of accessibility and transparency can inform RIA. In 2004, the GAO discussed two economic performance measures commonly used in the evaluation of regulatory programmes: net benefits and cost-effectiveness. Specifically, the discussion revolved around the use of economic analysis and performance measures in the comparison of programmes across government. The comparison can be flawed, owing to 'the lack of agreement about the values to be used for key economic assumptions' or because 'they are based on different assumptions for the same key economic variables' (GAO, 2005: 1).

In the context of a recent workshop with policy officers, think tanks and stakeholders, the GAO (2005) aired a number of proposals, including minimum standards of economic analysis in the official RIA guidance (e.g., discounting costs and benefits, summarising results in a one-page summary in which the baseline is clearly indicated, and using scorecards). One important point raised by the GAO is peer review. Expert and external review of economic analysis can enhance the coherence of economic performance measures.

In summary, in the USA, the quality assurance system draws on the use of performance measures. The administration makes use of simple indicators of real-world outcome, such as the total net benefits, as well as measures of the quality of the regulatory process.

Canada

Like the USA, Canada has a multifaceted system to evaluate the performance of regulatory programmes. Three elements characterise the Canadian

---

Box 4.2 Canadian guidance on the assessment of regulatory initiatives

Departments that have carried out reforms to major or significant regulations[2] that they administer, or that have introduced new regulations, must comment on the performance of those reforms by:

- reporting how regulations contributed to the overall departmental goals identified in their strategic outcomes (key results, commitments or business lines);
- focusing on the result or impact of the introduction of a regulation;
- identifying quantifiable results wherever possible.

At the department's discretion, a summary of these initiatives could be located in this section or given a reference to where in the departmental performance report they can be found.

The performance of these initiatives may be reported using the following table:

Performance of regulatory initiatives

Department/agency: *Purpose of regulatory initiative*	*Expected results*	*Performance measurement criteria*	*Results achieved*
1.			
2.			

When such initiatives overlap several departments, the lead department is responsible for reporting and ensuring appropriate horizontal coordination.

Source: Treasury Board of Canada (2003).

---

approach. Firstly, governmental departments report annually to parliament with the aim of demonstrating 'the links between policies and programs (including regulatory initiatives) and their actual outcomes' (Argy and Johnson, 2003: 106).[1] The government has developed (and revised) guidelines for these reports (Government of Canada, 2002a). An extract from the guidelines is presented in box 4.2. Moreover, the Treasury Board of Canada is setting up a format for the evaluation and reporting of the process (Government of Canada, 2002b; Argy and Johnson, 2003). Indeed:

> departments and agencies have undertaken an initiative to develop a common understanding of performance measurement in the context of the Regulatory Policy, to take stock of current 'regulatory performance measurement' practices in the management of regulatory programs and to identify potential indicators. The initiative will also identify existing work in pertinent domestic

or international institutions, including the identification of common aspects (e.g., performance indicators, approaches) and areas of marked differences and best practices. (Government of Canada, 2002a: unpaginated document)

There is an example of 'regulatory performance measurement' in the annual performance report of Environment Canada.[3] In this case, the performance measure is the rate of compliance with regulation – an indicator of real-world outcome. Among Canadian government departments, the criteria to assess the performance of regulation vary markedly. Indeed, the guidelines do not set stringent requirements in terms of measurement. The evaluation system is not systematic. One implication is that it is difficult to classify the indicators generated by the Canadian evaluation system according to the three dimensions (design, activity, outcome).

The second element is the role of the auditor-general of Canada, who – in 2000 – produced a review of federal health and safety regulatory programmes.[4] The auditor-general recommends objectivity in the assessment of regulatory impact, using the best available procedures. Furthermore, the regulatory policy should balance the protection of Canadians' health and wealth and the achievement of budgetary, economic and trade objectives (Government of Canada, 2002a). Another recommendation is to report annually to parliament on the overall effectiveness of health and safety regulatory programmes and the extent to which they have the necessary financial and human resources. In short, the auditor-general of Canada has formulated recommendations to enhance the quality of health and safety regulation, without proposing any indicator to measure it.

Finally, the oversight body is the Regulatory Affairs and Orders in Council Secretariat, within the Privy Council Office. This body has the responsibility of reviewing regulatory proposals and ensuring that there has been proper analysis, using credible methodologies. That Secretariat is also in charge of assuring compliance with the federal regulatory process management standards (see the definition of Canadian principles in chapter 2). These standards provide checklists for each stage of the regulatory process. In particular, the regulatory process terminates with regular internal self-assessments of performance and policy compliance (box 4.3). This system generates simple and categorical measures related to the activity and output dimension.

The Canadian government has set priorities in terms of measurement of quality since the 1990s. But the Treasury Board of Canada (1997a, 1997b) has acknowledged the impossibility of measuring the achievement of the key objective of regulatory policy: to maximise the net benefit to Canadians. Accordingly, it turned its attention to anecdotal evidence of the quality of regulatory decisions. For the Treasury Board it is more important to gauge whether departments have internalised the new regulatory culture than to produce a final indicator of success. Structured interviews of a sample of regulators have measured the change in their perception of the usefulness of RIA (in the context of a systematic external evaluation of RIA: Regulatory

**Box 4.3 Standards of regulatory process:
a self-assessment checklist**

Internal management reviews of the regulatory process are conducted on a regular basis

- Does your management system include regular assessments on whether your regulatory process complies with the regulatory process management standards?
- Do staff independent from the departmental regulatory units conduct these reviews?
- Do you use the Manual on Review, Internal Audit and Evaluation to structure the review process and identify performance measurements?

Regulatory program designs are periodically reviewed and improvements are made as a result

- Are risk-based reviews of regulatory programs conducted to determine whether the activities meet the program objectives and service standards?
- Are assessments by clients and staff systematically sought and used?

There is a system for verifying that managers address problems identified in reviews or by clients

- Are assessment results part of regular management reviews? Are they used to develop recommendations to improve adherence to the standards?
- Is there a system for ensuring that the results of regulatory program reviews are used to help reach goals and improve services in a timely manner?
- Does senior management verify that all policy requirements are met and initiate corrective action if needed?
- Do you use feedback from the complaint resolution system to improve regulatory programs and services?
- Is there a system to verify that these recommendations are implemented?

There is a system for verifying that staff are suitably trained in regulatory development skills and training is provided when appropriate

- Are there policies and procedures for assessing what competencies are required for each job, for assessing the competencies of incumbents and new recruits, and for training personnel when there are knowledge and skills gaps?
- Can managers verify whether any particular job is done only by trained people?

Source: Treasury Board of Canada (1996: 33–4).

Consulting Group and Delphi Group, 2000: 48–50). The interviews show that all regulatory departments appear to have accepted the principle that the economic impact of proposed regulations must be examined before the formulation of rules (Regulatory Consulting Group and Delphi Group, 2000: 5–6). The consideration of alternative options is another component of the emerging regulatory culture in Canadian departments. Nonetheless, there is evidence of regulatory decisions being taken without prior RIA.

The Canadian experience shows a possible approach to the measurement of cultural change. Most countries conduct surveys of businesses and (occasionally) citizens. Canada shows how structured interviews can be usefully employed to look 'inside' government rather than 'outside'. Items in interview schedules can be inserted in more comprehensive and systematic surveys of regulators and external evaluations. The reliability of these indicators increases with the repetition of surveys over time.

Australia

There are several Australian initiatives to evaluate quality. The system is composed of the following elements – described in a study published by the Productivity Commission (Argy and Johnson, 2003: 105):

- internal monitoring and evaluation systems within responsible departments and agencies;
- ongoing reporting by the Productivity Commission, including detailed information on how the 'regulation impact statement' shows compliance with federal regulatory policy;
- performance audits by the Australian National Audit Office;
- annual compilation and reporting by departments and agencies of 'regulatory performance indicators'.

An Office of Small Business has been established with the duty of developing a set of nine regulatory performance indicators and reporting annually on performance measurement. The indicator initiative is therefore a spin-off of a policy on small and medium-sized enterprises (SMEs). Indicators are inspired by the six objectives of regulatory policy:

1 delivering a net benefit to the community;
2 achieving regulatory objectives without imposing undue business restriction;
3 ensuring transparency and fairness in the regulatory process;
4 ensuring accessible and understandable information on regulation and how to comply with it;
5 creating a predictable regulatory environment, so that businesses can make decisions with some certainty about the stability of regulation;
6 ensuring an accessible and responsive consultation process.

Table 4.1 The nine Australian regulatory performance indicators

Key objective	Regulatory performance indicators
To ensure that all new or revised regulations confer a net benefit to the community	1 Proportion of regulations for which the regulatory impact statement adequately addressed the net benefit to the community *Monitored by ORR (Office of Regulation Review)*
To achieve essential regulatory objectives without unduly restricting business in the way in which these objectives are achieved	2 Proportion of regulations for which the RIS [regulation impact statement] adequately justified the compliance burden on business *(Monitored by ORR)* 3 Proportion of regulations which provide businesses and stakeholders with some appropriate flexibility (as defined) to determine the most cost-effective means of achieving regulatory objectives *Monitored by OSB (Office of Small Business)* A regulation would be regarded as providing flexibility if it had one or more of the following attributes: • it set a performance- or outcome-based standard without prescribing in detail steps which business must take in order to comply • it included provision for business to seek acceptance of an alternative compliance mechanism to that prescribed in regulation • it used a market-based mechanism such as tradable permits to allow businesses flexibility in determining a compliance strategy • it incorporated other means to ensure that businesses have flexibility in deciding what steps to take to comply with regulation
To ensure that regulatory decision-making processes are transparent and lead to fair outcomes	4 Proportion of cases in which external review of decisions (as defined) led to a decision being reversed or overturned *Monitored by OSB* External review for these purposes is limited to processes with the following characteristics: • review is carried out by a judicial body or any other review body which is either separate from the department or agency which made the decision or is set up by legislation and has a function of reviewing decisions made by the department or agency • the review body is empowered to reverse or overturn the decision • the department or agency is a party to the review 5 Proportion of regulatory agencies whose mechanisms for internal review of decisions meet standards for complaints handling outlined in Principles for Developing a Service Charter, published by the Department of Finance and Administration *Monitored by OSB*

To ensure that information and details on regulation and how to comply with it are accessible and under-stood by business	6 Proportion of regulatory agencies having communications strategies for regulation, or formal consultative channels for communicating information about regulation *Monitored by OSB* 　　Guidelines for this purpose should be documented.
To create a predictable regulatory environ-ment so business can make decisions with some surety of future environment	7 Proportion of regulatory agencies publishing an adequate forward plan for introduction and review of regulation *Monitored by OSB* 　　An adequate forward plan for regulation should include the following elements: 　• it should be published in a way which makes it readily accessible to the business community, for example in an annual report, on the Internet, or by distribution to relevant business organisations 　• it should outline planned or likely regulatory activity expected to occur within a specified period, and should be published before that period starts 　• it should include information about reviews of legisla-tion to be undertaken in the relevant period, including reviews underway at the beginning of the period 　• it should include information about policy development processes which will be taking place during the relevant period which could affect business regulation, where information about those processes is publicly available 　• it should include information about government deci-sions to develop or implement legislation during the relevant period to the extent where those decisions have been publicly announced
To ensure that consultation processes are accessible and responsive to business and the community	8 Proportion of regulation for which the regulatory impact assessment included an adequate statement of consultation *Monitored by ORR* 9 Proportion of regulatory agencies with organisational guidelines outlining consultation processes, procedures and standards *Monitored by OSB*

Source: Office of Small Business (2003).

Indicators are therefore explicitly linked to objectives. The Office of Regu-lation Review monitors three of the nine indicators. This body, which is within the Productivity Commission, is in charge of monitoring and reviewing the regulation impact statements; it also undertakes the appraisal required for primary or subordinate legislation proposals or quasi-legislation which directly affect business, and have a significant indirect effect on business or competition. The Office of Small Business monitors the other indicators. Some indicators are based on the approach of a quality assurance process (numbers 5, 6 and 7 in table 4.1). Regulatory performance indicator 4 is the only indicator measuring the intrinsic quality of regulatory decisions. A high number of regulations reversed or overturned by a judicial review is a measure of poor quality of decision and rulings.

In summary, Australia provides evidence of a small set of indicators that have four desirable properties: they are rich in information; they are easy to understand; they are monitored by the government; and they are clearly linked to the principles of regulatory governance. These properties mean that the indicators can be inserted 'organically' into better regulation policy.

The Netherlands

The Netherlands provides an approach to better regulation policy centred on administrative burdens. The policy goal is to reduce them by 25 per cent at the end of the legislative period. Nevertheless, the Dutch better regulation policy is not confined to tackling red tape. The RIA process is characterised by the flexible use of a three-pronged checklist covering different policy areas:

- Seven questions form the Business Effects Test (the BET checklist). They aim to identify the impact of regulatory proposals on the functioning of the market and socio-economic development.
- Four questions concern environmental consequences.
- Four questions deal with problems of feasibility and enforceability.

The checklist is a support in the preparation of the compulsory explanatory memorandum that accompanies bills and cabinet proposals. One manifestation of political attention to RIA is a study commissioned by the Ministry of Justice on how to improve the assessment of proposals through a 'scenario method'. Sets of scenarios are built with the objective of clarifying possible future contexts for the enforcement of new regulations (Janssen *et al.*, 2002).

Turning to the core of Dutch better regulation policy, that is, cutting red tape, the government encourages departments to respect ceilings of administrative burdens. The ceilings 'are being created for all departments as a fixed component of the budget and accountability system' (ACTAL, 2003: 7). The integration of cutting red tape into budget policy enhances accountability, since departments report systematically to the minister of finance for their plans. Consequently, the Ministry of Finance plays a major monitoring function, together with other departments. Indeed, responsibility for achieving targets is spread throughout departments. Departmental units monitor the steps towards goals, and also train and advise officials.

The Dutch Advisory Board on Administrative Burdens (ACTAL, established in 2000) monitors, advises and supports the government effort to achieve the quantitative target of reducing administrative burdens. ACTAL guides departments in administrative burden assessment, and proposes improvement when quality is weak, especially with reference to estimates.

In the period September 2003–December 2004, this advisory body planned to review 150 RIAs (ACTAL, 2003: 15) and proposed thirty-five recommendations to reduce administrative costs. Moreover, ACTAL conducts studies on specific aspects of simplification. ACTAL's officers are also involved in visits to other countries, in order to draw lessons from innovative methods developed elsewhere.

The strategy to reduce administrative burdens targets the stock of existing regulations as well as the flow of new regulations. In both cases the Dutch government uses a specific tool, the so-called 'standard cost model' (SCM). It quantifies administrative costs, as defined in chapter 3 (see figure 3.1), and divides them according to ministries (Legislative Burden Department, 2003: 17) and the origin of the regulation (EU directive, EU regulation or national regulation). In the case of ex-ante RIA, the SCM quantifies administrative costs per regulatory option, showing the lowest burden achievable.

Turning to the data collection methodology, the Legislative Burden Department (2003) (within the Ministry of Finance) has issued a guide for defining and quantifying administrative burdens for businesses. This guide lists seventeen different pieces of paperwork or 'information obligations'. Different administrative actions have been associated with each piece of paperwork. There are two steps to the calculation of the administrative burdens produced by a single regulation. Firstly, costs per administrative action are quantified. They are composed of three variables: the cost of a single action; the number of times a firm has to provide specific information in a year (the so-called 'frequency'); and the number of businesses affected by the regulation. The cost of a single action is given by the hourly labour cost and the time spent dealing with a specific information obligation per regulation. The guidelines provide several suggestions on how the data might be gathered. For example, hourly labour costs can be determined from wage statistics, which can be validated in business interviews. Time can be estimated through business surveys. Alternatively, an objective method can be used, the so-called 'stopwatch method', in which time is actually quantified by a simulation of an administrative action (Legislative Burden Department, 2003: 21–2). The quantification of costs hence can rely on subjective and objective measures. Secondly, as there are different 'actions' implied by each regulation, all costs are calculated to obtain the total estimated cost.

The process of estimating the administrative burdens is based on a set of assumptions and hypotheses. For example, the guide requires computation of the administrative costs with the compliance rate set at 100 per cent. It has been estimated that existing regulations have created €17 billion in administrative burdens. The burden generated by the Ministry of Transport is estimated at around €1.3 billion. This is a point estimate with some important limitations. Firstly, point estimations are often less informative than ranges supported by probabilities assigned to different points within the range. Secondly, this specific point estimation is based on 100 per cent compliance – a heroic hypothesis. Finally, the estimate does not account for the time profile of costs that are expected to decrease over time.

As mentioned, the results of the SCM are reported in the explanatory memorandum that accompanies proposals for legislation. Estimates for existing regulations, instead, are contained in an annual report that all ministries table to parliament. This document is an action plan to reduce administrative burdens. The strategy to reduce administrative burdens is buttressed by an information desk (within the Ministry of Economic Affairs), which collects opinions from businesses and citizens on burdensome regulations, and by the use of ICT to reduce red tape.

To summarise: the experience of the Netherlands provides an interesting approach to total measures of administrative burden. In terms of communicability, measures such as the total administrative burden created by, say, transport regulation score well and are easy to link to targets. As will become clearer, the SCM has now become a term of reference in the better regulation policies of European countries such as Belgium, Denmark, Sweden, Norway and, most recently, the UK and the EU itself.

However, the SCM does have some limitations. Firstly, it is based on unrealistic assumptions about compliance. Secondly, as mentioned, point estimates are often less informative than probabilistic ranges. Thirdly, administrative burdens are only one component of direct costs. The other important component is compliance cost. The risk is one of focusing the public debate on a limited type of regulatory cost. Public policy should target the wider regulatory burdens (for firms, citizens and the public sector). According to the standard terminology, regulatory burdens include both direct and indirect costs. Finally, there is the political risk of tilting the whole better regulation programme towards only one stakeholder, that is, the firm.

Belgium

Belgium, with its focus on simplification and reduction of administrative burdens, stands in contrast to North America and Australia, with their emphasis on RIA and the definition of quality as the maximisation of net benefit for citizens. At the federal level, the aim of Belgian better regulation policy is to simplify the regulatory environment and to reduce administrative burdens. Organisational structure follows these principles.

Since 1999, a specific body, the Agence pour la Simplification Administrative (ASA), has carried out the task of reducing paperwork burdens on citizens and businesses. Better regulation policy is also adopted at the regional level, where specialised units – like the Regulatory Management Unit in the Flemish region – have been active since 2002. The goals of the Regulatory Management Unit are to provide: administrative relief; judicial and technical simplification; transparency; and clarity of new and existing regulation. These goals are detailed in an annual action plan, which also contains structural reform initiatives and pilot projects (ninety-one in 2003). The structural initiatives in the Flemish region include: the formulation of better regulation principles; the development of a method to measure administrative burden;[5] the introduction of a 'compensation rule' (i.e., new administrative burdens cannot be introduced unless they are counterbalanced by an equal reduction in existing administrative burdens); and the introduction of RIA.

In the Walloon region, the institutional design revolves around two specific administrative bodies. The first body, dubbed 'Wall-on-line', focuses on e-government and the simplification of administrative formalities. The second body, the Commissariat à la Simplification Administrative, aims through a series of projects to cut red tape which burdens citizens and enterprises. By June 2004, twenty of the foreseen forty-three projects had been completed. In the future, the priority will be given to those projects focused on developing a methodology to 'track and trace' administrative procedures.

Moving on to federal policy, the ASA is in charge of implementing and monitoring the quality of ex-ante RIA, with emphasis on administrative burdens. In 2004, the ASA launched the 'Kafka test', a process structured in six phases. Each phase identifies a parameter relating to how administrative burdens affect citizens, businesses and non-profit organisations (ASA, 2004). In the first phase, regulators are called to identify the target group and to estimate the number of citizens, businesses and non-profit organisations affected by a regulatory proposal. Then, a description of the type of information obligation implied by the regulation has to be provided. The second step revolves around an inventory of the most common administrative duties. In the third step, the regulator establishes who triggers the information obligation – in some cases it is the public administration that sends forms and requests data, while in others it is the target group that contacts the administration requesting a subsidy or product licence and so on. The fourth parameter is related to the frequency of the proposed obligation. Another step required by the Kafka test is to identify the type of data and certificates required. Finally, regulators should describe how citizens, businesses and non-profit organisations would be able to send to the public administration the information required.

Essentially, the Kafka test is a tool to gather information on administrative burdens. It supports the decision-making process in the Belgian council of ministers by showing whether (and how) a new proposal is worsening the regulatory environment for citizens, businesses and non-profit organisations. This simplicity, however, has been achieved at the cost of limiting the scope of the assessment methodology. For instance, the test does not allow for a clear-cut comparison of regulatory options. Another point to bear in mind is that the Kafka parameters are not aggregated in a single index.

Beyond the Kafka test, in 2005 the ASA measured the reduction in administrative burdens resulting from simplification, in connection with the governmental objective to reduce burdens across the economy. The ASA makes use of the SCM and business surveys – using the methodology of expenditure studies mentioned in the previous chapter. Survey measures of the quality of the business environment are limited to costs, and there is no estimate of the net benefits (De Vil and Kegels, 2001). They capture the administrative burdens created by existing regulations. By October 2004, there were 119 simplification projects.[6]

Belgium has also focused on e-government initiatives in the context of the effort to reduce administrative burdens – exploiting ICT. One of the main projects, dubbed Banque-Carrefour des Enterprises, is to reduce the formalities necessary for enterprise start-up.[7] To measure this project's success, Belgium relies on the indicators recommended by Djankov *et al.* and the World Bank (see chapter 3), such as the time necessary for an entrepreneur to set up a new firm.[8]

Belgium represents a good example of coherence among the components of simplification policy. The goal of reducing administrative burden has been supported by a series of tools and measurements. This gives the government greater control. Moreover, the different measurement exercises reinforce each other. At the same time, this is an experience that narrows the scope of better regulation policy to simplification and administrative burdens. Wider principles of regulatory reform, such as introducing rules that deliver net benefits to the community, are ignored.

Denmark

In Denmark, there are two pivotal departments which coordinate and monitor the better regulation policy: the Ministry of Economic and Business Affairs, through the Danish Commerce and Companies Agency, and the Division of Better Regulation, within the Ministry of Finance. The former is in charge of new regulatory proposals, which are subject to mandatory consultation conducted by the Danish Commerce and Companies Agency. The Division of Better Regulation is responsible for the simplification of existing regulations and is also mandated to define 'good regulation' (Danish Commerce and Companies Agency, 2003: 139).

All regulatory proposals tabled to parliament have to be appraised through RIA, covering not only business administrative costs but also economic impact on citizens and the public administration, as well as any effects on the environment (Danish Commerce and Companies Agency, 2003: 140). However, the emphasis is on improving the regulatory environment for business. Indeed, the Business Test Panel is a distinctive element of the Danish approach to better regulation.

The simplification strategy is based on two approaches (or tools): a systematic simplification project – currently under way; and a new method to measure administrative burdens. The Ministry of Economic and Business Affairs, the Ministry of Finance and the Ministry of Taxation are developing a comprehensive process to review existing regulations. The purpose of the project is to set up a rolling programme for simplification, based on measurement methodologies. The collaboration between these three ministries is also targeted at operationalising three necessary steps to quantify and eventually simplify red tape:

- the selection of particular regulatory sectors for simplification;
- the production of a map of information obligations;
- the streamlining of administrative procedures.

The first step requires the estimation of business administrative costs in each regulatory sector. The aim of this activity is to select a regulatory sector in which simplification will be most efficient. The selection relies on information gathered by business surveys, the so-called 'model companies'. This model is based on a random sample of 1,000 firms. These are then surveyed on how the stock of regulation affects the daily administration of a company; this provides a quantification of the total administrative burden. It considers the representative sample according to business sectors and firm size. It is important to note that the 'model companies' approach has been used for different purposes. It has been used to evaluate the effect on administrative burdens of specific government initiatives, for instance the utilisation of ICT in public administration, as well as to provide data to the European Commission on the most cumbersome regulations affecting SMEs.

The second step draws on the SCM (see the above section on the Netherlands) in order to obtain a clear picture of actions associated with a specific information obligation.

The third step targets information obligations and ends up with suggestions for action. Specifically, the third step looks at the options of: abolishing or reviewing information obligations; bundling several obligations together in order to reduce the number of deadlines and forms to fill; and adopting ICT. The government will provide general guidance on these simplification tools in the context of the quantitative target to reduce administrative burdens by 25 per cent in 2010. An annual report on the achievement of this target is presented to the Danish parliament.

The Danish version of the SCM has been developed by the Ministry of Economic and Business Affairs, in cooperation with other ministries as well as stakeholders. The model makes it possible to estimate the costs related to specific administrative provisions. The measurement of the existing regulations is based on 'zero-base measurement'. The latter is an inventory of all information obligations and administrative activities grouped according to the responsible ministry.[9] The administration activities are then quantified.

The progress achieved in the simplification strategy is evident. Administrative burdens are now measured with a more objective method: the SCM (although the previous remarks on the limitations of the SCM apply to Denmark as well). This measurement method creates greater transparency and accountability (since, as a general rule, each ministry is responsible for reducing administrative burdens by up to 25 per cent by 2010) and facilitates a systematic review and simplification of regulations.

Simplification policy is characterised by frequent consultations with business. Indeed, business surveys measure administrative costs either for a specific industry or across specific kinds of firms, such as the sole proprietor company.

Denmark is one of the EU countries focused on a specific definition of better regulation policy – the improvement of the business environment. Two different methods of measuring administrative burdens coexist. There is no specific system of indicators covering all tools, but, as is the case with the Netherlands, the total administrative burden per sector and across the economy is known.

Sweden

Sweden is yet another country wherein better regulation is linked to the government's commitment to improve the regulatory environment for SMEs. As a result, RIA targets direct business compliance costs, especially for SMEs. Since 2002, there has been political momentum for a reduction in administrative burdens. In December 2002, a parliamentary resolution called for 'effective simplification', and required the government to review and simplify business regulations, set a quantitative target for simplification and set a time limit within which government agencies would answer requests or deal with specific cases. Further to the resolution, the government has adopted two main measures. The first is an action plan to reduce administrative burdens. The action plan requires forty-six public agencies, selected according to the impact of their regulatory activities on the business environment, and all ministries to review all existing regulations that affect business. In doing so, ministries and agencies can count on two tools: the simplification of existing regulations; and improved access to public administration services and regulation via ICT. Agencies should propose simplification plans at the end of the review.

The other measure is related to the administrative burdens. The methodology has been developed in cooperation with Denmark and the Netherlands, starting from the SCM. It relies on a survey of 'average' enterprises (the median firm in terms of efficiency in compliance) within a 'target group'. When the administrative cost triggered by new activities is gathered through a survey, the new figures are validated against the time spent on activities similar to the new one.

Having explained the recent evolution of better regulation in Sweden, let us turn to the experience of RIA appraisal. Here stakeholders have provided fresh ideas by turning the Swedish principles of better regulation into indicators. The Board of Swedish Industry and Commerce for Better

Regulation (NNR) has conducted a study on how agencies, committees and commissions of enquiry,[10] as well as government offices, comply with Swedish regulatory policy. In developing its analysis, the NNR draws on three major landmark rules (ordinances) for the regulatory process. To begin with, the Government Agencies and Institutes Ordinance (no. 1322 of 1995) requires regulatory agencies to analyse the impact of their proposals. The analysis:

> includes an account of existing problems, the aims of the proposal, alternatives to regulation and the financial impact on companies affected by the proposal. The parties concerned are entitled to express their views on the matter and on the RIA. (NNR, 2002: 4)

Secondly, an ordinance on the special impact analysis of rules on small businesses (the so-called 'SimpLex Ordinance', no. 1829 of 1998) requires an RIA be performed when the proposal is likely to affect SMEs. This RIA is presented to parliament in the explanatory memorandum that accompanies legislative proposals. The emphasis given to the regulatory business environment is also reflected in the design of the RIA process. Within the Ministry of Industry, Employment and Communications, the SimpLex Team is the oversight body (of the regulatory process) and must be involved at an early stage of the law-making process. This is an obligation spelled out in the Cabinet Office's guidelines for the preparation of new laws and regulations. The Team reviews and approves RIAs of legislative proposals. In doing so, a checklist based on the OECD reference checklist for regulatory decision-making is used. The twelve questions of the Swedish RIA checklist are presented in box 4.4. The SimpLex ordinance is also applied to regulatory agencies when a regulatory proposal may be deemed to affect SMEs. To some extent, the SimpLex ordinance covers the same issue of RIA required by the Government Agencies and Institutes Ordinance.

Thirdly, the Committees Ordinance obliges parliamentary committees and commissions to analyse the impact of their proposals in an RIA format.

The NNR has developed eleven quality indicators on the basis of these three ordinances (see box 4.4). The indicators are designed to measure outputs and are 'classic' indicators of a quality assurance process (see chapter 3). They are simple and expressed in a yes/no format.

The NNR has proposed additional indicators, such as business survey measures. Some of them are useful for a subjective assessment of the quality of consultation. The NNR has also argued for the systematic incorporation of OECD and large-scale comparative surveys (OECD, 2001) in the analysis of domestic output (NNR, 2003).

The NNR (2003) provides the following data on the quality of eighty consultations in Sweden:

- in 25 per cent of cases, agencies quantified administrative costs;
- in 14 per cent of cases, the number of companies affected was not specified;

Box 4.4 The NNR regulation indicators for 2003 and SimpLex checklist

The NNR indicators

1 Summary. Has the regulator summarised the case and described its content in the proposal?
2 Previous regulations. Is there a description of previous regulations?
3 Alternatives described. Has the regulator described the alternatives to a new or amended regulation?
4 Early consultation. Were the parties affected, or their representatives, consulted before the proposal was presented?
5 Number of companies. Is there an account of how many companies and which sectors are affected by the amendment or the new statutory requirement?
6 Companies' costs. Has the regulator calculated the cost incurred by those affected as a result of the proposal?
7 Total costs. Are there any estimates of costs incurred by the whole business collective concerned?
8 Clarification of competition aspect. Have the regulators analysed competition issues?
9 Goldplating. In the implementation of an EU decision, it must be made clear whether, and if so why, the Swedish regulation is more far-reaching than the EU decision.
10 Period of circulation for official comment. Is the period of circulation for official comment at least three weeks?
11 SimpLex analysis. Has the regulator carried out a SimpLex analysis?

The 'SimpLex' checklist

1 What is the problem to be solved by regulation and what happens if regulation does not take place?
2 Are there any alternative solutions?
3 Which administrative, practical or other measures must small businesses take as a consequence of the regulation?
4 How much time would be needed for small businesses to comply with the regulation?
5 Would regulation lead to additional costs for wages, other expenses or stress resources for small businesses?
6 Can regulation distort competition to the disadvantage of small businesses or otherwise decrease their competitiveness?
7 Will the regulation affect any other aspects of small businesses?
8 Is it possible to control compliance with the regulation, and how will regulatory effects on small businesses be observed and reviewed/scrutinised?
9 Should the regulation be in force only for a limited period, to prevent possible negative effects on small businesses?
10 Do particular concerns arise for small businesses in relation to the regulation coming into force?
11 Are any special information measures needed?
12 How has the necessary business and authority consultation been done and what significant points of view have been put forward?

Source: NNR (2002, 2003: 194).

- in 21 per cent of cases, the results of consultation produced an overall decrease in the information requirement of the final regulation;
- in 24 per cent of cases, requests for information and other formalities were eliminated;
- in 53 per cent of cases formalities were simplified.

This kind of database can be a measure of how and to what extent the interaction between consultation and simplification can produce results. It also shows the importance of integrating tools of better regulation.

On balance, Sweden is a country focused on simplification and administrative burdens, with special emphasis on the problems encountered by SMEs. Stakeholders assess the quality of governmental efforts, propose indicators and suggest improvements.

The UK

In the UK, better regulation policies have developed around the pivotal role of RIA. Regulators must identify and quantify, where possible in monetary terms, any (direct and indirect) costs and benefits that may fall on consumers, the environment or citizens in general.

An RIA is required in the appraisal of new regulations, as well as the simplification of existing regulations. In both cases, the Cabinet Office's 'Public Service Agreement' has specific quantitative targets. In the appraisal of new regulations, the Better Regulation Executive (before May 2005 the Regulatory Impact Unit), the oversight regulatory body, has the target of full compliance with the RIA process by departments and agencies for every regulatory proposal that may affect business, charities or voluntary organisations (NAO, 2004: 11). A Cabinet Office statement declares that in 2004 and 2005 the level of compliance was 100 per cent.[11]

The other quantitative target was to deliver over sixty drafts of regulatory reform orders by 2006 (House of Commons, 2003). Regulatory reform orders are proposals to simplify existing primary law under the Regulatory Reform Act 2001. This Act enables departments to amend legislation in order to reduce administrative burdens. The UK has not used this quantitative target to develop specific indicators.

The UK approach to the design of quality control mechanisms is based on different layers of monitoring, evaluation and quality appraisal. There is an internal layer of quality assurance mechanisms based on departmental units, a level of coordination of quality policies within the executive based on the Better Regulation Executive in the Cabinet Office, mechanisms based on bodies at arm's length from the Cabinet Office – notably, the Better Regulation Task Force, a body (established in 1997) with a mission to make the voice of stakeholders heard in the UK's regulatory process, which in January 2006 became the Better Regulation Commission – and, since 2001, the external appraisal performed by the NAO.

The other oversight body of regulatory process is the Small Business Service, an executive agency of the Department of Trade and Industry. It focuses on the impact of regulation on SMEs and promotes 'horizontal' policy on a better regulatory environment for the economic development of SMEs.

External and independent scrutiny has been made possible by recent developments in the RIA process that make the assessment exercise more open and transparent. The Better Regulation Commission oversees the quality of RIA and defines the principles of better regulation. It reviews specific regulatory areas in order to suggest improvement and change. Both the degree of acceptance and the time taken to respond to the Commission's recommendations may be considered indicators of activity.

In 2003, the Better Regulation Task Force listed ten examples of poor-quality RIAs, and challenged departments to make them all so good that the next report would not list any RIAs of this type (Better Regulation Task Force, 2003: 13). Seven of these examples of poor RIAs were used by the NAO to review the quality of RIA.

The role of the NAO in the quality assurance process has become more important since 2001. In that year, the NAO produced a report on good RIA practice, drawing some lessons from a review of a sample of twenty-three RIAs (NAO, 2001). The NAO has also covered the quality of RIA guidance. One interesting feature of the work conducted is that desk analysis of specific RIAs is accompanied by semi-structured interviews within the departments and with staff at the Better Regulation Executive. Since 2002, the NAO has used a set of criteria to assess the quality of RIA (box 4.5). Work by the NAO (2005: 3) shows the different types of RIA in the British political system.

Scorecards are commonly used by both stakeholders and academics. The British Chambers of Commerce (Ambler *et al.*, 2004) collected information on aggregated costs and benefits quantified in RIAs. The report shows the total sum of costs and benefits identified by RIA in a year.[12] This analysis leads to simple measures of output, such as percentages of RIAs that: present a summary of consultations; illustrate how proposed regulations have changed in response to consultation; consider non-regulatory options; include sunset clauses; quantify costs, on business, environment, citizens and government; quantify benefits, for business, environment, citizens and government; quantify net benefits; and report measures of compliance costs for SME. These are useful indicators. They represent a stripped-down version of the indicators of quality of RIA suggested by economists, and add some dimensions of learning and good governance – such as data on how consultation really affects the formulation of new regulations. A score-card on the quality of RIA in the UK has been discussed by Jacobs (2005). It is a simpler version of the scorecards used by academics in the USA (see chapter 3).

Box 4.5 The NAO checklist on regulatory impact assessment

Was the preferred regulation chosen by appropriate analysis/process?

1 Was the RIA process started early enough?
   - Did the department have clear objectives for the regulation?
   - Did the department allow a realistic timetable for the RIA process?
   - Did the department consider the risks?
   - Did the RIA consider a range of options?
   - Were alternatives to regulation considered?
   - Were alternative regulatory tools considered?

2 Was consultation effective?
   - Was effective consultation started early in the process?
   - Did the department use appropriate consultation techniques?
   - Did the department explain clearly the impact of the regulation?
   - Did the department consult all interested groups of stakeholders?
   - Did the department consider the impact on small businesses?
   - Were the results of the consultation used well in formulating the regulation?

3 Did the RIA assess costs thoroughly?
   - Were the implementation and policy costs on all those affected taken into account?
   - Did the department identify all parties on whom costs would fall?
   - Did the department consider the costs to small businesses?
   - Did the department identify all likely costs?
   - Did the department assess the costs of all options?

4 Did the RIA assess benefits realistically?
   - Did the department identify all parties who would benefit?
   - Were the benefits realistic and relevant to the regulation?
   - Was the methodology for quantifying/scoring the benefits robust?
   - Did the department assess the benefits of all options?

5 Did the RIA realistically assess compliance?
   - Was possible non-compliance factored into the analysis?
   - Did the department assess the existing level of compliance?
   - Were ways of increasing compliance considered?

6 Will the regulation be effectively monitored and evaluated?
   - Did the RIA contain procedures for monitoring and evaluating the extent to which the regulation meets its objectives?

Source: NAO (2004).

Turning to consultation, the Better Regulation Executive's Code of Practice on Consultation sets minimum standards based on the following six criteria:[13]

1 Consult widely throughout the process, allowing a minimum of 12 weeks for written consultation at least once during the development of the policy.
2 Be clear about your proposals: who may be affected, what questions are being asked and the timescale for responses.
3 Ensure that your consultation is clear, concise and wisely accessible.
4 Give feedback regarding the responses received and how the consultation process influenced the policy.
5 Monitor your department's effectiveness at consultation, including through the use of a designated consultation coordinator.
6 Ensure your consultation follows better regulation best practice, including carrying out an RIA.

The Better Regulation Executive has produced a self-assessed questionnaire in order to assess the compliance of departments with the Code of Practice. The assessment has been performed annually since 2001.[14] There were 609 written consultations in 2004; 622 in 2003; 349 in 2002; and 356 in 2001. In 2004 and 2003, 79 per cent of written consultations complied with the requirement to grant at least twelve weeks to interested parties to express an opinion on policy options (see above). Some departments have designated a 'consultation coordinator'. The 2002 report on consultation included simple indicators, such as:

• the number of complaints on consultation (e.g., the length of consultation period, or the omission of groups from a consultation list);
• the number of complaints concerning the content of the consultation (e.g., the clarity of background documents, or the availability of a consultation document in other languages, such as Welsh translations);
• the number of comments provided by stakeholders that have been used to improve consultation.

The UK experience has developed from an early start in the 1980s based on compliance cost assessment. Over the 1990s, the approach to better regulation policy was widened. RIA has now become the cornerstone of the regulatory process (Baldwin, 2005). In connection with the emergence of RIA, increasing attention has been given to the principles of risk analysis (Black, 2005) and to the principle that meta-regulation should be used to deliver net benefits to the economy and society.

More recently, however, the political drive has been towards simplification and targets for the reduction of administrative burdens. An influential report on regulatory enforcement (the so-called 'Hampton review' – HM Treasury, 2005) has been flagged up by the British executive as an example of how to step up the initiatives for simplification and for improving the business environment. The report of the Better Regulation Task Force (2005) *Less Is More* had been requested in October 2004 by the prime minister. It was endorsed publicly by the prime minister – with a letter sent to the chair of the Task Force in July 2005 – and the chancellor of the exchequer. The report draws explicitly on the SCM (one chapter of *Less Is More* is entirely dedicated to the Dutch methodology). It recommends the identification and setting of quantitative targets for the reduction of administrative burdens via the SCM. It also makes the controversial proposal to adopt a drastic 'one in – one out' approach to the management of regulatory burdens.

The 'recalibration' of bodies such as the Regulatory Impact Unit (now the Better Regulation Executive) and the Better Regulation Task Force (now the Better Regulation Commission) was a consequence of a new focus on targets for simplification and burdens. Paradoxically, perhaps, the UK is moving from a broad and multi-stakeholder paradigm to a policy confined to burdens and business. It is a case of convergence with the other countries that have adopted the SCM – possibly in connection with a successful campaign by the 2004 Dutch Presidency of the EU to adopt a common method across the Member States and at the EU level.

The technical limitations of the 'burdens' approach to better regulation have already been exposed. One of the challenging tasks of the Better Regulation Executive is to estimate the total level of burdens, otherwise targeted reduction cannot be delivered. But, for the UK, legitimacy issues can be even more important. Until recently, better regulation had been presented as a policy benefiting a large set of stakeholders, but the political attention (since *Less Is More*) has now turned to business. This may create a controversial debate on 'better regulation for whom?' in the future. Further, it is not clear to what extent the RIA-based strategy pursued during the 1990s is compatible with a focus on burdens. The RIA principle is that regulation is good if its benefits justify the costs. As mentioned in chapter 2, quality of regulation should not be confused with quantity. The presumption behind *Less Is More* is that burdens should be cut, in line with a target, but these targets are not necessarily set by balancing administration costs and regulatory benefits.[15]

Conclusions

This chapter has illustrated how governments monitor and measure quality and the specific initiatives under way. Setting quantitative targets is a popular option, at least in Europe, to encourage the public administration to implement measurement systems (as shown by Belgium, Denmark, Sweden, the Netherlands and the UK). Some countries have gone further than that, by introducing measures of quality and/or systematic reviews and monitoring tools based on quantifiable variables.

In fact, the number of countries with measurement initiatives is increasing. The OECD (2004: 10) lists nine of its Member States as having some experience in the evaluation of RIA output. Moreover, in 2004 a specific OECD questionnaire on 'ex-post evaluation of regulatory tools and institutions' was sent to the national directors or experts of better regulation. The results from this self-assessment questionnaire are interesting: eight out of twenty-two OECD Member States recorded 'an explicit and current policy/ strategy on ex-post evaluation of regulatory tools and institutions'; three out of the twenty-two reported that this policy or strategy was in preparation. Our data on this issue are presented in chapter 5. But one striking fact is that even European countries with information that can be potentially turned into systems of indicators (as opposed to the use of a single target) are not aware of this potential, or, if aware, they have not started activity along these lines.

Another interesting result is the systematic incorporation of stakeholders' needs into quality assurance systems and tools of better regulation like RIA and simplification. Surveys of stakeholders have been refined over the years, and have improved the overall accuracy of estimates. Some EU governments are developing their methodologies with the input of stakeholders. In other cases, stakeholders are not formally part of the process, but contribute ideas and suggestions to the development of methods and techniques. This happens eminently in the area of administrative burden.

Quality assurance systems seek to change the culture of regulators. Canada provides an example of using semi-structured interviews to measure changes in the attitudes of civil servants towards regulation. One can see how indicators of quality can be developed along these lines by replicating interviews and even surveys over the years, although this exercise does not come cheap.

This review has covered five of the twenty-five EU Member States, as well as Canada, Australia and the USA. These eight countries can be divided into two groups, according to how they approach RIA and its evaluation: those targeting administrative burdens, and those seeking quality across a broader range of RIA issues. Indeed, there is an interesting correlation between an approach to RIA and quality assurance structures based on a sophisticated monitoring system. Table 4.2 shows this correlation. Australia, Canada, the UK and the USA have a robust network of quality assurance actors and also look at RIA beyond the issue of red tape – with some qualifications regarding the recent political enthusiasm for a reduction in administrative burden in the UK.

By contrast, Belgium, Denmark and the Netherlands focus on administrative burdens and are characterised by a simpler system of monitoring. Should the UK move to this group of countries, there would be some incoherence between a narrow focus on burdens and the sophisticated institutional arrangements for quality assurance. In Sweden the design of the quality

Table 4.2 Correlation between quality assurance systems and approach to regulatory impact assessment

	Simple quality assurance	*Sophisticated quality assurance*
Administrative burdens	Belgium, Denmark, the Netherlands, Sweden	
Analysis of costs and benefits (net-benefit principle of impact assessment)		Australia, Canada, the UK, the USA

assurance system is similar to the one adopted in the other countries in the cell. However, the involvement of stakeholders provides additional elements of robustness to the overall quality assurance process. The NNR indicators, although not formally adopted by the government, go well beyond the analysis of administrative burdens.

No systematic evidence in our sample points to the use of aggregate measures, as described in chapter 3. Even the simplest of indexes, comprising time and costs to comply with regulation of entry (Djankov *et al.*, 2001), is not currently used. Nevertheless, countries that focus on the reduction of administrative burdens rely on simple measures amply discussed by the literature, such as the time spent to deal with information requests, and hourly costs.

Considering that most EU Member States are targeting red tape and that the literature has discussed several indexes, there is considerable potential for a closer dialogue between policy-makers and social scientists. For example, Djankov *et al.* (2001) developed an index ranking all the costs of specific actions to be undertaken in order to set up a new firm (as a percentage of GDP) (see chapter 3). This index can provide policy-makers with a shortlist of administrative burdens for which simplification is more cost-effective.

Governments tend to use simple measures. The most widely used measure is the yes/no format to assess the degree of compliance with RIA guidance and simplification. Moreover, the only example of simple consultation measures is in the UK. Few indicators refer to the 'access' dimension. Table 4.3 shows examples of indicators currently in use.

Table 4.3 Indicators currently in use

Tool of better regulation	Activities and outputs	Real-world outcome
RIA	Australia • Regulatory performance indicators Canada • Regulatory process standards UK • Time to implement independent audit body's recommendation UK and Sweden (NNR) • Scorecard to assess the compliance with impact assessment guidelines USA – PART • Is the programme's purpose clear? • Is the programme designed to make a significant impact in addressing the interest, problem or need? • Did the programme seek and take into account the views of affected parties including state, local and tribal governments and small businesses, in drafting significant regulation?	Australia • Regulatory performance indicator: proportion of cases in which an external review led to a decision being reversed or overturned Canada • Performance measurement: rate of compliance • Change in regulators' behaviour assessed through semi-structured interviews in the context of external evaluation USA – PART • Were programmatic goals (and benefits) achieved at the least incremental cost to society and did the programme maximise net benefits? • Does the performance of this programme compare favourably with other programmes with similar purposes and goals?

Consultation	Denmark • Number of companies systematically surveyed Sweden (NNR) • Administrative costs avoided through consultation conducted before new information obligations were issued UK • Scorecard to assess compliance with written consultation guidelines • Percentage of consultations granted in the required time to stakeholder • Number of complaints about the consultation process • Number of useful comments to improve consultation	Sweden – OECD survey • Percentage of small businesses that believe that agencies consult the business sector before taking decisions on new regulation
Simplification	Various countries • Administrative costs associated with a single regulation	Various countries • Administrative costs of all existing regulation (through a standard cost model or business survey) • Number of forms to communicate data to public administration • Cost of filling in forms
Access		Various countries • Administrative costs to have access to regulations (via standard cost model)

Notes

1 There is also a more strategic document to be tabled to the parliament each year: the *Report on Plans and Priorities*. Some departments, for example Environment Canada, include a regulatory agenda in this document.

2 A 'major' regulation is one that costs more than C\$50,000,000 or costs between C\$100,000 and C\$50,000,000 and has a low degree of public acceptance. A 'significant' regulation is one that: has an annual impact on the economy of C\$10,000,000 or more; or adversely affects a sector of the economy, productivity, competition, jobs, the environment, public health or safety, provincial, local or Aboriginal governments; or creates a serious inconsistency or otherwise interferes with an action taken or planned by another federal department or agency; or materially alters the authorised levels of departmental (or the budgetary impact) of entitlements, grants, user fees and loans programmes, or the rights and obligations of recipients thereof; or raises novel legal or policy issues arising out of legal mandates or the government's priorities.

3 The performance reports are available on-line at www.ec.gc.ca/dpr/index_e.htm.

4 See chapter 24 of the review at www.oag-bvg.gc.ca/domino/reports.nsf/html/0024ce.html.

5 According to the 2003–4 action plan, the method had been applied in sixteen pilot projects aimed at reducing administrative burden. With this method, it will be possible to monitor a clear and quantifiable target: a €100 million reduction in the administrative burden.

6 See the press release 'Kafka Marche – L'index Kafka est a 46% après 1 an', 22 October 2004, available at http://www.vbo-feb.be/index.html?file=625/.

7 Also in this context, the Carrefour de la Sécurité Sociale has been established with the aim of providing citizens with a social security identification – an electronic card used in all health transactions.

8 In a press note dated 22 October 2004, the ASA emphasised the successful results of the simplification action plan, with reference to the *Doing Business* World Bank indicator. The latter measures the number of days it takes to set up an enterprise. In one year, this indicator had decreased from twenty-two to three to set up a small or medium-sized enterprise, and from fifty-six to thirty-three to set up a big enterprise.

9 This methodology is common also in the Netherlands.

10 These bodies examine the issue or problem the regulation aims to solve. The findings of the analysis, together with consultations, are the basis of government's proposal for new regulation.

11 See www.cabinetoffice.gov.uk/regulation/ria/compliance/index.asp.

12 The study collected 165 of 197 RIAs performed by government departments.

13 The Code of Practice is available at www.cabinetoffice.gov.uk/regulation/documents/consultation/pdf/code.pdf.

14 Reports on these assessments are available at http://www.cabinetoffice.gov.uk/regulation/documents/consultation/pdf/2001.pdf through to /2005.pdf.

15 We are grateful to Robert Baldwin for this comment.

5

The results of the questionnaire

Introduction

As mentioned throughout this volume, the profile of better regulation in the EU is still quite varied. Chapter 4 and the recent report from the Directors of Better Regulation (DBR, 2004) confirm that national contexts are still different. The emphasis on various principles and tools is not the same in all EU countries. Yet chapter 4 has also provided evidence of limited clustered convergence. The main purpose of the questionnaire used in the present study was to ascertain whether the Member States are converging in terms of the definition of regulatory quality principles, use of tools and measures of better regulation policy.

In chapter 4, we found a cluster of countries working on measures of regulatory quality in the context of sophisticated quality assurance processes, which were characterised by the pivotal role they afforded RIA. Another cluster adopts the same approach to indicators in the context of a lean quality assurance process with emphasis on administrative burdens and simplification. These were the major results of the research conducted during the first semester of 2004, including consultation with the support network (described below) and correspondence with experts from several countries. The questionnaire results helped us to identify a third cluster of countries, with no systematic experience of quality indicators, limited investment in quality assurance and a basic approach to RIA. The questionnaire has been an indispensable tool to map out the specific details of better regulation policies and what progress has been made in terms of measures of regulatory quality.

In designing the questionnaire we drew on our framework of dimensions and tools of better regulation. The questionnaire is not the usual 'tick the box' exercise. It served the following purposes:

- To illustrate how the framework we have used for the review of initiatives in chapter 4 can lead to the design of indicators. Hence we started from the definitions and principles of better regulation, looked at quality assurance systems, and showed the implications in terms of measuring activity and outcome.

• To test the support network on the meanings of quality and possible indicators. The questionnaire enabled us to determine the level of convergence in Europe around principles of better regulation, quality assurance approaches and of course indicators. We asked the support network whether they agreed on definitions and concepts, and invited them to formulate alternative proposals if they thought that our approach missed some dimensions.

• To measure the progress made by Member States since 2000 and to find out whether progress also means convergence in Europe – on the direction and targets of initiatives.

• To invite the support network to formulate proposals for the development of EU-level indicators.

• To illustrate how indicators can be developed. In this respect, the questionnaire served an educational purpose.

One point to stress is that the questionnaire was not intended to provide data in order to derive indicators. We think that the first step should be a thorough discussion of the indicators proposed in this volume – including a reflection on how data can be gathered and used. Only after having 'absorbed' the proposal contained in chapter 7 will the Member States and the Commission be able to discuss whether a series of different sets of indicators can be used to monitor and evaluate the quality of regulatory governance in the EU.

The questionnaire contains eighteen questions. It is shown in full in appendix 1. It is divided into two basic parts, with two supplemental questions. Drawing on the previous discussion on principles of regulatory quality, the first part (from question 1 to question 10) deals with the preconditions for effective better regulation policy. In consequence, the questionnaire emphasises quality definitions and specific principles adopted to achieve it. Since we intend to propose indicators, the questionnaire then turns to a set of questions on quantifiable goals, targets and the link between performance management systems and better regulation goals.

One innovative feature of the questionnaire is that quality is not considered exclusively 'tool by tool'. It is also related to the integration of different tools of better regulation, such as RIA and consultation. Our review of the experience of Member States has shown some interesting examples of integration. In Sweden, consultation is used in the approach to simplification. Belgium, Denmark, the Netherlands and Sweden use ICT to increase access to legislation and reduce administrative burdens, thus integrating the tools of simplification and access. The UK reviews legislation through RIA – an example of how simplification can benefit from the systematic use of economic analysis.

The second part of the questionnaire (from question 11 to question 16) is on real-world outcomes and initial ideas for the development of EU-level indicators. Knowing that these indicators do not exist in Europe, we asked some hypothetical questions about how long it would take to collect them and whether such collection is feasible at all. This section provides some questions on economic analysis applied to the regulatory process, such as quantification of lives saved and illness reduction, as well as quantification of the costs and benefits related to the regulations issued in a specific year. This is also a way of showing how indicators of real-world outcome may look.

Finally, question 17 aims to gather respondents' opinions on what should be the key activities within better regulation in the near future. Question 18 asks the support network to contribute ideas to the discussion about what should be measured at the EU level, and how.

In May 2004, the questionnaire was sent to members of a support network specifically created by DG Enterprise at a meeting held at the Hague in January 2004. The support network was composed of government officials in charge of better regulation policy as well as four members of organisations representing business interests. Additionally, the questionnaire was sent to directors of better regulation for those countries not participating in the support network.

This has yielded reliable answers, even if respondents have faced some difficulties in coordinating different levels of public administration in countries where data and information are not held by a central unit but are dispersed across departments. However, a degree of subjectivity, present in every questionnaire, should be taken into account. This subjectivity is also due to the format of the questionnaire – it is not based exclusively on 'yes/ no' answers: several questions are open. The last few questions for example ask the support network to provide specific comments on the project and its analytical framework.

Response rate

The response rate was quite satisfactory. In total, we received twenty-two responses. There were fourteen respondents among the fifteen 'old' Member States of the EU.[1] Five of the ten new Member States answered. Finally, the support network included Bulgaria (among the new candidate countries) and Norway (a member of European Economic Area) and both countries answered the questionnaire. A member of the support network representing business interests, that is, the NNR, answered and provided additional comments and background papers; however, because many of the questions pertain to national government, for the most part it is not included in the sample reported on below. Table 5.1 provides information on the respondents. The remainder of the chapter looks in turn at the responses to the respective questionnaire items.

Table 5.1 Respondents to the questionnaire

Country	Old Member State	New Member State	Candidate countries	Support network
EU Member States				
Austria	Yes	No	No	Yes
Belgium	Yes	No	No	Yes
Czech Republic	No	Yes	No	No
Denmark	Yes	No	No	Yes
Estonia	No	Yes	No	Yes
Finland	Yes	No	No	Yes
France	Yes	No	No	No
Germany	Yes	No	No	Yes
Greece	Yes	No	No	No
Hungary	No	Yes	No	Yes
Ireland	Yes	No	No	No
Italy	Yes	No	No	Yes
Latvia	No	Yes	No	Yes
Luxembourg	Yes	No	No	No
Netherlands	Yes	No	No	Yes
Poland	No	Yes	No	Yes
Spain	Yes	No	No	No
Sweden	Yes	No	No	Yes
UK	Yes	No	No	Yes
Other countries				
Bulgaria	No	No	Yes	Yes
Norway	No	No	No	Yes
Other				
NNR (Board of Swedish Industry and Commerce for Better Regulation)	–	–	–	Yes

Objectives of regulatory quality

The first question is on better regulation policy. Figure 5.1 groups respondents according to the objective they selected as best describing their country's approach to regulatory quality (one answer only was permitted).

Having effective and efficient regulations was the most common objective among our sample (eight respondents). Cost-effectiveness was the second most common aim, chosen by six countries, followed by the minimisation of administrative burden (four countries). Norway had the objective of achieving a better regulatory environment for business and trade.

In Belgium, regulatory quality objectives varied according to the level of government. Indeed, if at the federal level and the Walloon region the objective

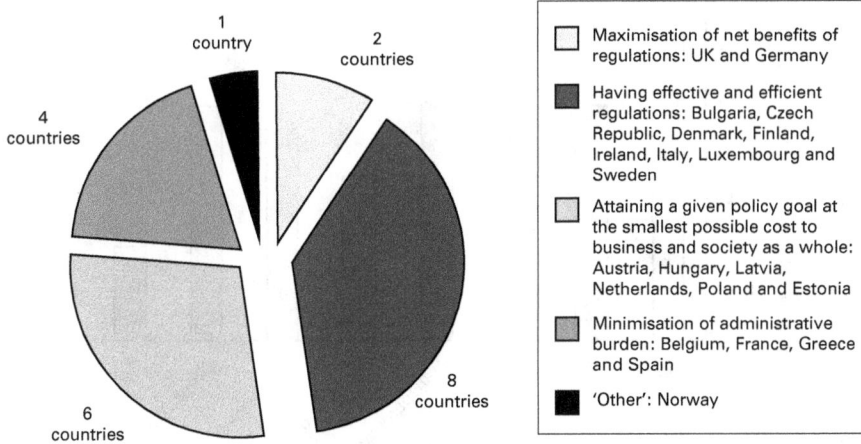

Figure 5.1 Chief objectives of regulatory quality in Europe. One of the possible responses, 'Maximisation of citizens' wealth', was not endorsed by any country.

was to minimise administrative burdens, in the Flemish region the objective was broader: apart from simplification, there was also the goal of implementing RIA. Here we have classified Belgium according to its federal objective.

Our sample did not provide evidence of convergence around the broadest possible objective of 'maximisation of the net benefits of regulatory measures' (two respondents) or 'maximisation of citizens' wealth' (0 respondents). For the reasons discussed in chapters 1 and 2, we include these two objectives in our system of indicators and propose measures of net benefits and quality of regulation from the point of view of the citizen.

Principles of regulatory quality

We asked the respondents to identify principles of regulatory quality set within the better regulation policy. The list of the possible answers was drawn from the principles established in the Mandelkern report (2001) and Hellenic Presidency report (2003). Respondents had the opportunity to indicate alternative options, and more than one response was allowed.

Explicit commitment to regulatory quality principles was common in European countries (figure 5.2). Fourteen countries had these guiding principles: Belgium, Czech Republic, Estonia, Finland, France, Greece, Hungary, Ireland, Italy, Latvia, Norway, Poland, Sweden and the UK. Remarkably, all the 'new' Member States in our sample, with more recently introduced better regulation policies, had established principles of regulatory quality. On the other hand, Austria, Bulgaria, Denmark, Germany, Luxembourg, the Netherlands and Spain did not have specific principles of good regulation.

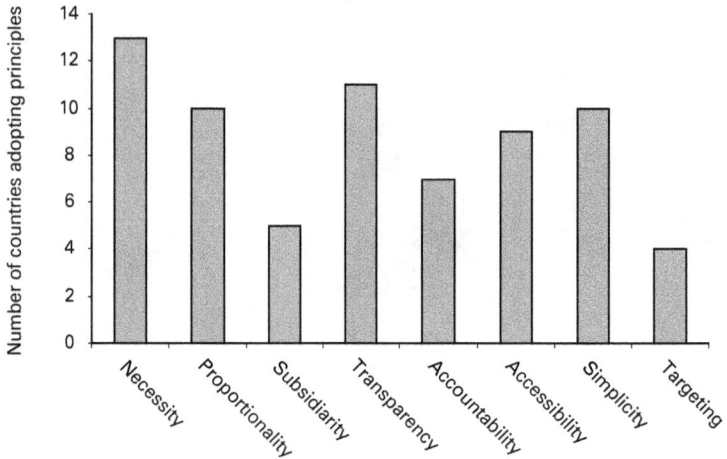

Figure 5.2 Principles of regulatory quality.

The principles presented in the Mandelkern report had been quite diffusely adopted among the European countries. However, two of these principles were not so common. Indeed, accountability was present in seven countries and subsidiarity in only five. The principle of having targeted regulation, which was not included in our questionnaire's list of possible answers, had been established in four countries: Belgium, Ireland, Sweden and the UK. Belgium's response also reported the principles established by the Flemish government: necessity, proportionality, relevance and actuality of regulation.

Coordination between levels of government

We asked the respondents about the existence of a specific process for systematic coordination between the national-level governmental bodies in charge of regulatory quality policy and different levels of governance, namely the EU, independent regulators, regional authorities and local authorities. The results showed that this dimension of regulatory quality was under-developed. Indeed, only thirteen countries had adopted a coordination system with the EU. Coordination with independent regulators was carried out in nine countries. The regional level was considered in nine countries, while only seven countries coordinated their better regulation initiatives with the local authorities. There was a large variation in the answers to this question. Austria, Bulgaria, Denmark, the Netherlands and Spain had no system of coordination with any of the levels of governance. On the other hand, Hungary, Italy and Sweden reported comprehensive coordination among all levels of regulatory governance.

Tools

Let us turn to the diffusion of the four better regulation tools identified by this project. Respondents gave a value from 1 to 5 according to the perceived importance of the tools within the better regulation policy. Additionally, respondents told us if the importance of tools had increased over the previous five years (see table 5.2).

The questionnaire left respondents free to insert alternative tools other than the four we identified in chapter 1. This further information can be useful to understand the content of policy adopted by governments.

The choice of tools also reflects administrative tradition. In Ireland, for instance, the use of 'proofing mechanisms' was spread across areas such as gender impact assessment, rural development and poverty issues. In other words, there were tests appraising the impact of policy on specific population groups. Codification and quality of drafting were two other tools identified by the respondent. They could be included, however, in the more comprehensive tool of 'accessibility and transparency'.

The tool whose importance was reported to have grown most over the last five years was RIA (sixteen respondents), followed by simplification (twelve respondents), consultation (eleven respondents) and access (ten respondents). This confirms the pivotal role of impact assessment in better regulation policies.

Guidance

Government guidance on regulatory tools may be made available in different forms: handbooks, guides, checklists, minimum standards and so on. Respondents were also asked to indicate the year of the current guidance document.

Figure 5.3 shows the numbers of countries with published guidance on each regulatory tool. Fourteen European countries and one region (the Belgian Flemish region) had published guidelines on RIA. These publications were quite recent: between 2000 and 2004. In Sweden, the guidelines for regulatory agencies were constantly updated.

Publishing guidance was an element of the simplification strategy in twelve countries. The publication year varied between 2001 and 2004. In Belgium, the Walloon region and the federal government published guidelines in 2004, the Flemish region in 2003. Ten of the fourteen countries that had published guidance on RIA had also published guidance on simplification.

Guidance on consultation had been published in twelve countries. In this case, too, there was a clear relationship between the publication of RIA guidance and consultation regulation, in that all twelve which had published guidance on consultation had also produced guidance on RIA. The relationship between consultation and simplification was less evident

Table 5.2 Regulatory quality tools

Country	Regulatory impact assessment (RIA)	Importance of RIA has increased	Simplification	Importance of simplification has increased	Consultation	Importance of consultation has increased	Accessibility	Importance of accessibility has increased
Austria	2	Yes	4	n.a.	5	n.a.	5	n.a.
Belgium	3	Yes	5	Yes	3	Yes	4	Yes
Bulgaria	1	n.a.	5	n.a.	3	Yes	2	Yes
Czech Republic	1	Yes	2	Yes	2	Yes	4	No
Denmark	4	Yes	4	Yes	5	n.a.	3	n.a.
Estonia	3	Yes	3	n.a.	4	Yes	5	Yes
Finland	3	n.a.	1	n.a.	4	n.a.	4	n.a.
France	3	Yes[a]	5	Yes[b]	n.a.	n.a.	5	Yes[c]
Germany	4	n.a.	5	n.a.	4	n.a.	3	n.a.
Greece	5	n.a.	5	n.a.	4	n.a.	4	n.a.
Hungary	3	Yes	4	Yes	3	n.a.	3	n.a.
Ireland	5	Yes	5	Yes	4	Yes	3	Yes
Italy	4	Yes	5	Yes	3	Yes	3	Yes
Latvia	4	Yes	2	n.a.	5	Yes	5	Yes
Luxembourg	1	n.a.	2	n.a.	4	n.a.	5	n.a.
Netherlands	1	Yes	2	Yes	3	n.a.	4	n.a.
Norway	4	Yes	4	Yes	4	n.a.	4	Yes
Poland	5	Yes	3	n.a.	4	Yes	4	n.a.
Spain	n.a.	Yes	5	Yes	3	Yes	4	n.a.
Sweden	4	Yes	4	Yes	5	Yes	5	Yes
UK	5	Yes	3	Yes	4	Yes	3	Yes

Note: 1 indicates the lowest level of importance, 5 the highest.

n.a. = no answer.

[a] Importance had increased since 1998.
[b] Importance had increased since 2002.
[c] In particular, codification.

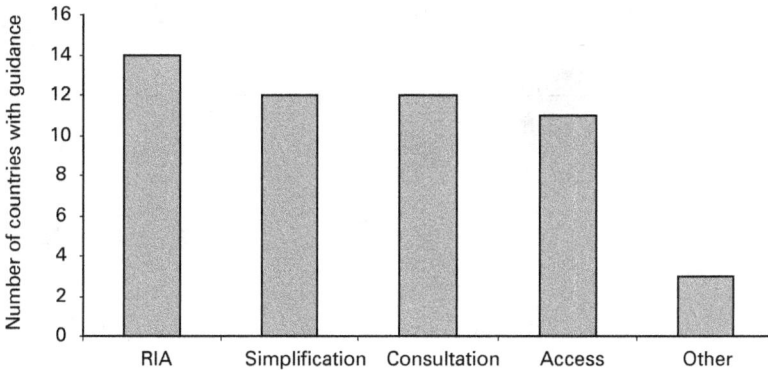

Figure 5.3 Guidance on regulatory tools.

(eight cases). The four countries with guidance on simplification but not on RIA did not have guidance on consultation. Consultation was integrated into the RIA process for most European countries.

Guidance on access was the least common among our respondents (eleven countries). Overall, seven countries had published guidance on all four regulatory tools. Respondents remarked the following on specific themes:

- in Ireland, the government published its guidelines on principles of better regulation in 2004;
- in Belgium, the federal government published guidelines on the quantification of administrative burdens in 2002;
- in the Flemish region, the regional government produced guidelines on regulatory management in 2004.

Quantifiable targets

Quantifiable targets are an important aspect of policy design. Clear policy targets allow ex-post evaluation via appropriate indicators. Table 5.3 shows which countries had adopted quantifiable targets and when they were established.

Twelve respondents gave a positive answer to this question. There were three groups of quantifiable targets. The first group covered administrative burden (four countries). The second group was composed of another five countries targeting administrative simplification through the reduction of procedures or time to get licences. The last group aimed at full compliance with the requirements of RIA; two countries had set this specific target. In Latvia quantifiable targets on better regulation are embedded in a more general performance measurement framework. In the context of the strategic planning process, each ministry sets its own budget programme with outcomes and

Table 5.3 Diffusion of quantifiable targets

Country	Quantifiable targets	Year
Austria	No	
Belgium	Yes	1999
Bulgaria	Yes	2002
Czech Republic	No	
Denmark	Yes	2002
Estonia	No	
Finland	No	
France	Yes	n.a.
Germany	No	
Greece	Yes	2001
Hungary	No	
Ireland	No	
Italy	Yes	1997
Latvia	Yes	2004
Luxembourg	No	
Netherlands	Yes	1994
Norway	No	
Poland	Yes	1998
Spain	Yes	2000
Sweden	Yes	n.a.
UK	Yes	2003

n.a. = no answer.

sub-programmes with output indicators. The respondent, however, was not able to define any specific quantifiable target or indicator on better regulation. Table 5.4 reports the details given by respondents to explain how their quantifiable targets relate to regulatory objectives and principles.

Monitoring

There were different monitoring systems in place across Europe (figure 5.4). Interestingly, six countries had implemented more than one system. The UK had three systems: self-reporting of the central unit in charge of monitoring the better regulation policy; reporting to the prime minister's office, and reporting to parliament. In Belgium, the monitoring system included reporting to the 'social parties' (unions and employers' organisations). In Denmark, reports were tabled in parliament and were made available to the general public. In Italy, legislation required reports to be sent to the prime minister's office and parliament; in addition there was monitoring via independent bodies. The Netherlands used self-reporting, reporting to parliament and monitoring via

Table 5.4 Quantifiable targets

Country	Year of introduction of the first target	Description of target
Belgium	1999	2004: Reduction in the number of days needed to create a new economic entity 2003: Use of on-line tax forms 2003: Reduction of administrative burden by €100 million (Flemish region) 2001: Number of on-line administrative forms (Walloon region) 1999: Global reduction (25 per cent) in administrative burden (government agreement)
Bulgaria	2002	20 per cent reduction of the existing regulatory regimes corresponding to administrative burdens
Denmark	2002	In its growth strategy of 2002, the government put forward a goal of reducing administrative burdens on companies by 25 per cent by 2010 (compared with 2002)
France	n.a.	200 measures of simplification
Greece	2001	• To reduce the number of necessary documents (in the case of services provided) • To reduce the number of days (in the case of complaints) • To reduce the number of unnecessary organisational structures (in the case of services provided)
Italy	1997	Targets, principles and criteria for simplification
Latvia	2004	Since 2004 each ministry has had its own budget programme with outcomes and sub-programmes with output indicators
Netherlands	1994	Net reduction in administrative burdens by 25 per cent between the end of 2002 and 2007
Poland	1998	The Law of Economic Activities has introduced a target to reduce administrative burdens
Spain	2000	Reduction of the days necessary to set up a business
Sweden	n.a.	Full compliance with RIA requirements
UK	2003	The UK Cabinet Office has a Public Service Agreement (PSA), approved by HM Treasury, during the current Spending Review period, to ensure departments deliver better regulation through: • full compliance with the RIA process; • delivering the commitments in the Regulatory Reform Action Plan, including over 60 Regulatory Reform Orders, by 2005

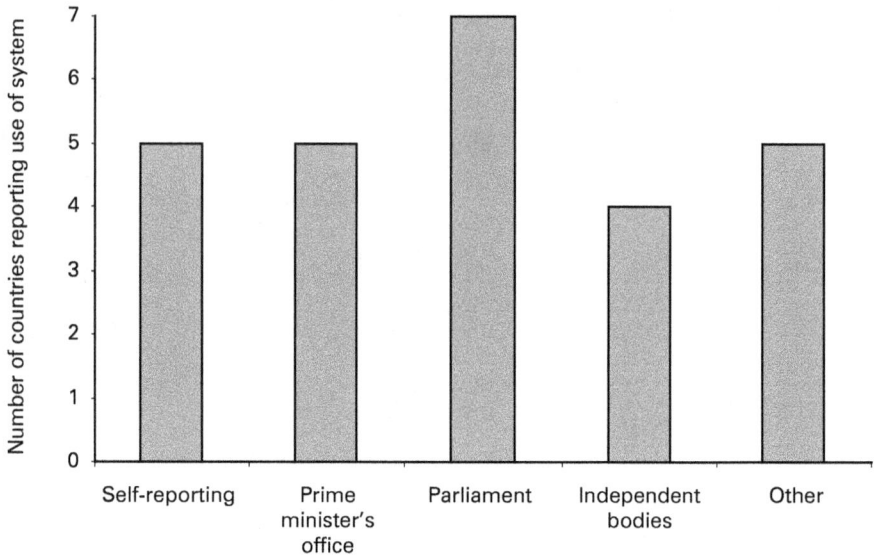

Figure 5.4 Monitoring of targets. (Note that some countries use more than one system.)

independent bodies. Among the five new Member States that responded to the questionnaire, Poland was the only one with more than one monitoring system – namely, self-reporting and reporting to independent bodies.

Performance measurement

Is better regulation policy linked to the performance management systems generally embedded in other policies, such as budget policy? Figure 5.5 shows that ten governments required ministers to measure the performance of better regulation policy. There were five models for this:

1 within budgetary policy (the most common);
2 through national audit offices;
3 by quality control (conducted internally or by a central overseeing authority);
4 within 'modernisation programmes' undertaken by the public administration;
5 as part of a government programme (one country had included performance measurement as part of a coalition agreement).

On balance, there was evidence of linkage mechanisms between budgetary policies and better regulation policies.

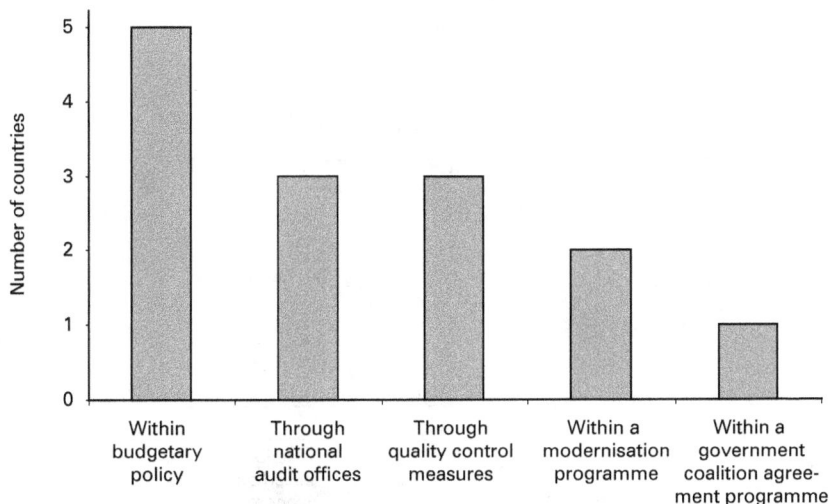

Figure 5.5 Performance measurement.

Financial resources

Our questionnaire featured this item on whether budgetary resources for better regulation policies had increased in the previous five years, with reference to the budget for RIA, resources for specific training on better regulation tools and the overall budget for better regulation. The idea was to measure the dynamics of better regulation policies rather than providing a static picture.

In eleven countries, the budget for RIA and for specific training (on RIA, consultation and drafting) had increased. The number of positive answers went up to fourteen in the case of the total financial resources for better regulation. The numbers of respondents stating that 'there is no dedicated budget' for RIA, specific training or better regulation policy were respectively eight, seven and five. Two respondents were not able to answer the question. The overall picture, in conclusion, was one of increased commitment, in terms of financial resources and training, to better regulation policies and specific tools.

Regulatory agendas and coordination of tools

To what extent are better regulation tools coordinated? In several countries, citizens had the right to access the documents underpinning a regulatory decision. This is an example of integration between RIA and access.

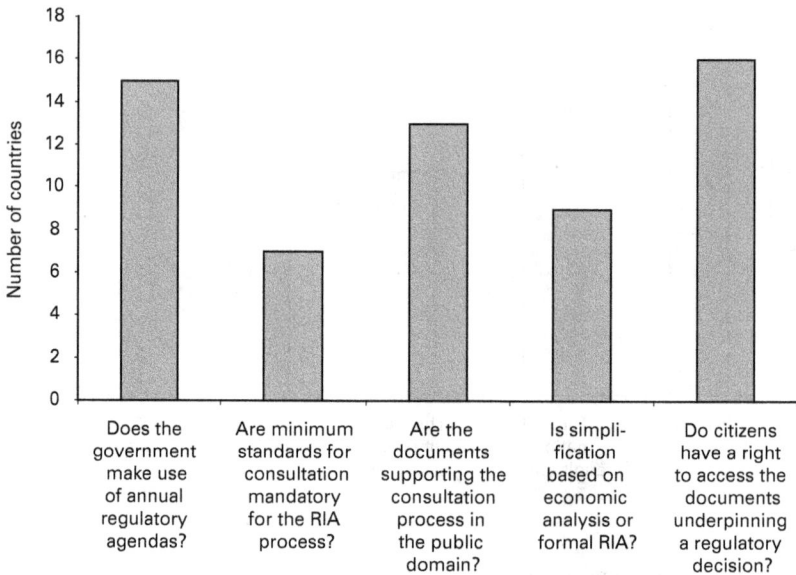

Figure 5.6 Coordination in use of tools.

Regulatory agendas (possibly the most efficient approach to the integration of tools) and access to documents supporting consultation were also quite common. Minimum standards for consultation and economic analysis within simplification policies were not yet popular. Looking at figure 5.6, the picture is one of interesting connections among tools.

Indicators of activity

Have governments designed and implemented better regulation policies in a way that allowed them to monitor the final outcome of the process in quantifiable terms? Figure 5.7 shows the responses to the following questions:

- How many regulations were cost assessed in 2002 and 2003?
- How many regulations were cost–benefit assessed in 2002 and 2003?
- How many procedures were simplified in 2002 and 2003?

These are challenging questions, given the development of better regulation policies in Europe. Furthermore, there is a fundamental difference between the North American and the European approaches to impact assessment: cost–benefit analysis plays a pivotal role in the former but not in the latter. In Europe, the thrust of impact assessment is to provide evidence regarding the major trade-offs in policy formulation – the Commission's system is a case in point. Even in the USA, however, as shown by Hahn on several occasions

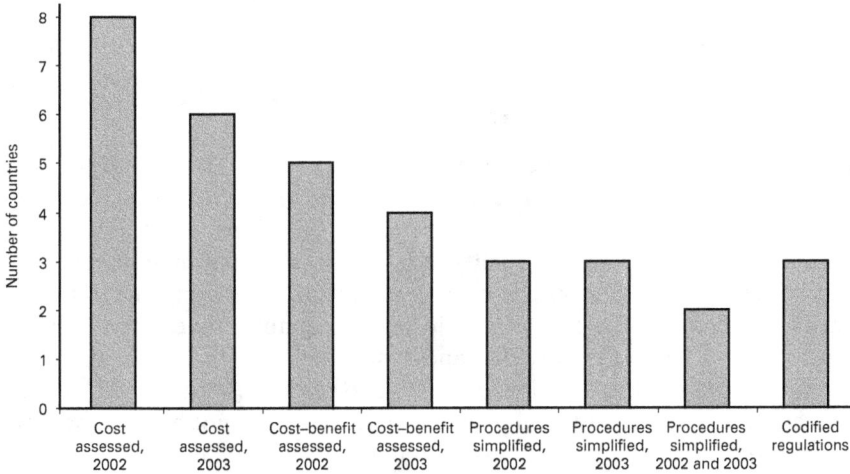

Figure 5.7 Indicators of activity: number of countries that were able to count the numbers of regulations subject to cost and cost–benefit assessments in 2002 and 2003, the numbers of procedures simplified in 2002 and 2003, and to estimate the proportion of regulations in force that had been codified and/or consolidated.

(see Hahn and Sunstein, 2002), the diffusion of full cost–benefit analysis does not match the guidelines set by the executive. For these reasons, it was of interest to see whether governments know the number of regulations subject to a cost (or cost–benefit) assessment in a year, without implying that all regulations should be so assessed (figure 5.7). The 'quality' we were looking at with this question concerned data on activities.

The results show that this dimension of regulatory quality was still underdeveloped in many European countries. Only four governments had implemented a system to count regulations assessed in terms of cost–benefit in 2003. The situation was somewhat better in the case of regulations that were cost assessed: eight respondents were able to quantify them in 2002 and six in 2003. Just three respondents quantified the number of procedures simplified or the percentage of regulations that had been codified. In Sweden, a quantification of regulations that had been cost assessed was provided by the NNR.

Time and/or cost savings achieved through the use of the various tools

Simple measures of real-world outcome are the time and costs saved as a result of better regulation policies. The choice of the single measure to cover both time and cost saving allowed us to cover all countries – not just the ones with a fully fledged RIA system. At the same time, this was a difficult indicator to collect data on. Unsurprisingly then, only four of the twenty-one country respondents answered this question positively.

Quantification of simple measures

The next four questions of the questionnaire focused on classic indicators of real-world outcomes (simple measures). As already specified in the introduction to this chapter, the goal of this series of questions was to assess the feasibility of some regulatory quality indicators that were not actually in use at the time. For this reason the questions asked, considering the data and statistics available, how long it would take to quantify lives saved, illness reduction, and regulatory benefits and costs stemming from a new regulation introduced in 2003. Figures 5.8, 5.9, 5.10 and 5.11 show the results.

Overall, it is apparent that European countries were not able to estimate and quantify benefits and costs associated with new regulations in a defined period of time.

Key activities and indicators of regulatory quality at the EU level

In the final section of the questionnaire, we asked respondents to make suggestions and proposals. Let us start with the key activities that respondents felt the Commission should track over the next five years (figure 5.12).

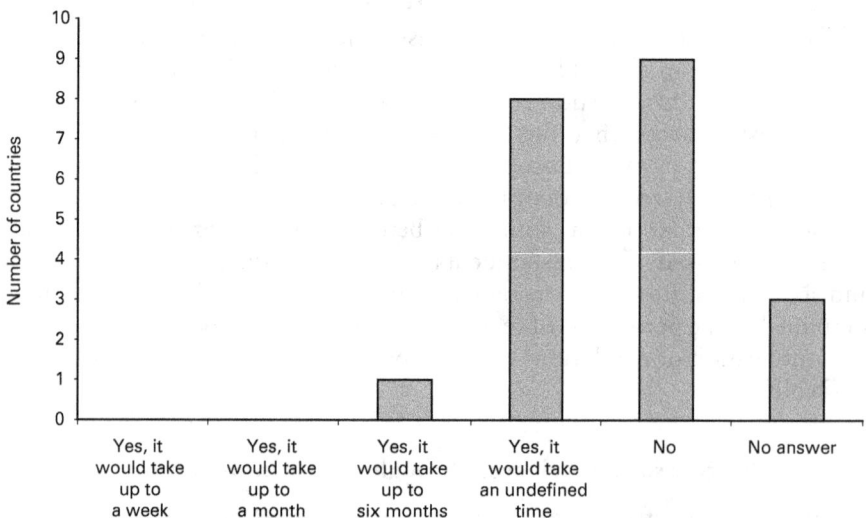

Figure 5.8 Number of countries that would be able to quantify the lives saved through new regulations issued in 2003.

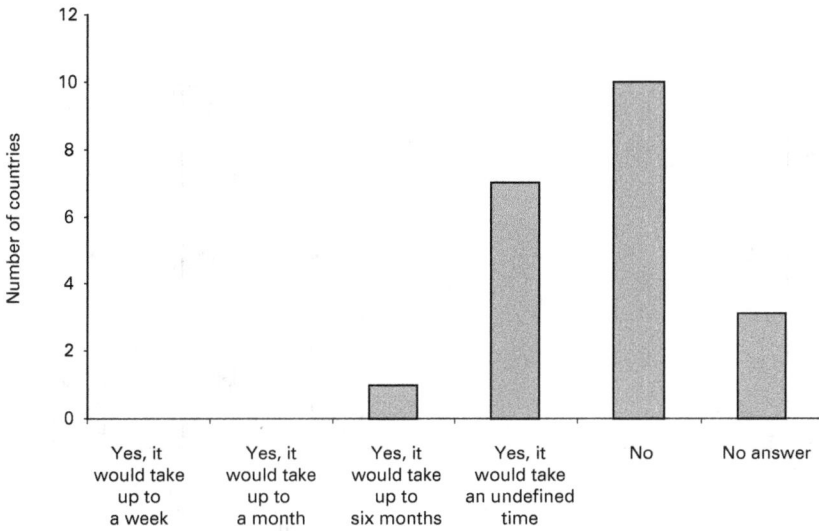

Figure 5.9 Number of countries that would be able to quantify illness reduction arising from new regulations issued in 2003 (cancer related to smoking).

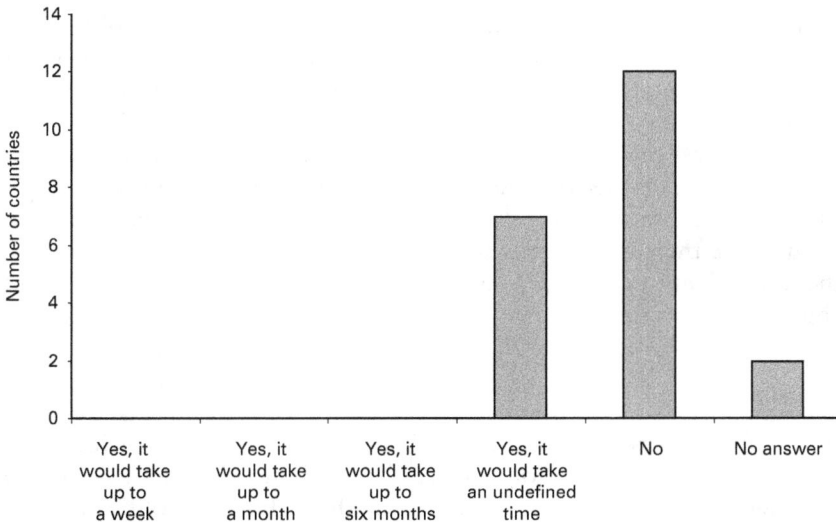

Figure 5.10 Number of countries that would be able to quantify the regulatory benefits delivered by new regulations issued in 2003.

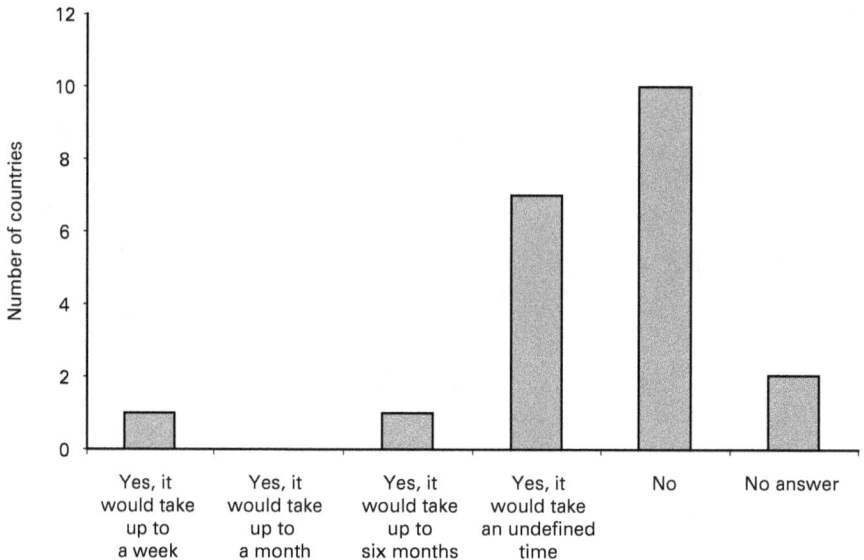

Figure 5.11 Number of countries that would be able to quantify regulatory costs (as a percentage of national GDP) arising from new regulations issued in 2003.

The four regulatory tools chosen to define regulatory quality in the present study were quite broadly accepted by respondents. Indeed, RIA, simplification and consultation were the top key activities. Our fourth tool (access) scored pretty well, if we include codification and recasting as elements of a broader horizontal strategy to facilitate accessibility and transparency of regulation.

There are three other key activities that were quite widely endorsed by our support network: market-friendly instruments, 'sun-setting' and updating of single-market legislation. These activities relate to the business environment. Consequently, these suggestions from the support network were indicative of the respondents' priorities in terms of an efficient regulatory environment for business across the EU.

Conclusions

The support network provided a clear message in terms of principles and objectives of better regulation. Generally speaking, the message of the Mandelkern (2001) report had been diffused throughout the 'old' and 'new' EU Member States. Our sample shared relatively broad objectives, but there was still limited convergence around the 'maximisation of the net benefits of regulatory measures' (two respondents) and 'maximisation of citizens'

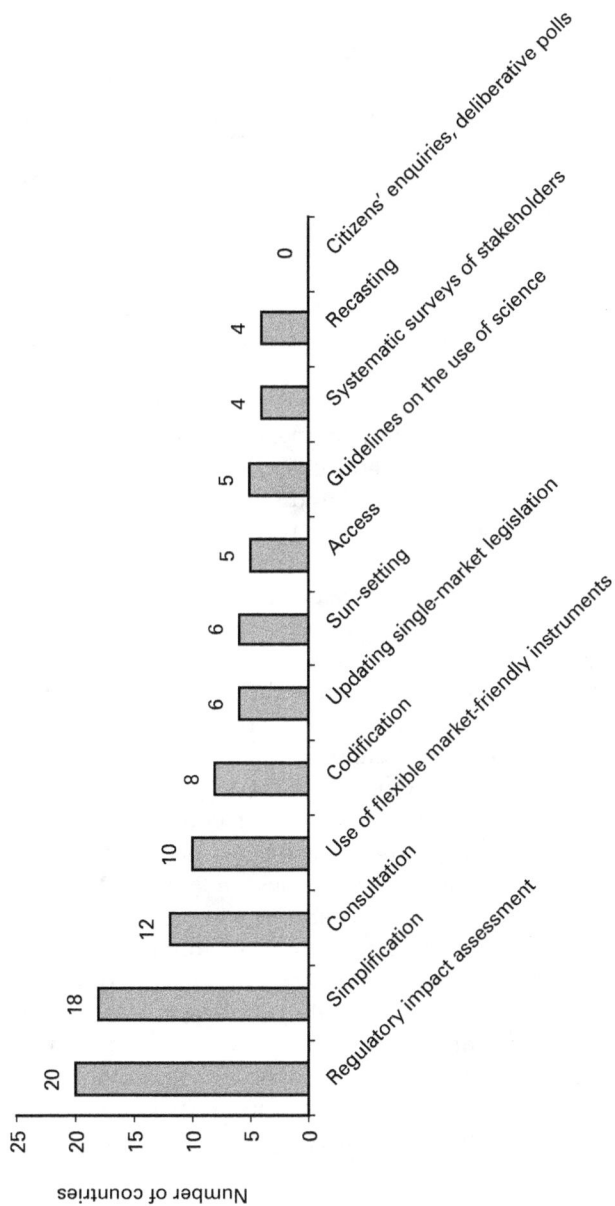

Figure 5.12 Number of countries indicating which key activities should be tracked at the EU level over the next five years.

wealth' (no respondents). This chimes with the limited diffusion of full cost–benefit analysis as the cornerstone of regulatory quality. When we probed the support network on indicators of quality arising out of a cost–benefit approach to better regulation, we found no evidence of countries pursuing cost–benefit assessment of regulation as the major pathway to quality.

The picture was varied, with different approaches to regulatory quality. One belief was widely shared, however. The respondents agreed on the objective of efficient and effective regulation. This is a broad but sufficiently precise objective to start a focused discussion on indicators of better regulation policy, preferably in the context of open processes of coordination (see chapter 7).

Resources for better regulation policies had increased over the previous five years in fourteen countries. Better regulation policies were also embedded in other policies, especially budgetary policies. Coordination of tools was still limited, but instruments like regulatory agendas were becoming more popular. In federal countries like Belgium, all levels of governance were investing resources in the measurement of better regulation.

The support network confirmed the pivotal position of RIA in better regulation policies noted by previous EU and OECD studies. It also confirmed the importance of the tools selected for this project, with the qualification that, according to the respondents, more emphasis should be put on tools that target explicitly the quality of the business environment.

Although the sample showed variability, a group of countries had made the initial and fundamental steps towards the measurement of better regulation. Eleven countries had quantifiable targets in their better regulation policies. The specific details of the approach to measurements varied within the clusters we have identified in chapter 4.

Overall, the data confirm that there was convergence at the level of clusters. The previous chapter revealed the existence of a cluster with the broad objective of better regulation policy and sophisticated quality assurance systems. This chapter has revealed that these countries tended to be more ambitious in terms of measurement. In contrast, countries with a 'lean' system of quality assurance tended to focus on targets confined to administrative burden – the second cluster in our sample. Finally, there was a cluster of countries where the tools of better regulation were still at the stage of pilot projects, and no systematic measurement of better regulation had been undertaken. The presence of three clusters suggests three systems of indicators, so that each country can measure progress in relation to its capacity and 'stage' of better regulation policy. We introduce the three systems in chapter 7.

Note

1 Portugal did not respond to the questionnaire.

6

The state of play in the EU

Introduction

Although better regulation programmes in the EU date back to the early 1990s, the activity of monitoring the results is more recent. This chapter presents the initiatives launched since around 2001. Its main thrust is to look at better regulation tools, current practice in the Commission and other EU institutions, quality assurance mechanisms and pilot projects on quality measurement undertaken by academics and stakeholders. We show how they provide either conceptual foundations or information that can be used in the design of indicators. Put differently, the idea is to map out institutions and better regulation activities and draw as much as possible on what exists in order to propose indicators. In doing so, we also avoid the risk of reinventing the wheel. This chapter and the next illustrate how existing information may be used more efficiently, and how different projects and initiatives 'in the pipeline' may be brought together.

Another aim in this chapter is to provide a clear picture of the EU institutions' own standards of regulatory quality. There are many ways to design the conceptual foundations of indicators. One is to look at the economic literature (see chapter 3). Another is to consider how a government approaches the issue of quality within technical guidelines and standards for better regulation tools, and derives indicators from the government's explicit policy and standards (discussed country by country in chapter 4). The next sections provide the foundations for the latter approach at the EU level.

In 2002, the Commission launched an ambitious action plan for better regulation, a new integrated system of impact assessment (IA)[1] and minimum standards for consultation. Simplification policy has been enhanced by the action plan (covering the period February 2003–December 2004) (European Commission, 2002a). The plan (articulated in phases) provides a comprehensive strategy to reduce administrative burden. In March 2005, the Commission launched a 'package for better regulation' with the slogan 'less red tape = more growth'. The innovative part of this package is the set of pilot projects to develop a methodology for measuring and reducing administrative burden.[2] In October 2005, the Commission presented a proposal for a common method to address burdens, drawing on the results of the pilot projects.

Regulation 1049/2001 (on public access to European Parliament, Council and Commission documents) completes the picture of tools which have been redesigned in order to deliver on the better regulation action plan. Each EU institution has drafted internal rules in order to comply with the public access directive. In particular, the Commission has issued a specific Decision[3] to identify standards for access to documents supporting regulatory decisions.

After a brief introduction to the inter-institutional agreement on better regulation and quality assurance issues, we discuss the IA process as defined by the Commission's internal guidelines. Specifically, attention is paid to procedural steps that can lead to performance measurement. As think tanks and the academic community have already proposed their own analyses of the Commission's IA reports, we also look at the criteria and measures proposed by these external observers. Overall, the procedures which are already in place and the suggestions coming from think tanks and academics provide useful inputs for the design of better regulation indicators.

In a further section we move on to discuss consultation and look at possible measures of quality within existing practices. In the case of consultation, the task of identifying indicators revolves around the 2002 minimum standards (European Commission, 2002e). They provide the Commission's own benchmark and therefore lend themselves quite naturally to possible measures of the outcomes of consultation. Another section is dedicated to the simplification action plan, with emphasis on its performance in the reduction of administrative burden. Finally, we look at access and transparency in the EU regulatory process and summarise the main initiatives.

How EU institutions manage better regulation tools

The EU institutions (Council, European Parliament and Commission) are committed to a common approach to better regulation policy via the 2003 inter-institutional agreement (Council of the European Union, 2003: 4). The importance of the agreement lies in the shared vision and principles and in the commitment of all institutions to make the tools of better regulation work. Progress (or lack of it) with the agreement is crucial, otherwise the results achieved by one institution run the risk of being nullified by what the other institutions do or fail to do.

The inter-institutional agreement defines quality. High-quality regulation is clear, simple and effective (Council of the European Union, 2003: 4). Another dimension of quality is the transposition of EU legislation within given deadlines. Consequently, the agreement introduces a control mechanism: the Commission will produce an annual report showing the transposition rates of each Member State. In turn, Member States are encouraged to present reports on their efficiency in the transposition process (Council of the European Union, 2003: 4). Currently, the Single Market Scoreboard annually reports the transposition rates as notified by Member States. This specific dimension of regulatory quality is discussed in the broader approach pursued by the Mandelkern (2001: 70) report. Correct transposition is obviously more important than transposition *per se*: 'Correct transposition means that the national transposition legislation is in accordance with the European legislation' (Mandelkern, 2001: 66). The report adds: 'Member States should consider their position very carefully before introducing extra requirements in the legislative measures that they adopt' (Mandelkern, 2001: 74). In fact, stricter national measures are justified only when they do not restrict trade or negatively affect the internal market (Mandelkern, 2001: 69).

The agreement specifically mentions two better regulation tools: consultation and IA. In addition, one important transparency principle is contained in the agreement: that IA should be 'fully and freely available' to interested parties and citizens.

Turning to the procedural aspects, the agreement establishes that 'the Commission will take due account in its legislative proposals of their financial or administrative implications, for the Union and the Member States in particular'. The Commission is also called to illustrate in the explanatory memorandum that accompanies each piece of legislation how IA has influenced the formulation of the proposal and the final result (Council of the European Union, 2003: 4).

As mentioned, the presence or absence of joint commitment is crucial. In the context of the co-decision procedure, the agreement states that:

> the European Parliament and Council may, on the basis of jointly defined criteria and procedures, have impact assessments carried out prior to the adoption of any substantive amendments, either at first reading or at the conciliation stage. (Council of the European Union, 2003: 4)

In order to achieve a common methodology, the three EU institutions are engaged to 'carry out an assessment of their respective experiences'.

Methodology is obviously a vital component of the whole exercise. The progress made by the three main EU institutions on the development of common methods is still embryonic, as shown by the problems experienced by the Council in handling IA of substantive amendments to a Commission proposal. For example, in 2004 the Council started a pilot project on a Commission proposal (on batteries and accumulators) that had been substantially amended. The Dutch Presidency prepared a draft of the Council's IA, in which it took:

> political responsibility for the assertion and assumptions contained [in the report]. The General Secretariat of the Council assisted the Presidency with

the handling and drafting of the impact assessment. The Commission helped by granting access to material used to produce its impact assessment. (Council of the European Union, 2005b: 3)

Notwithstanding the perceived usefulness of the IA for clarifying the positions of the delegation on the draft directive:

the Presidency announced in Coreper [the Committee of Permanent Representatives] that the pilot project was over and that it did not intend to carry out any further work on the impact assessment. It would be for the next Presidency to consider lessons to be learned and the next steps. (Council of the European Union, 2005b: 4)

The reason for this partial failure has been attributed to the dispute over the political conclusions being drawn from the IA and its contents (Council of the European Union, 2005b: 4). The Secretariat-General of the Council reported that the IA pilot project 'provided for more structured discussion and helped delegations to clarify their views. However, it does not seem to have significantly modified delegations' position' (Council of the European Union, 2005b: 5).

The road towards a streamlined better regulation policy across the three main institutions is still quite rough. General principles for a common approach to IA were agreed by the Council, the European Parliament and the Commission in 2005.[4] In May 2006, the Secretariat-General of the Council sent the national delegations a document on how to handle IA in the Council's working parties (Council of the European Union, 2006).

Let us turn to operational management. A typical problem of EU better regulation policies is the weakness of management and overall quality assurance (within the Commission and at the inter-institutional level). What are the principal bodies and working groups currently involved in IA?

The inter-institutional agreement on better regulation has set up a specific high-level technical working group for inter-institutional cooperation. It is in charge of monitoring the implementation of the inter-institutional agreement. This inter-institutional working group convened for the first time in June 2004. Beyond this group, however, each EU institution has created bodies and/or working groups on better regulation. The very presence of so many groups raises questions about operational management.

Within the Council there is the High Level Group on Competitiveness, which has recently turned its attention to how the Commission makes use of IA.[5] In particular, the Competitiveness Test Subgroup has looked at the IA process in connection to the competitiveness dimension launched by the Lisbon strategy (on which, see chapter 1). In June 2004, this Subgroup proposed the following recommendations (Council of the European Union, 2004b: 5–6):

- a requirement for policy makers to highlight Lisbon impacts (positive and negative across the 3 pillars) in assessments;

- a global perspective – comparing the EU policy framework to those in key competitor economies, looking at relative impacts and successful, competitive approaches;
- an assessment of the (economic) employment impacts;
- analysis of new policy proposals in terms of the existing regulatory framework, including the scope for attendant simplification and reduction of administrative burdens;
- making explicit to decision makers the framework used to identify trade-offs between policy options and conflicting objectives, and the value judgements and reasoning behind the selection of the preferred option; and
- continuing development of practice in quantifying impacts, including in monetary terms where possible, to enhance the data on the benefits and costs of proposals.

There are other more, informal groups at Council level, such as the Directors of Better Regulation (DBR), an informal inter-governmental group of senior officials responsible for better regulation policy at the national level. The DBR supports (at the technical level) the High Level Group on Competitiveness. It has discussed methodological issues related to the input provided by Member States in the assessment of EU legislative proposals. In March 2005, the Commission issued a communication linking better regulation policy to the Lisbon agenda for 'growth and jobs' and making the case for more coordination between the EU and the domestic level. Specifically, the Commission recommended that Member States follow its 'national better regulation strategy' – a fundamental component of the 'Lisbon Action Plan'. 'The Commission proposed also to set up a group of high-level national regulatory experts, to develop a common Better Regulation agenda.' These are champions of better regulation who advise the Commission and provide 'an interface between the Commission and key governmental authorities' (European Commission, 2005a: 10).

Within the European Parliament, the Committee on Legal Affairs has overall responsibility for better regulation. This Committee is responsible for:[6]

1 the interpretation and application of European law, compliance of European Union acts with primary law, notably the choice of legal bases and respect for the principles of subsidiarity and proportionality;
2 the interpretation and application of international law, in so far as the European Union is affected;
3 the simplification of Community law, in particular legislative proposals for its official codification.

In March 2004, one of the members of this Committee, Mr Bert Doorn, prepared a report on IA (European Parliament, 2004). The Doorn report proposes that 'any legislative proposal by the Commission should be accompanied by a global estimate of the costs of that legislation on social, economic and environmental aspects'. The proposal envisages an audit body 'reporting directly to the President of the Commission' (European Parliament, 2004).

This audit body would monitor the quality of the IA process and outcome. Moreover, it would be in charge of carrying out the IA on the European Parliament's amendments to regulatory proposals. Parenthetically, there have been other proposals for audit bodies. In a report on better regulation, the European Policy Centre (Allio *et al.*, 2004) recommends the establishment of a regulatory quality unit within the Secretariat-General and an audit body in the European Court of Auditors. One problem with the idea of taking on board the Court of Auditors for regulatory quality audits is that the Court has more expertise in financial audit than in performance audit.

Turning to the Commission, the Secretariat-General has an important role in the coordination of IA and the relationship between IA and the broader strategic planning and programming cycle. Its role in the coordination and quality assurance system extends to the organisation of training, the publication of technical guidelines and 'monitoring of the final quality of the impact assessment carried out' (European Commission, 2002b: 8–9). Coordination at the Commission level is based on a specific working group on IA chaired by the Secretariat-General. Currently, the working group includes officials from DG Enterprise, DG Internal Market and Services, DG Employment, DG Environment, DG Economic and Financial Affairs and DG Budget. The group has a mandate: to coordinate the initiatives on IA; to follow European Parliament and Council initiatives; and to reflect on how to improve IA procedure and methodology (European Commission, 2004a: 10).

Within DG Internal Market and Services, there is an advisory body working on better regulation: the Internal Market Advisory Committee (IMAC). It is composed of officials – from both Member States and the Commission – and provides 'input into Commission initiatives and acts as the interface between Commission and Member States' initiatives' (European Commission, 2004a: 10). In 2004, IMAC was engaged in the design of 'better regulation indicators'. The IMAC approach is twofold: one dimension of the indicators looks at the administrative structure and the regulatory process; the other attempts to assess the real-world impact, via surveys of business – an activity presently carried out by the European Business Test Panel (see below, under the heading 'Consultation'). In particular, the first dimension relies on a self-assessment by the DBR and intends to measure whether essential structures and conditions are in place to produce high-quality regulation. This is a clear yes/no answer format for indicators of design. Box 6.1 shows the indicators being discussed within IMAC at the time of writing.

The indicators listed in box 6.1 can be applied to the EU institutions, the Commission in particular, as well as to the Member States. They cover different tools of better regulation. The questions under the first heading, 'Assessment methods and obligations', are related to IA. The second question is particularly innovative. It brings the idea of having a sort of 'single-market test' into the (R)IA process at national level. The second heading

('Structures') covers indicators of design. They are the typical questions of 'who is doing what?', in this case referred to a quality assurance central body. The third section ('Stakeholder information') looks at access and regulatory transparency. The fourth heading ('Improving stakeholder access to existing legislation') covers simplification tools. Finally, the last heading covers indicators of access and regulatory transparency at the consultation phase. Furthermore, a self-assessment questionnaire discussed by IMAC includes some indicators of activities and outcomes of better regulation policy (see box 6.2).

Apart from IMAC's initiatives, there are two surveys on regulatory quality as perceived by European businesses. We briefly review them here, before we sum up our thoughts on IMAC. One interesting survey was conducted in 2001. Its results are contained in *Internal Market Scoreboard No. 9* (European Commission, 2001b).[7] This survey covered over 4,000 firms in all fifteen 'old' Member States. Businesses were asked to rate the quality of regulation (without distinguishing between Community and national rules) and its impact on business activities. The survey identified the following:

- percentage of businesses that are dissatisfied with the quality of the regulatory environment;
- regulatory areas where compliance was considered to be the most costly and burdensome;
- unnecessary compliance costs as a percentage of total compliance costs;
- percentage of companies willing to be consulted;
- percentage of companies which think that their national government authorities show good judgement and a sense of proportion when applying legislation;
- percentage of companies which indicate that the laws and regulations affecting their company had been simplified only marginally, or not at all;
- countries with the easiest regulatory environment to trade with.

The second survey was conducted by the European Network for Social and Economic Research in 2002. It targeted a sample of European SMEs on the major constraints on business performance. Administrative burdens arising out of environmental and health and safety regulation came out as one of the most important factors hindering SMEs' performance, in terms of the percentage of firms endorsing that view. That percentage, though, varied greatly among the fifteen 'old' Member States: only 2 per cent of Greek and Spanish SMEs perceived administrative regulation as a major constraint, against the 20 per cent of German or the 19 per cent of French SMEs. This real-world indicator of regulatory quality is presented also in the 2003 *Benchmarking Enterprise Policy*, a report published by DG Enterprise (European Commission, 2003a).

Box 6.1 IMAC indicators of better regulation policy design

Assessment methods and obligations

- Are regulators required to use standard criteria (e.g., cost–benefit analysis) to determine whether government action is appropriate?
- Is there a requirement to consider the impact of regulatory/legislative action on the functioning of the internal market and the effects on companies operating from other Member States?
- Are regulators required to consider alternatives to regulation?
- Are regulators required to calculate/estimate compliance costs for new rules? If yes:
  - ○ Do regulators use a standard methodology by which compliance costs are calculated/estimated?
  - ○ Is there a standard requirement to conduct an RIA in the case of new legislation? If yes:
    - ❏ Is there a defined period within which an assessment must take place?

Structures

- Is a specific government body responsible for ensuring that the above 'good' practices are followed? If yes:
  - ○ Can this body take concrete action if regulatory authorities do not respect provisions and practices?
  - ○ Can third parties (like businesses and business organisations) present comments to this body?
  - ○ Are there any exceptions to these obligations?
- Is there a specific body responsible for coordinating initiatives aimed at improving the quality of the regulatory framework? If yes:
  - ○ Does this body operate directly under the control of the 'political' level (i.e., prime minister's office or of another senior minister)?

Stakeholder information

- Is there any systematic mechanism, besides the official publication of new rules, whereby stakeholders are informed about the goal of new legislation, the responsibilities of those involved and the distribution of possible (side) effects?

Improving stakeholder access to existing legislation

Consolidation of law.
- Is there any structural mechanism whereby consolidation options are examined?

Codification of law.
- Is there any structural mechanism for regularly codifying rules in force?

Simplification of law.
- Is there a structural mechanism for regularly simplifying current rules? If yes:
  - Is there an explicit programme aimed at reducing compliance costs (e.g., administrative burdens and obtaining business licences and permits)? If yes:
    - Does the programme include quantifiable targets?
    - Has a system for measuring administrative burdens been established?
    - Have existing administrative burdens of legislation been fully quantified?
- Is there a national better regulation plan setting out objectives for better regulation? If yes:
  - Is there a system to monitor progress, and if so are the results made public?

Facilitating compliance
- Is there a strategy to increase the use of e-government to facilitate compliance with the rules? If yes:
  - Have targets been set?
- Is there a facility which keeps track of total legislative output?
- Is there a published consolidated register of all regulations currently in force?
- Can the public search the register electronically?
- Are there one-stop shops to help companies meet regulatory requirements? If yes:
  - Do these one-stop shops cover all of the requirements, a substantial part of the requirements, or only some of the requirements?
- When proposing new legislation, are parties likely to be directly affected always consulted?
  - If no, for what proportion of new regulations are consultation opportunities available?
  - If yes, does this include companies operating from other Member States, for example by making draft rules available in other languages?
  - Are consultation opportunities publicised on government websites?
  - Can any stakeholder choose to participate in the consultation?
  - What is the average time available for providing responses?
  - Is there a minimum delay for providing responses?
  - Are responses published?
  - Must regulatory authorities take account of comments made during consultations?

Source: European Commission (2004d).

Box 6.2 IMAC indicators to monitor legislative output

- What proportion of new legislation has been subjected to extended impact assessment?
- What proportion of new legislation has been subjected to preliminary impact assessment?
- What proportion of staff has been trained on impact assessment techniques?
- How many laws were adopted last year (total number of laws and total number of pages)?
- How many laws were repealed last year (by number and pages)?
- What percentage of the laws in force have been codified and/or consolidated?
- How many laws were simplified last year?
- How many laws were changed in 2003 specifically as a result of programmes to reduce administrative burden?
- How many laws were repealed in 2003 specifically as a result of such programmes?

Source: European Commission (2004d).

IMAC's indicators cover efficiently two specific dimensions: real-world indicators based on businesses' perceptions; and indicators based on governments' self-assessment. In terms of data gathering, IMAC draws on feasible and well known approaches to indicators of regulatory quality, that is, self-assessment and surveys. In terms of cost, surveys are obviously more expensive than self-assessments. Further, as previously mentioned, we have some doubts about the capability of SMEs to distinguish between specific types of regulations affecting the firm.

Additionally, since one important aim of the IMAC project is to measure the quality of administrative processes at national level, obviously some indicators appear too generic. Indicators measuring the quality of the RIA process should be based on the most important methodology requirements of a specific country. For instance, if the guidelines of a given country require a discount on multi-annual effects, it is quite important to identify the portion of RIAs that comply with this specific requirement. On this matter, we now briefly turn to review the process of the EU IA system.

Impact assessment: the quality criteria identified by the Commission

The new system of IA is built upon the basis of three documents: the inter-institutional agreement on better regulation (Council of the European

Union, 2003); the communication of the Commission on IA (European Commission, 2002b); and the Commission's internal guidelines on IA (European Commission, 2003b, 2003c, 2005b, 2005c).

Communication on impact assessment
The communication set out the design of a new, integrated system of IA at the EU level for regulatory and policy measures in 2002. The system is characterised by an 'integrated' approach for evaluating economic, social and environmental impacts. The integration of economic, social and environmental policy goals is an element that distinguishes the Commission's approach to better regulation (and IA in particular) from the one pursued by the majority of the Member States – focused on the economic dimension. The aim of this system of IA is to have a broad, encompassing, ex-ante evaluation of policy initiatives, contained in a unique document identifying 'trade-offs in achieving competing [policy] objectives' (European Commission, 2002b: 2).

Although the Commission had developed experience with the assessment of proposed regulation since the early 1990s, the new integrated system introduced in 2002 is qualitatively different in several respects. To begin with, whereas previous initiatives targeted one category of stakeholders, such as the business community, the new approach refers to a broad range of stakeholders. Secondly, whereas the previous experiments and pilot projects produced results that were difficult to transfer across DGs and different policy areas, the new approach is based on a single template applicable to all policy proposals and managed by a network of specialists from different DGs and the Secretariat-General of the Commission. Thirdly, although previous experience was essentially limited to the Commission, the new system of IA has potential for integrating the European Parliament and the Council as users of the assessments conducted by the Commission. The potential for streamlined inter-institutional relations in the EU policy process is therefore increased by the adoption of a single template for IA. Finally, in the past, companies (Union of Industrial and Employers' Confederations of Europe, 1995), national research institutes (see the TMC Asser Institute Report, Kellermann *et al.*, 1998) and think tanks (European Policy Centre, 2001; Pelkmans *et al.*, 2000) complained that the quality of IA varied too much from one DG to another. Another point raised by several commentators in the past was that the Commission had considerable experience with single-sector types of assessment, but needed to coordinate partial assessments in an overall strategy of regulatory management (Radaelli, 1999).

The new integrated system addresses these concerns. It replaces (and integrates into a new tool) all previous requirements for business IA, environmental assessment, compliance cost assessment for SMEs, gender assessment and trade assessment (European Commission, 2002b: 3). Of course, the methodologies and scope of the various types of assessment vary according to the substantive policies examined. Proportionality is a guiding principle. It makes sense to invest in deeper analyses only when the importance of the proposals under scrutiny justifies it (European Commission, 2002b: 8).

The Commission has also taken some organisational steps to perform IA. The 2002 communication establishes that IA is the responsibility of the DG in charge, but (as mentioned above) in the context of an organisational network. The latter includes the Secretariat-General (with major responsibility for coordination of the overall support structure for IA) and the 'most concerned DGs' (European Commission, 2002b: 8). As a result, the new 'integrated' system of IA is a pivotal tool for implementing three ambitious policy strategies at the EU level: the Gothenburg Council strategy of sustainable development; the Lisbon agenda for competitiveness; and EU-wide better regulation policy.

The communication on IA calls for the participation of other EU institutions as well as Member States. Member States' initiatives for IA of their own legislation is obviously important for the overall efficiency of assessment methodologies across levels of governance. Additionally, Member States can contribute to the quality of the IAs in different guises.[8]

In what cases is IA required?

> A formal IA is required for *items on the Commission's Work Programme* (WP). All regulatory proposals, White Papers, expenditure programmes and negotiating guidelines for international agreements (with an economic, social or environmental impact) put on the WP are concerned. In addition, the Commission may, on a case-by-case basis, decide to carry out an impact assessment of a proposal which does not appear on the WP. (European Commission, 2005b: 6, emphasis in original)

The Commission's work programme is established in the strategic planning and programming cycle. IAs are well suited to the analysis of directives and regulation. However, other initiatives (such as communications and recommendations) were made subject to IA in 2003, the first year of experience with the new system of IA. Moreover, the IA communication envisages that other proposals – the 'White Papers, expenditure programmes and negotiating guidelines for international agreements' from the extract above – may be subjected to IA.

The communication mentions what may be excluded from the IA regime. These are the following (European Commission, 2002b: 5–6):

- green papers and proposals for consultation with social partners;
- periodic Commission decisions and reports;
- proposals following international obligations;
- executive decisions, such as statutory decisions, technical updates and reports on technical progress;

- circumstances of *force majeure*, as in the case of emergencies, international obligations, human rights, security and safety issues.

The Commission makes a distinction between the early-stage appraisal of proposals (the 'road map') and the final IA report.[9] The road map provides a concise analysis of the problem, the alternative policy options (including the option of preserving the status quo) and the sectors affected. It also indicates which impacts warrant further analysis, outlines the consultation plan and indicates whether an inter-service steering group will be established – a compulsory requirement under the new (2005) guidelines. With the aim of improving the participation of stakeholders, the road maps are published along with the Commission's legislative and working programme.

There are two purposes to the IA reports. The first is to have an in-depth analysis of the regulatory impact on the economy, society and the environment. The second is to consult widely with interested parties – in line with the minimum standards (see under 'Consultation', below). The report is tabled for inter-service consultations on regulatory proposals (European Commission, 2002b: 10). It should be sent to other EU institutions 'as a working document when the proposal is adopted by the Commission' (European Commission, 2002b: 8), although 'each institution is responsible for carrying out impact assessments in their respective areas of responsibility' (European Commission, 2005b: 15). Moreover, the explanatory memorandum contains a summary of the IA report.

The 2005 internal guidelines on the IA procedure also define a quality control mechanism:

> Since the Secretariat-General will consider the quality of the IA report as part of the formal Inter-Service Consultation procedure, it is important that it is kept up to date with progress on the IA throughout the process, either as part of the Inter-Service Steering Group or on an *ad hoc* basis. If the IA report subjected to Inter-Service Consultation does not reach a satisfactory level of quality, a suspended or unfavourable opinion may be issued. Once over the hurdle of Inter-Service Consultation, the IA report accompanies the draft proposal submitted to the College of Commissioners. It also possible that one or more of the Groups of Commissioners will examine the draft proposal and the impact assessment prior to the College's deliberation. (European Commission, 2005b: 14–15)

The main results of quality assurance are communicated to the public via the annual *Better Lawmaking* report. The 2003 report identified five areas for improvement in the quality of IA (European Commission, 2003d: 36):

1 the social and environment impacts;
2 a broader discussion of the principles of subsidiarity and proportionality;
3 assessment of more than one policy option;

4 quantification and monetisation of the options;
5 accessibility of the IA formats.

Moreover, the 2004 *Better Lawmaking* report mentions that, in 2003, the first trial year, 'the rate of completion remained below 50%' (European Commission, 2005d: 5). The report goes on to state that the overall quality of IA has improved, 'particularly with respect to the range of options reviewed and the information on the consultation processes feeding the analysis'. However, it also confirms that the weaknesses in assessing the social and environmental dimensions and in the quantification of 'likely impact' still persist (European Commission, 2005d: 5).

The internal evaluation system of IA is still to be developed, but the fundamentals are there. In October 2003, the Secretariat-General circulated among the DGs and heads of service a questionnaire on quality and accessibility of regulation, with questions on public consultation, the collection and use of expertise, and the choice of instruments. Interestingly, the questionnaire asked respondents to quantify regulatory proposals that had been withdrawn. In this context, in September 2005 – after completing the screening of 183 proposals for EU laws pending the agreement of the European Parliament and Council – the Commission announced the withdrawal of more than a third.

Academics and think tanks have made proposals for the assessment of the quality of IA. They are reviewed below, after we have turned to the current Commission guidelines (European Commission, 2002c, 2003b, 2003c, 2005b, 2005c).

The Commission's internal guidelines
In this section we highlight the main criteria built into the technical guidelines.

Chain of objectives – and indicators   'Objectives are ideally expressed in terms of the expected effect of the policy on the situation it is meant to influence' (European Commission, 2003b: 10). They should be defined in a way that makes it possible to verify their achievement. Objectives are distinguishable on three levels. The first level is the general objective to which are associated outcome or impact indicators. The latter are usually general indicators, such as rates of economic growth or unemployment. The second level refers to specific objectives and results indicators. They 'are expressed in terms of the direct and short-term effects of the policy' (European Commission, 2003b: 10). The third level of objectives refers to the operational as well as output indicators. Here the achievement of these types of objective is directly related to the policy and the chosen option. The design of objectives and associated indicators should be based on the following principles (European Commission, 2003b: 12):

- they should be specific (the objectives should be precise and concrete);
- they should be measurable;
- they should be accepted by the affected parties;
- they should be realistic;
- they should be time dependent (the objectives must be related to a temporal dimension).

This guideline requirement for a 'chain of objectives' and related indicators is important in relation to the evaluation of the success of policy options in reaching the desired outcomes. It is a foundation for ex-post evaluation of individual IA.

Baseline The analysis of policy options should be based on the 'no policy change' baseline, which should nevertheless take into account 'the future trends of the main variable likely to be relevant, such as demographic, technological, and economic variables' (European Commission, 2003b: 13).

Policy options Annex 2 of the internal 'technical' guidelines (European Commission, 2005c) lists several policy options, namely: status quo (option zero); regulatory watch (monitoring self-regulation); information and guidelines; self-regulation;[10] open methods of coordination; framework directives; prescriptive regulatory action ('command and control'); market-based instruments, such as permits to pollute, taxes or charges, limits to price and/or quantity; direct public sector financial interventions; and co-regulation.[11] The selection of the most relevant policy options is based on three principles: efficiency, effectiveness and consistency (European Commission, 2005b: 25).

Methods of identifying possible impacts The guidelines illustrate three methods of listing and screening the possible impact of a policy option. The first relies on an 'impact matrix': the policy options considered in the assessment are collocated in the rows of the matrix; the main types of impacts are collocated in the columns. Each cell shows the likelihood of the impact (certain, probable, unlikely) and the type of impact (positive or negative). The last stage of the analysis consists in specifying the affected parties and the timescale over which the impacts are expected to occur (European Commission, 2005b: 35). The second method consists of a qualitative assessment. Essentially there are two dimensions to assess: the likelihood (low, medium or high probability) and the magnitude of each impact (low, medium or high) (European Commission, 2005b: 33). The third method relies on the so-called 'causal model'. In this method, the starting point is the identification of impacts that would arise from the policy options. These impacts can then form the basis for identifying further rounds of impacts, and so on. A flowchart or map of impacts sketches out the cause–effect linkages between each of the policy options/instruments and their impacts (European Commission, 2005b: 27). The 2005 guidelines propose the use of separate tables for the economic, environmental and social impacts.

Measuring impacts   The guidelines acknowledge that are three possible ways to describe the impacts of policy options: qualitative, quantitative and monetary. For the last, the analyst should consider all the values in real terms, adjusting them for inflation. Moreover, the monetary value that occurs in different time periods should be discounted. The real discount rate is 0.4 (European Commission, 2005c: 39). The guidelines require an assessment of 'the impacts in qualitative, quantitative and monetary terms where possible and appropriate' (European Commission, 2005b: 26). As a result, the Commission's approach does not consider quantification and monetisation as the *sine qua non* of IA methodology.

Integrating economic, social and environmental impacts   The guidelines propose a wide range of approaches, including (European Commission, 2005c: 22–5): computable general equilibrium models; sectoral models; macro-econometric models; environmental IA models; micro-simulation models; and projects and programmes. The main methodologies available to compare impacts are (European Commission, 2005c: 42–4): cost–benefit analysis; cost-effectiveness analysis; multi-criteria analysis; and risk analysis. Other methodologies can be used when necessary, such as 'compliance cost assessment, risk–risk assessment, and cost–risk assessment' (European Commission, 2005c: 59; see also the previous guidelines, European Commission, 2003c: 27). The guidelines require a specific assessment of administrative costs. The latter are defined as:

> the costs incurred by enterprises, the voluntary sector, public authorities and citizens in meeting legal obligations to provide information on their action or production, either to public authorities or to private parties. (European Commission, 2005c: 35)

The reference to several stakeholders (including citizens) shows that the approach to administrative burdens is not limited to a reduction of costs for the business community. The guidelines recommend the SCM formula, essentially based on the costs of human resources (see the section on the Netherlands in chapter 4). However:

> other types of costs will be taken into account where appropriate. For instance, in the case of an obligation to inform all customers by mail, the time spent by staff in drafting the leaflet is generally marginal compared to the printing and mailing costs. (European Commission, 2005c: 35)

Consultation   'Consultation [of interested parties and experts] can be used to validate existing data and analysis' (European Commission, 2002c: 32).

The consultation strategy must comply with the minimum standards of consultation (see below) and the guidelines on the use of science and experts' advice (European Commission, 2002d).

Uncertainty   Sensitivity analysis is recommended in the case of highly uncertain cases. Moreover, when risks cannot be estimated properly, then a scenario analysis should be provided (European Commission, 2005c: 44).

Distributive effects   The IA should take into account the 'adverse impact on particular social group, sector, or region, including impacts outside the EU' (European Commission, 2005b: 26).

Ex-post monitoring   The IA should show how to monitor the implementation of the proposal. 'Procedures for evaluating the proposal, the timing of the evaluation, their focus, and the responsibility of their organisation should be defined.' 'Within the framework of the analysis, an attempt should be made to define some core indicators for the main policy objectives and to outline the monitoring and evaluation arrangements envisaged.' Such indicators should provide information on the extent to which 'a policy has been properly implemented and its objectives achieved' (European Commission, 2005b: 45). The analyst should describe briefly how to collect data on indicators and outline the nature, frequency and purpose of the monitoring. Moreover, the IA report should contain (European Commission 2005c: 46):

- an analysis of 'the soundness and reliability of the proposed methods and instruments for collecting follow-up data, storing and processing this data and ensuring its validity';
- a monitoring system that ensures data from Member States or other institutions will be collected reliably and smoothly.

Quality of EU IA: the view from academia and think tanks
Academics and think tanks have reviewed the quality of IAs. We present in this section two studies conducted by scholars at the University of Manchester and at the University of East Anglia and two studies carried out by think tanks, namely the Institute for European Environmental Policy and the European Policy Forum.

Table 6.1 presents and compares the methods used in these studies to assess the quality of IAs performed by the Commission, the specific aspects of IA considered for the analysis (e.g., sustainable development, or business competitiveness), the main conclusions and finally the recommendations. A column of the table highlights whether the recommendations have been taken into account in the 2005 revised IA process (European Commission, 2005b).

Table 6.1 Summary of the four evaluation studies on the Commission impact assessment

Study	Methods	Specific aspects of the IA process considered	Main conclusions	Recommendations	Are recommendations met in the 2005 guidelines?
Lee and Kirkpatrick (2004)	Scorecard and grading system	Overall quality of content (of impact assessment report) and quality of the process	The quality findings are marginally disappointing considering that 2003 was the first year of adoption of the IA process	• Guidance should require a non-technical summary; training should be designed in order to allow practitioners to learn from practical experience of colleagues	No
European Policy Forum (Vibert, 2004, 2005)	Scorecard (yes/no format)	Overall quality but with emphasis on competitiveness	2004 The overall assessment is positive, but there are areas for further progress 2005 Commission's IA may be vulnerable to the criticism of 'window dressing'; however, transparency has increased. On balance, there is room for improvement. An independent body should be introduced	2004 • Improve the consultation process • Strengthen market analysis • Strengthen the support from the Council and from the European Parliament 2005 • Establishment of a system for independent peer review outside the Commission • Judicial review of IAs • Guidelines should properly address any concern about 'confirmation bias' • Among the non-legislative alternatives, greater prominence should be given to market analysis	 Partially No No Yes[a] No No No

Source	Format	Focus	Overall assessment	Recommendations	
Institute for European Environmental Policy (Wilkinson *et al.*, 2004)	Yes/no format checklist	Sustainable development	Overall poor quality due to: the lack of control mechanisms; the limited resources for undertaking assessment, and for provision of advice and guidance; and the absence of an institutional framework within which learning by doing can take place	On design:	
				• More political commitment	No
				• More resources and better training and guidance	No
				• Enhancing the transparency and accessibility of the IA process	No
				• Council and Parliament can reject poor-quality IA	No
				On IA process:	
				• Elimination of selection criteria (all proposals should be assessed) and revision of two-stage process (initial checklist for scoping the assessment required)	Yes[b]
				• Infrastructure for systematic collection and analysis of data	No
				• Involvement of Member States in the IA process	No
				• Network of national experts	Yes
				On guidelines:	
				• Regular review and revision	Yes
				• Guidance on sustainable development assessment	Partially[c]
				• Guidelines should regard IA as a process rather than a one-off event	No
Opoku and Jordan (2004)	Scorecard with a grading system (0–4)	The external dimension (that is, extra-EU) of IA and sustainable development	The process is not leading to an adequate information flow among policy networks	• Central steering	Partially[d]
				• Improvement in the guidelines	No
				• Major consideration of the external dimension of EU policies	No
				• Enhance consultation within the IA process, in particular taking into consideration developing countries, development non-governmental organisations and DG Development	No
				• Transparent application of selection criteria	Yes

[a] The Commission has proposed the establishment of a group of external experts who will support the analysts in drafting IAs.
[b] The procedure designed by the 2005 guidelines requires that all proposals inserted in the Commission work programme should pass the IA test.
[c] Environmental indicators have been developed.
[d] An inter-service group is now compulsory.

Table 6.1 shows that all four studies relied on checklists and scorecards. Lee and Kirkpatrick (2004) developed a 'review package', applied to a small sample – six out of a total of twenty-three IAs concluded in 2003. The 'review package' is a scorecard based on both the quality of content (of the IA) and quality of the process. On content, Lee and Kirkpatrick review three sections or 'areas': description of the problem, policy objectives and policy options; description of options analysis methodology and findings; and presentation of report findings. The quality of an IA is measured by two overall measures (Lee and Kirkpatrick, 2004: 42), one associated with the quality of the IA report and the other with the quality of the IA process. The measures, however, are simply in the form of an A–F overall grade for the quality of the content and the process. This is a limitation of the scorecard as it now stands. The clarity of the information provided to the reader and the quality of analysis that can be performed would be greater if the grading system were turned into a numerical format. Once turned into numbers, the grades of individual aspects of IA would enable a precise analysis of correlation. For example, it would be possible to measure the correlation between content and process, or whether weaknesses in one specific element of IA are correlated to problems in other elements. Another limitation of the scorecard is the mixing of objective and subjective information. The basic grades are aggregated by using subjective weights. Although the weights are discussed by the two reviewers, they are based on subjective assessments of how important any particular element is in a given IA. On balance, however, the Lee–Kirkpatrick review package provides valuable insights on quality variables, in line with the best international literature on the quality of IA and project evaluation.

Frank Vibert reviewed twenty IAs performed in 2003 (Vibert, 2004) – the first year of the implementation of the IA system – and another twenty-eight IAs performed in 2004 (Vibert, 2005). His scorecards provide food for thought for the elaboration of indicators across three quality dimensions: the quantification of costs and benefits; the procedural aspects of assessment; and the extent to which IA fosters learning. In developing his 2004 score-card, Vibert (2004: 3) relied on the OECD (1995) checklist and the OMB (2001) guidelines on regulatory analysis. Good economic analyses – Vibert argues – are those that succeed in quantifying and monetising regulatory costs and benefits. When monetisation is not possible, quantification should be pursued in a standardised way. For instance, the benefits of health and safety regulatory provision should be expressed in quality-adjusted life years (QALYs) and disability-adjusted life years (DALYs). Moreover, it is desirable that the quantification is shown 'as a central "best estimate" with uncertainties being expressed as inner and outer bounds' (Vibert 2004: 4). Another aspect of IA quality is to take into account the distributive effects (the so-called salient populations) and the way risk is handled. Risk–risk analysis is an essential element of the appraisal of health and safety regulation.

In 2005 Vibert focused on three other areas: the description of the issue or problem; the quality of consultation; and the selection of instruments to achieve a policy goal. According to Vibert, these are the useful dimensions to gauge the existence of a 'confirmation bias'. The latter:

> refers to situations where people look for and select evidence and views that confirm their initial preconceptions or their desires. It means that people hear and see what they want to see, regardless of contradictory or ambiguous evidence in front of their eyes or ears. (Vibert, 2005: 2)

Under certain circumstances IAs can be considered 'window dressing'. They can become 'tools for the manipulation and selection of evidence and opinion in way that then provide a more elaborate justification of the conclusions sought in the first place' (Vibert, 2005: 2–3).

Turning to procedural aspects, Vibert considers four elements: selection criteria (economic significance, use of external advice); framing of the enquiry (discussion of issues, explicit analysis of alternatives, assessment of market alternatives to traditional regulation); data sourcing (consultation of affected parties); and review of the IA. In 2004, the last item referred to the validation of science used in IA. The credibility of the Commission's new system hinges on how economics and the natural sciences as used in IA are validated and by whom. The quality criteria proposed by Vibert (and common to the North American experience) include the reproducibility of models and key findings, and the systematic use of peer review.

In 2005, Vibert shifted his attention to institutional design, proposing an independent review body that 'would aim to make the proposals of the Commission more open to judicial review', since 'it would identify any grounds for subsequent judicial review stemming from any procedural or factual shortcoming in an impact assessment' (Vibert, 2005: 30–1).

Vibert looks also at the role of IA in the regulatory process. In line with international experience, Vibert observes that there are two ways to consider the 'outcome' of the exercise: one is to ascertain whether IA delivers net benefits to the community; the other refers to learning. Do IAs change the behaviour of regulators? Vibert operationalises learning in terms of IAs leading to the rejection of a proposal, or to major redesign. Another operationalisation is the number of IAs that take explicit account of fundamental EU goals in the assessment of proposals.

Vibert makes the important point that outcome and real-world impact can be measured in terms of changes in the behaviour of the regulators. This is a notion of outcome that (as observed in previous chapters) is more manageable and more useful for the goals of this project than the notions proposed by economists. The operationalisation of learning and the points about the validation of the scientific components of IA are also useful. At the same time, Vibert's scorecard is much less sophisticated than the one proposed by Lee and Kirkpatrick. It does not lend itself to in-depth understanding of what goes wrong in specific IAs. This, however, is compensated for by its great advantage in terms of the communicability of results. In fact, the main limitations are elsewhere. In particular, Vibert's operationalisations are somewhat crude. Finally, and paradoxically, Vibert's rating system does not provide a final score for the IAs. Although one can see how the raw measures used by Vibert could easily be developed into a real scorecard (and standard indicators of average quality, variance and so on could be calculated) the papers by the European Policy Forum deliver something less than this.

The Institute for European Environmental Policy (Wilkinson *et al.*, 2004) analysed eight IAs from 2003 in order to assess whether and how sustainable development had been factored in. The main conclusions and findings are summarised in table 6.1. The review of the Commission's IA was fourfold. Firstly, the study looked at the quality of the guidelines. The second aspect was related to the operations of the IA system such as – *inter alia* – publication of IA reports, criteria for selecting regulatory proposals, consultation within the Commission inter-services groups and among stakeholders, and involvement of Member States in the IA. The third aspect revolved around the quality of the IA report in all its elements (form, structure and contents). The final dimension of quality concerned whether existing methods and models to identify or quantify economic, environmental and social impacts had been used. The eight selected reports were assessed through a yes/no format checklist. This is not the most adequate instrument to measure the quality of a regulatory programme (see also the critics of the OMB's PART instrument in chapter 4). However, Wilkinson *et al.*'s (2004) review embeds the consideration of sustainable development in all four of their elements of quality of IA system (guidance, operations, IA report and economic, environmental and social assessment). This aspect has been neglected in the other studies.

Finally, Opoku and Jordan (2004) focused on a specific aspect of sustainable development: the potential impacts of EU policies beyond the Union's borders, in particular on developing countries (Opoku and Jordan, 2004: 2). The two academics assessed the totality of IAs performed in 2003 and 2004. Although limited by their narrow perspective, Opoku and Jordan draw two interesting conclusions. The first concerns the control mechanism within the IA process. The lack of involvement of other DGs in drafting IA reports and their poor quality indicate that the Commission's self-steering network is ineffective (Opoku and Jordan, 2004: 22). The second conclusion is a corollary of the first:

> [Because of the] Commission's preference for voluntary coordination through self-steering networks … [the] IAs are, on the whole, being constructed within the same sectoral boundaries that characterise the Commission and have led to the present state of policy incoherence. (Opoku and Jordan, 2004: 22–3)

Turning to assessment method, the scorecard used by Opoku and Jordan was not structured to capture the complexity of the IA process and contents. Indeed, the scorecard is composed of only nine items to ascertain the external impact of EU regulation in the IA report. Another methodological flaw is related to the assumption that all EU policy and/or regulation has a 'significant' impact on the sustainable development of countries outside the EU. It seems improbable that this is so. Consider, for instance, the following directives and decisions drafted in 2003 and 2004: a groundwater directive, a directive on services in the internal market, a decision establishing the 'Culture 2007' programme, and the framework decision on procedural rights in criminal proceedings throughout the EU.

While the four studies formulated a series of recommendations to improve the IA system, table 6.1 shows that a very limited number of these were taken into account in the drafting of the 2005 guidelines. This is evidence of limited learning on the part of the Commission.

Consultation

What is the definition of high-quality consultation provided by the Commission? Does it shed light on the design of indicators? In this section we turn to the major master document on consultation, that is, the communication of the Commission on the minimum standards for consultation of interested parties (COM(2002)704). This communication defines consultation as 'processes through which the Commission wishes to trigger input from outside interested parties for the shaping of policy prior to a decision by the Commission' (European Commission, 2002e: 15–16). Consequently, it does not cover consultation in the context of international agreements, comity procedures or Treaty-based consultation requirements.

Beyond the communication on minimum standards, the protocol on the application of the principles of subsidiarity and proportionality calls on the Commission to conduct a wide consultation 'before proposing legislation and, wherever appropriate, publish consultation documents' (protocol no.7 annexed to the Amsterdam Treaty). Moreover, the 2003 *Better Lawmaking* report recaps the overall approach to consultation by stating that:

> the Commission is required to consult widely before proposing legislation; to justify explicitly the relevance of its proposals in the accompanying explanatory memorandum; and to take into account the burden falling upon the Community, national governments, local authorities, economic operators and citizens. (European Commission, 2003d: 17)

The white paper on governance stipulates that consultation cannot replace the procedures and decisions of legislative bodies (European Commission, 2001a; see also European Commission, 2002e: 4).

Let us now turn to the communication on minimum standards. The main principles enshrined by the minimum standards are (European Commission, 2002e: 15): participation; openness; accountability; effectiveness; and coherence, in terms of transparency of the consultation process, allowing interested parties an opportunity for feedback, evaluation and review.

The communication goes on to highlight the key five aspects of a good consultation process (European Commission, 2002e: 19–22):

1 defining the content of the consultation process;
2 identifying target groups for consultation;
3 publication;
4 setting time limits for participation;
5 allowing acknowledgement and feedback.

These standards, however, do not address the question of when a high-quality consultation should start.

The first step in the consultation process is to define its content, which principally involves drafting documents to support consultation. 'All communications relating to consultation should be clear and concise, and should include all necessary information to facilitate responses' (European Commission, 2002e: 19). The minimum standards detail the type and the contents of documents necessary to achieve an efficient consultation (European Commission, 2002e: 19), notably: summary of context; scope and objectives of consultation; details of any hearing, meeting or conferences; contact details and deadlines; explanation of the Commission's processes for dealing with contributions, what feedback to expect and details of the next stages involved in the development of the policy; and reference to related documentation.

The second step is to define the target groups. In this case 'the Commission should ensure that relevant parties have an opportunity to express their opinions' (European Commission, 2002e: 19). To achieve this goal, an 'adequate coverage' should be assured for those interested parties that: are affected by the policy; are involved in the implementation of the policy; or have objectives linked with the policy. In the selection of the parties to consult, the following characteristics should be taken into account (European Commission, 2002e: 19–20): wideness of the policy impact; need for specific experience, expertise or technical knowledge; need to involve non-organised interests; the record of participants in previous consultation; and balancing the representatives in terms of social and economic bodies, large and small organisations or companies, wider constituencies and specific target groups, and organisation in the EU and those in non-member countries.

The third stage is the publication of documents. Here the minimum standards require that the consultation documents be available on-line through a specific 'single access point'.

The fourth stage deals with the time limits allowed to interested parties to participate. The time limit is eight weeks in the case of written consultation and twenty working days for meetings.

The last step of the consultation process is to acknowledge the contributions, which should be displayed on websites:

> Contributions will be analysed carefully to see whether, and to what extent, the views expressed can be accommodated in the policy proposals. Contributions to open public consultations will be made public on the single access point. Results of other forms of consultation should, as far as possible, also be subject to public scrutiny on the single access point on the internet. (European Commission, 2002e: 21–2)

Adequate feedback should be given by the Commission in the explanatory memoranda. The latter should contain: the results of consultation, and an explanation of how this was conducted and how the results were taken into account in the proposal. 'In addition, the results of consultations carried out in the Impact Assessment process will be summarised in the related reports' (European Commission, 2002e: 22). The principles and minimum standards of consultation should be incorporated in 'extended' IAs. This makes the link between consultation and IA clear. One could easily develop scorecards and indicators by checking whether an extended IA has followed the minimum standards in the five stages described above. However, the minimum standards of consultation go well beyond IA. For instance, they should be taken into account in the case of green papers, since they are typical consultation tools.

According to the Commission, there are essentially seven consultation tools (European Commission, 2003d: 32): green papers; white papers; communications; fora; workshops; consultations on the internet; and the European Business Test Panel (EBTP). Of these, it is worth focusing on two innovative consultation tools, namely the EBTP and consultation on the internet, the so-called 'interactive policy-making'.

The EBTP is a panel of 3,700 European companies (from Member States plus Norway and Iceland). It supports IA processes and identifies specific regulatory provision to simplify (in this context, the Commission has launched a 'red tape observatory').[12] The Commission expects around six to eight EBTP consultations per year. These will be conducted on-line through an electronic and structured questionnaire, mostly using multiple-choice questions and some 'free text' answer options. EBTP consultation 'should be conducted at a sufficiently early stage'.[13] Moreover, questionnaires will be structured 'to gauge views on alternative options and cost–benefit analysis' of regulatory proposals for the single market. Consequently, the EBTP is a consultation tool that supports the IA of internal market regulatory proposals. Another important rule of the game concerns access to results. Each panellist will be informed of the result of a questionnaire within four weeks of the conclusion of the consultation. Additionally, and more importantly, panellists will know how the Commission has taken their views into account.

The Commission aims to develop communication from interested parties to Brussels via interactive policy-making, through the collection of spontaneous feedback via intermediaries, notably the Euro Info Centres. The idea is to integrate feedback from economic operators into the policy-making process. It complements the more traditional modes of consultation. Since the interactive policy-making project envisages a structured database, it can be useful to have some measurement of the real-world impact of the regulatory environment. A possible indicator is the change (in percentage) of firms that believe the Commission is not taking their views into account (see chapter 7).

To sum up, the minimum standards provide the Commission's own benchmark for high-quality consultation. As they are fairly precise in terms of what is expected from each step of the consultation process, they can be used to develop indicators and scorecards. Consultation indicators can also assist in the design of indicators of the quality of IA, as consultation is a fundamental aspect of assessment. In terms of data-gathering, the EBTP and interactive policy-making (when fully implemented) will be useful sources of data for subjective indicators of real-world outcome.

Simplification

The Commission carried out an action plan to update and simplify the regulatory environment (European Commission, 2003e). The plan covered regulations, directives and decisions. Its aim was to achieve a clear, under-standable, up-to-date and user-friendly *acquis*, in order to enhance the competitiveness of the European economic system as set out in the Lisbon strategy.

The stock of *acquis* in force at the EU level amounted at the end of 2002 to 14,500 legal acts and some 97,000 pages of the *Official Journal* (European Commission, 2003e: 5; 2003f: 5, note 3). This is a basic (yet efficient – see chapter 3) indicator. The Commission used this indicator (i.e., reduction of the number of pages) to measure the success of any efforts at simplification. At the Laeken European Council, the Commission undertook a commit-ment to reduce the number of *Official Journal* pages by at least 25 per cent by January 2005 (European Commission, 2001c: 5).

The simplification action plan was structured as six objectives and six lines of action (namely simplification, consolidation, codification, repeal, obsolescence, and organisation and presentation of the *acquis*). The action plan was set as three phases (European Commission, 2003e):

- phase 1, February 2003–September 2003;

- phase 2, October 2003–March 2004;
- phase 3, April 2004–December 2004.

The first objective was to identify specific regulatory sectors which need to be simplified. To do so, the Commission drew up a list of 'prioritisation indicators' to select regulatory sectors in which to start and how to utilise resources better. Box 6.3 presents these eight indicators.

These 'indicators' should be more accurately referred to as a checklist for the identification of priorities. By using this checklist, one can easily get to some real-world outcome indicators already used either by governments or by economists (see chapters 3 and 4), notably the following:

- number of legal acts;
- number of *Official Journal* pages;
- number of infringements, even if their significance is not defined;
- number of complaints received from citizens or businesses about the complexity of a piece of legislation;
- number of responses to consultation;
- compliance costs, even if the assessment methodology is not given.

The Commission in its first report on the simplification action plan recognised that:

> strict application of the prioritisation indicators and selection of policy sectors for screening has proven a relatively weak point. Although work is progressing, a more structured and consistent application of the methodology set out would have been desirable. (European Commission, 2003f: 13)

Objectives 2, 3 and 4 of the simplification action plan described the measures that would be adopted to simplify and update the *acquis*. The specific simplification tools were consolidation, codification and reviewing the organisation and presentation of the *acquis*. The tools can be grouped in two categories according to their capacity to modify the substance of regulation.

The first group of tools does not affect the substance of the underlying policy. Two policy tools are included in this definition of simplification: consolidation and codification. Consolidation integrates legislative amendments into the text of the piece of law that is being simplified. Codification brings together (i.e., unifies), in a new legal act, all the provisions of an act together with any subsequent amendment. The result of this exercise is a single text, achieved by 'deleting obsolete and overlapping provisions, harmonising terms and definitions, and correcting errors without substantive change' (European Commission, 2003e: 12).

The second approach to simplification is more dynamic: it addresses the substance of a policy, with a view to modifying its objectives and scope (European Commission, 2003e: 6). 'Recasting involves substantial

Box 6.3 The prioritisation indicators of the Commission's simplification action plan

A Importance of a particular policy area, assessed thorough two specific indicators:
  1 The policy areas' relative importance within the European economy and the EU internal market in terms of growth, competitiveness and jobs.
  2 The weight of a particular policy area represented in terms of its share of the EU secondary Community law and how significantly its functioning is influenced by EU legislation (for example indicated by the number of legal acts and *Official Journal* pages) and the level of technical details included in the existing acts in force.

B Where there are indications of potential problems with existing legislation:
  3 Where there are difficulties in implementing the legislation because of successive amendments, overlapping or conflicting requirements and potential legal uncertainty resulting from inconsistent definitions or terminology, or as a result of Member States' transposition, which has itself added unnecessary, complicated, detailed or excessive provisions.
  4 Where experience has shown that administrative implementation and compliance costs appear disproportionate in relation to the benefits sought by the European Community legislators and achieved, and/or the potential for legislation (and policy) simplification is considerable.
  5 Where there are potential major risks (fundamental rights, the environment, consumers, health or safety, industries or services, etc.) that are not satisfactorily targeted by existing legislation but which could be addressed in a simplification initiative rather than in a new legislative proposal.

C Where new political initiatives or evolving regulatory practices may justify a legislative update and consequently an opportunity to simplify the *acquis*:
  6 Where the application of horizontal initiatives (sustainable development, environmental concerns, safety, fundamental rights, etc.) require updating and amendments in respect of a particular sector.
  7 Where the legislative approach may no longer be appropriate and could be replaced by more efficient, flexible and proportionate instruments (e.g., framework directives, new approach directives or 'softer' regulatory alternatives). In addition, evaluation of Community policies should be more systematically used to establish the possible need for simplification.
  8 Where new obligations (e.g., resulting from international agreements) require updated legislation or changes to the legislative format chosen in order to exploit more effectively the potential synergies between overlapping regulatory regimes, or where European legislation refers to international agreements and annexes such agreements to Community legal acts.

Source: European Commission (2003e: 7).

modification of the basis legal act' (European Commission, 2003e: 12–13). Repeals can be classified as another policy tool that modifies the substance of the *acquis*; repeals eliminate obsolete legal acts. The Commission adds that the accuracy, quality and user-friendliness of CELEX, the Directory of Legislation in Force and EUR–Lex can be improved (European Commission, 2003e: 15). This can lead to the formulation of indicators linking simplification and access.

Objectives 5 and 6 defined the political and technical control of the simplification process (European Commission, 2003e: 6). The Commission established a summary scorecard. It tracked progress on consolidation, simplification and repeals (European Commission, 2003e: 16). The scorecard provided information on 'the evolution of the stock of Community law and, in particular, the progress being made with regard to the simplification, codification and repeals targets' (European Commission, 2003e: 17). The scorecard was both a management and a communication tool (directed towards interested parties and the public). Table 6.2 shows the section of the scorecard dedicated to the codification of the Commission's acts.

The Commission monitors its simplification action plan through two indicators: the number of legal acts, and the reduction in the number of pages of the *Official Journal*. They are measures of output.

Beyond the scorecard, what are the results achieved by the simplification action plan? In 2003, the Commission collected some useful measures (European Commission, 2003f):

- Around 170 directives and regulations had been identified to be simplified.
- Of twenty-three planned simplification proposals for the first phase (February–September 2003), fourteen had been adopted and four more were planned before the end of 2003.
- The consolidation programme was completed in mid-2003. Consolidated texts are now available on-line.[14]
- There has been a reduction of about 20,000 pages of the *Official Journal* as a consequence of consolidation (European Commission, 2003e: 11).
- Although the Commission had proposed 217 codification initiatives, in the first phase only seven codified acts were adopted.
- Some thirty obsolete legal acts were eliminated.

A subsequent Commission communication on a strategy for the simplification of the regulatory environment summarised some other results of the 2003–4 simplification action plan:

> As a result of the screening of 42 policy sectors, the Commission identified more than 200 legal acts with a potential for simplification and has adopted more than 35 initiatives with simplification implications. To date, 15 legislative simplification proposals are still pending before the legislator. In addition,

Table 6.2 Scorecard of the codification of the Commission's acts. Results of the first phase (February–September 2003)

DG	February 2003 commitments (SEC(2003)165)						Progress[a]											
	Regulations		Directives		Decisions		Regulations				Directives				Decisions			
	No. of acts	No. of OJ pages	No. of acts	No. of OJ pages	No. of acts	No. of OJ pages	No. of acts			No. of pages	No. of acts			No. of pages	No. of acts			No. of pages
							A	B	C		A	B	C		A	B	C	
Agriculture	48				3		3	41	4	681						3		20
Health	3		7		52			3		32		5	2	254	2	45	5	814
Enterprise																		
Environment																		
Transport	2				1			2		9						1		4
Justice																		
Internal market																		
Employment																		
Taxation	2							2		30								
Competition																		
Eurostat	1				3		1			14					1	2		44
Total	56		7		59		4	48	4	766	0	5	2	254	3	51	5	882

[a] A = Operation completed (codification adopted by the Commission); B = Operation in progress; C = Project dropped from the programme: abandoned or not relevant.

Source: European Commission (2003f).

to improve the accessibility, readability and consistency of the Community *acquis*, considerable work has been done to produce consolidated and codified texts. Besides, several hundred repeals and declarations of obsolescence have significantly contributed to further reducing the volume of the *acquis*. (European Commission, 2005b: 3)

The number of *Official Journal* pages is a basic indicator that can be used in a distorted way. For example, in order to achieve the target, a DG could simplify only directives covering many pages, without considering perhaps more relevant directives. Moreover, the objective to reduce the number of pages could lead to an excessive reduction in the length of a piece of legislation, worsening the comprehensibility of a text.

Access and regulatory transparency

The main innovations on public access and transparency of documents are the following (European Commission, 2001d: 1):

- access is extended to documents originating with third parties, for example the Member States or other EU institutions;
- time limits for replies to citizens' queries have been reduced to fifteen days;
- a document register is available to facilitate the search for documents of public interest.

The Commission's documents can be classified as published or unpublished. Preparatory documents on Commission decisions and policy initiatives such as preliminary drafts, interim reports, draft legislative proposals or decisions are typical unpublished documents. IA reports are unpublished documents. The web-based document register facilitates access to IA documents. Obviously, an on-line single point of access to IA documents, as well as to all documents related to the IA process, for instance the documents supporting the consultation process, is a better solution. The Secretariat-General launched the IA website at the end of 2004.[15] On 17 November 2005, the website showed the links to twenty-one reports performed in 2003, thirty in 2004, and thirty-eight in 2005. In this specific context, the benchmark is the e-docket of the US regulatory agencies, where all documents related to a regulatory proposal are classified, numbered and available on-line in a specific section of the agencies' websites.

Finally, transparency is also granted by article 207 of the Amsterdam Treaty. This article requires the Council to grant access to documents relating to legislative activities. A minimum requirement is that votes, explanation of votes and statements in the minutes must be made public.

Conclusions

This chapter has reviewed the progress made by the Commission and other EU institutions in terms of measures of regulatory quality. One prerequisite for any quality assurance system is institutional design. The EU's main attempt to streamline institutional relations and design is the inter-institutional agreement on better regulation. Additionally, specific communications and action plans define the institutional context in which tools such as simplification and IA are used.

Within the Commission, the Secretariat-General is the body in charge of horizontal coordination of better regulation tools. An important task for the future is to foster the development of similar approaches (to better regulation tools) across the institutions. The working parties of the Commission, the Parliament and the Council in charge of defining common approaches to tools like IA have a crucial mission to accomplish.

Although the results reflect the trial-and-error nature of a classic learning stage, the potential is high. We base this conclusion on evidence pointing to the difficulty of handling the assessment of substantive amendments to the Commission's proposals, the high number of bodies and technical groups on better regulation active within the institutions, and the volatile nature of the Commission's guidelines. On the last point, we observe that while the frequent changes to the technical guidelines and the communications produced between 2002 and 2005 are the result of learning from experience, they may not help the institutionalisation of better regulation policies in the EU. Moreover, the revised guidelines consider only a few of the many recommendations of academics and think tanks on streamlining IA methodology and procedure.

The Commission's approach to IA therefore represents something of a moving target. It does not provide a stable reference, neither for those governments that are looking to Brussels for inspiration and guidance on better regulation, nor for those Member States that, drawing on their considerable experience with better regulation, have specific models to propose for adoption and would like to see whether the Commission is going down one particular path (e.g., the SCM) or another. The explanation of this state of affairs lies in the political nature of better regulation policies, with all the obvious pressures in the Council and on the Commission to respond to different opportunities and constraints, and in the sheer complexity of handling better regulation across the three very different institutions (i.e., the Commission, the Council and the Parliament) that share the EU's legislative function.

All the same, the Commission's approach to IA has great potential. It is based on a consistent assessment of a range of costs and benefits, in line with the most advanced experience in the Member States. Further, it takes on board and operationalises the ideas put forward by the Mandelkern report. More importantly still, it combines the focus on the economy and competitiveness with the goal of social cohesion and sustainable development.

The overall quality assurance system is not as sophisticated as the one we found in some countries reviewed in chapter 4. There is no audit body in charge of regulatory performance evaluation. Some have suggested the creation of a regulatory audit body (Allio *et al.*, 2004; European Parliament, 2004; European Policy Centre, 2001; Vibert, 2004, 2005) in the Court of Auditors. One problem associated with this argument is that the Court of Auditors has not developed much in the direction of performance evaluation. Its methods are rooted in the continental tradition of financial evaluation. We return to this point in chapter 7, in the context of external evaluation. But our review shows that there is plenty of evidence of stakeholder-driven evaluations of the Commission's IAs. This is a very good indicator of 'pluralistic evaluation', with private sector think tanks and academics engaged with various methodologies in the appraisal of the quality of consultation, the Commission's own numbers and the overall approach to better regulation.[16] In terms of quality assurance, the existence of pluralistic and society-driven external evaluation is perhaps more important than establishing a new body in the European Court of Auditors.

A second element of weakness in terms of quality assurance is the lack of mechanisms for the validation of scientific analyses used in regulatory decisions. The Commission has not scored well in terms of the replicability of models used in IA, use of robust peer review mechanisms, and reliance on panels of external advisers for the purpose of validation (Vibert, 2004). However, the preconditions for a better system are there. One possible step towards improvement is to make systematic use of the guidelines on the use of experts' advice and the role of science (see European Commission, 2002d; Liberatore, 2001).

A third problematic element concerns the robustness of the design. So far the Commission is the body that has developed most in the direction of units with horizontal coordination tasks, like the Secretariat-General. However, the Commission is not an executive and the role of the Secretariat-General is by no means comparable (in terms of power and reach) to a better regulation unit located within a national cabinet office. Accordingly, it is crucial that the other institutions develop their own quality assurance units and that all the units interact, for example by promoting convergence of methods and by improving data collection. The Council's new groups working on the competitiveness dimension of IA and better regulation programmes can be seen as embryonic organisational efforts to address the problem. To conclude on this point, the challenge for the future is to move from institutional awareness to the creation of institutional capacity to use better regulation tools and to monitor their results.

One promising feature of broad quality assurance is the involvement of stakeholders in the discussion of simplification and IA. This is the consequence of specific efforts made by the Commission to increase the awareness of stakeholders and academics. To illustrate, in December 2003 the Commission organised a pan-European conference on integrated IA with academics and private sector think tanks.[17] The conference assembled some 100 academics and practitioners. Nowadays, reports on the quality of IA in the EU are being debated throughout Europe.

Turning to indicators, there are several initiatives under way which can directly or indirectly lead to measures of quality. Projects like IMAC have gone as far as to propose specific lists of indicators. The Commission's reports on better regulation tools include interesting measures, although some indicators, such as the reduction in the number of pages in the *Official Journal*, should be treated with caution.

One important result of our review is that some data collection instruments are already available, or almost so. These include the EBTP, the Eurobarometer and other instruments to collect the views of stakeholders. In terms of objective measures of regulatory quality, the Commission has already discussed some useful indicators, although the discussion of how to gather the data is less developed. The Commission has asked the group of national experts who advise Brussels on IA to agree on a set of objective indicators and start collecting them – but the response has been lukewarm. The European Parliament seems to argue that quality assurance should be entirely delegated to an audit body, but the debate on where the audit body should be located is still in its early days. Neither has the discussion on purposes (i.e., why indicators are collected) progressed beyond an embryonic stage. For the success of quality assurance systems, the three components of indicators, data gathering and design (who collects what and for what purposes) should proceed hand in hand. Chapter 7 considers how indicators can be collected on the basis of a limited number of tools. The idea is to make the most of existing data collection instruments and to integrate them in relation to the system of indicators we present in that chapter.

There are two problems with the current state of play. Firstly, reporting and measures of quality are not organised in a specific system of indicators covering the whole spectrum of better regulation tools. The individual proto-systems working in IA, consultation, simplification and access do not speak to each other. Secondly, there is a danger of an uncontrolled proliferation of indicators. There is no need to produce yet another set of *ad hoc* indicators. Rather, the challenge is to coordinate efforts and to weed out redundant measures.

Notes

1   In this chapter we use the term 'impact assessment' instead of 'regulatory impact assessment' in order to conform to the Commission's terminology. This term reflects the fact that the EU impact assessment system appraises regulatory proposals and other policy proposals, such as spending programmes.

2 Two pilot projects address administrative burden for construction products and statistics.

3 Decision 2001/937/EC, of 5 December 2001, published in the *Official Journal* on 29 December 2001. See also http://europa.eu.int/eur-lex/pri/en/oj/dat/2001/l_345/l_34520011229en00940098.pdf.

4 The document, entitled 'Inter-Institutional Common Approach to Impact Assessment (IA)', is available at http://ec.europa.eu/governance/impact/docs/key_docs/ii_common_approach_to_ia_en.pdf.

5 Within the High Level Group on Competitiveness there are more specific subgroups: the subgroup responsible for evaluating the IA on the draft service framework directive, the subgroup on cumulative burden on the automotive sector, and that on competitiveness testing.

6 See the Committee's website, www.europarl.europa.eu/committees/ uri_home_en.htm.

7 The survey had been conducted by EOS Gallup Europe within its Single Market Monitor Survey.

8 As mentioned, this collaboration is now effective, with the formation of the two subgroups of the High Level Group on Competitiveness that are dealing with specific IAs.

9 In 2005, the Commission revised the IA process. Brussels recognised that the appraisal procedure is not neutral from the point of view of resource allocations. It also affects the programming cycle of the legislative process. To tackle this problem, the Commission adopted a simplified process. 'The previous preliminary Impact Assessments will be replaced by Roadmaps' (European Commission, 2004b: 6). The term 'extended' impact assessment has been replaced in the second step by the simpler 'impact assessment', in order to better reflect the principle of proportionate analysis and the fact that certain IAs may remain relatively limited also in the second stage (European Commission, 2004b: 10).

10 'Self-regulation' is defined as the possibility for economic operators, the social partners, non-governmental organisations or associations to adopt among themselves and for themselves common guidelines at the European level (particularly codes of practice or sectoral agreements).

11 'Co-regulation means the mechanism whereby a Community legislative act entrusts the attainment of the objectives defined by the legislative authority to parties which are recognised in the field (such as economic operators, the social partners, non-governmental organisations, or associations)' (Council of the European Union, 2003: 7).

12 The 'red tape observatory' initiative was included in the Internal Market Strategy 2003–6. The aim of the observatory is to identify administrative requirements that are particularly burdensome. It is a joint tool to be used by the Commission as well as Member States in order to achieve a better regulatory environment for business. The observatory will take the form of an on-line questionnaire to be used by businesses to shed light on specific rules that need to be simplified. The observatory will indicate broad criteria to be applied in selecting complaints for follow-up.

13 See the EBTP's website, http://ec.europa.eu/yourvoice/ebtp/index_en.htm.

14   See portal www.europa.eu.int/eur-lex/en/consleg/index1.html.
15   See http://ec.europa.eu/governance/impact/index_en.htm.
16   See Allio *et al.* (2004) for a comprehensive assessment of EU better regulation programmes.
17   Documentation available at: http://europa.eu.int/comm/enterprise/regulation/better_regulation/impact_assessment/ia_conference.htm.

7

Better regulation indicators

Introduction

In this chapter we propose indicators of better regulation policy, drawing on the previous discussion of the notion of quality, the role of different actors, the suggestions arising out of the literature, the initiatives of Member States and EU institutions and the data discussed in chapter 5. We present three systems of indicators, show how they can be gathered and explain their relationship with better regulation tools. One argument made in this chapter is that the Member States and the EU institutions should select specific indicators and take decisions about aggregation. We do not make this selection; neither do we produce aggregations, because this is a process that belongs to 'knowledge utilisation' (i.e., how policy-makers use knowledge and information) and not to 'knowledge production' (i.e., knowledge produced by the social sciences).

Put differently, it is an issue for the 'demand side' of indicators rather than the supply side. The demand side (i.e., why governments and EU institutions want indicators) is still quite diverse. It would be dangerous to neglect complexity by suggesting that our selection of indicators can be a sort of 'one size fits all' approach to quality. It is only via a political process that convergence across the EU can be achieved. This leads us to the link between the design of indicators and their utilisation. We therefore illustrate how indicators can be used in the EU with reference to the open method of coordination – defined by the European Council in the context of the so-called Lisbon agenda for competitiveness.

It is useful to recall the relationship between indicators, regulatory policy and outcomes. In this book, indicators are used in the first place to appraise better regulation policies. These policies revolve around meta-regulation – the rules of the regulatory policy process. In turn, high-quality meta-regulation is a necessary condition for high-quality rules governing the environment, the economy and so on. Finally, regulation contributes to economic outcomes, although the relationship can be difficult to pin down, as discussed in chapter 3. Our indicators cover design, activity (or output) and outcomes. The outcomes of better regulation policies provide empirical information on the economic impact of regulation. It is difficult to establish a clear causal link between input, activity, output and impact, however. Thus, when we discuss real-world indicators of impact, we clarify the causal chain and explain whether this is a weak or a strong one.

We conclude this section with a caveat. The relationship between better regulation programmes, the quality of regulatory policies and economic outcomes is not straightforward – and indicators should not be used to make claims that there is a direct causal impact of programmes on policies and outcomes. It would be wrong to attribute all improvement in terms of outcomes to policy. There is also the paradox of indicators showing real-world improvement when in reality the overall degree of regulatory complexity is the same. For example, if a government employs more people to issue licences, business surveys will probably show that it takes less time to get a licence. However, in this case the real-world outcome indicator will obfuscate the fact that regulatory complexity has not decreased. This is yet another reason for considering *systems* of indicators – to compensate for the limitations of individual measures.

The purposes of indicators and their selection

Indicators represent, gauge and verify changes. What is actually measured by an indicator can vary – an objective or goal, a result or an effect. There is the same variance in the purposes or functions of an indicator system. 'Indicators can also help in producing results by providing a reference point for monitoring, decision making, stakeholder consultations and evaluation' (Sandhu-Rojon, 2003). In particular, according to Sandhu-Rojon, indicators: measure progress and achievements; clarify consistency between inputs, activities, outputs, outcomes and goals; and ensure legitimacy and accountability to all stakeholders by demonstrating progress. Moreover, a system of indicators 'can be used to identify what would have happened in the absence of the policy (the counterfactual)' (Tavistock Institute, 2003: 130).

This is not to say that indicators are panacea. Their limitations are well known. To begin with, indicators determine that a change has occurred, but they do not explain why (Mayoux, 2002; Sandhu-Rojon, 2003). Consequently, 'indicators constitute only one part of the logical and sub-stantive analysis' (Mayoux, 2002: 4). Put differently, a system of indicators is not a stand-alone evaluation tool.

The second limitation of indicators is that they are often silent about context. They are decontextualised data. Accordingly:

> indicators need to be used in conjunction with qualitative findings. To interpret indicators, it is necessary to consider the context as a whole, the factors which

help to facilitate or hinder the performance of the programme, the rationales of the programme, and the process of implementation. (Tavistock Institute, 2003: 142)

The third limitation does not arise out of indicators *per se*, but from their usage. The number of indicators (a few or many) does not reflect the quality of the evidence gathered. The idea of using a large number of different indicators has no merit in itself. The key to good indicators is their *credibility* and *legitimacy* – not the volume of data. Credibility can be achieved through the continuous improvement of the technical quality of indicators. But it also requires agreement on a process through which policy-makers and stakeholders probe indicators, select them and review their performance.

Types of indicators

The standard quality criteria of individual indicators are validity, reliability (two different people working under identical conditions should provide the same measurement), availability of data over time, sensitivity to a policy intervention and normativity (indicators should relate to outcomes that can be judged to be satisfactory or not; Tavistock Institute, 2003).

Quality criteria applicable to a system of indicators establish that a good system should: cover a sufficiently large number of elements or dimensions of the phenomena to be observed; balance different categories and types of indicators; be simple and selective; and be relevant, that is, the indicators chosen should have significance for decision-making (Tavistock Institute, 2003).

Indicators can be classified according to: the nature of the information (qualitative or quantitative indicators); the source of the information (objective or subjective indicators); the relation with the observed phenomena (direct or proxy indicators); and the extent of aggregation (single or composite indicators).

Qualitative indicators are expressed in verbal form and refer to observation of facts, ideas or attitudes. Qualitative indicators come in two types: those in a yes/no format, and those that are ranks, categories, assessments or opinions. Both types can be categorised and enumerated, and finally transformed into quantitative indicators; for instance, a value of zero can be attributed to a 'no' answer, a value of one to a 'yes' answer. Quantitative indicators are expressed in numerical form. They differ by the nature of quantification and degree of precision. They are expressed in simple numbers, percentages or ratios. A number can be transformed into a percentage or ratio by putting the element or problem into a broader context. A significance test can be used to determine whether the problem is evenly spread or concentrated in certain groups.

Objective measures are constructed from indisputable facts. Typical examples of objective measures are: the presence or absence of a published programme promoting regulatory quality, formally endorsed by the executive; the level of financial resources dedicated to regulatory tools; and the presence of an administrative unit in charge of better regulation policy. Subjective measures are based on the perceptions or views of respondents. Our indicators are designed to differentiate the source of perception. We distinguish between a system of indicators called 'internal evaluation' and a system for 'external evaluation'. The former is based on the assessment provided by the Commission or (in the case of domestic better regulation programmes) Member States' governments. By contrast, external evaluation is based on appraisals conducted by professional evaluators.

Simple measures are expressed in individual numbers or variables. A composite measure or index is a 'mathematical combination (or aggregation as it is termed) of a set of indicators' (Joint Research Centre of the European Commission, 2002: 5). Aggregation is performed by weighting sub-indicators. Unfortunately, there is no obvious and objective way to aggregate simple measures. For this reason our choice is to identify a range of simple indicators, without attempting to perform any kind of aggregation. More fundamentally, aggregation in the context of EU regulatory quality is possible only if there is convergence on the objectives, principles and purposes of better regulation programmes and tools. We look into this issue in the next section. At this stage, we make the point that simple measures are very useful for open coordination processes at the EU level (described below) – whereas reliance on one composite measure would make agreement over open coordination impossible, given the diversity of preferences across the Member States. All the same, a few composite indicators, currently gathered by the Commission and the OECD, are suggested. They seek to capture the impact of better regulation programmes in terms of real-world impact. The latter is a complex concept that includes several variables. Hence composite measures are an appropriate tool to reduce the complexity of information, provided that they are used to complement sets of simple measures rather than substituting for them.

The political level: indicators, open coordination and regulatory quality

The indicators of better regulation presented here have been developed for both the EU level and the Member States. One reason for doing so is that better regulation policy is not the exclusive responsibility of the Commission and other EU institutions. It involves different levels of governance, and Member States as well as local governments have their own responsibility. Indeed, when one measures better regulation via surveys, the stakeholder cannot possibly distinguish between EU-level regulations, domestic implementation of Community rules and rules produced by national and local governments. What matters is the real-world impact of regulation on business activity, the level of protection delivered to the citizens and so on.

Additionally, one important target for the EU and its Member States is competitiveness. The latter cannot be achieved by focusing exclusively on the EU dimension. In consequence, indicators should be used to measure quality both at the EU level and at the level of domestic better regulation policies. There is no need to discuss here whether the Lisbon agenda to make Europe the most competitive knowledge-based society is excessively ambitious, whether it is on the right tracks or not and how it should be redefined. It is sufficient to stick to the empirical observation that competitiveness has become a priority for the EU.

Better regulation is a fundamental component of the competitiveness strategy (with the qualifications we add in chapter 8). The commitment to better regulation is widely shared (although this does not mean convergence of policies). Indicators should reflect this joint commitment. They should also assist in the development of a common language and in the convergence of specific initiatives. On convergence, the conclusions of the Lisbon European Council (23–24 March 2000) established the coordinates of a new mode of governance, called the open method of coordination. There is a lively debate on what the open method of coordination can achieve in the context of the Lisbon strategy (Borras and Jacobsson, 2004). There are also political and academic discussions on the potential for the method in terms of governance (as shown by the discussion of the so-called Kok report – High-Level Group of Independent Experts on the Lisbon Strategy, 2004). The literature has found limited results of the method as far as cross-national learning is concerned (Radaelli, 2003).

Here we look at the open method of coordination as a mechanism of cross-national diffusion and policy transfer. There are several mechanisms of governance in the EU. Bulmer and Padgett (2005) mention hierarchy, negotiation and facilitated coordination (the most important example being the open method of coordination). We are well aware of the current disillusionment with facilitated coordination. But here the issue is not to probe the efficiency and legitimacy of different modes of governance. Rather, the issue we face is to suggest a mode of governance that, broadly speaking, may become a (politically acceptable) institutional support for the choice of indicators.

In this vein, both the treaty limitations and the political nature of better regulation policy make negotiation of Community measures and hierarchical solutions impossible. One cannot imagine how the classic Community method can be applied to better regulation. This is not an area where the EU can proceed by dint of directives and legislation. The implication is that, although the open method of coordination is facing several limitations, hierarchy and negotiation within the classic Community method would encounter even more formidable obstacles. On balance, if indicators have to be situated within a mode of governance, we would opt for the softest choice, that is, open coordination. The latter is no panacea, but it is the only realistic institutional vehicle to carry forward the discussion on regulatory quality. Let us now look at the open method of coordination.

Open coordination involves the following steps:[1]

- fixing guidelines for the Union combined with specific timetables for achieving the goals ... in the short, medium and long terms;
- establishing, where appropriate, quantitative and qualitative indicators and benchmarks against the best in the world and tailored to the needs of different Member States and sectors as a means of comparing best practice;
- translating these European guidelines into national and regional policies by setting specific targets; and
- periodic monitoring, evaluation and peer review organised as mutual learning processes.

The open method, therefore, includes the following components:

- guidelines;
- benchmarking and sharing of best practices;
- multilateral surveillance;
- indicators;
- iterative processes;
- implementation through domestic policy and legislation (this means that no EU legislation is needed).

Although there is no fully specified open coordination process for better regulation, some essential steps have been taken *de facto*. We can therefore talk of an open coordination process 'in the making' in the case of better regulation. Let us look at the individual components of this open method, commencing with guidelines. The Mandelkern (2001) report, the Commission's action plans on better regulation, and the inter-institutional agreement on better regulation (Council of the European Union, 2003) reviewed in chapter 6, provide the general guidelines for such a process.

On benchmarking and best practice, several initiatives were promoted by the Commission in the 1990s – and most recently by the informal meetings of the DBR[2] – to discuss the progress made by individual Member States and debate how the Mandelkern principles can be specified in national programmes. A set of criteria for best practice in impact assessment has been produced (DBR, 2004). Both the Commission and DBR have engaged in multilateral surveillance of the progress made. This has happened in a 'soft' form, typically by convening meetings and workshops in which data provided by Member States on specific projects are circulated and discussed.

Looking at the future, one can envisage an intensification of this embryonic open coordination in a way that would include indicators, national action plans and an iterative process in which guidelines and indicators are reviewed periodically on the basis of the experience accumulated and the results achieved. To get there, a common set of indicators is the crucial step. But one has to be aware of the risk of hindering learning by adopting the wrong approach to monitoring and convergence. The process selected for the use of indicators can either ease or aggravate the trade-off between learning and monitoring. As such, it is crucial.

This trade-off was originally identified by Charles Sabel (1994). Both learning from experience and monitoring progress towards convergence are essential features of the open method of coordination, although, as mentioned, the empirical evidence for learning via the open method is scarce. One reason for that is that monitoring is based on predictability, the reporting of tasks well specified in advance, whereas learning is essentially disruptive of regularity and may lead to the breakdown of 'monitorability' (Sabel, 1994). In EU processes, Member States often make a commitment to measure progress towards common goals, but are then reluctant to talk about their problems with reforms, why they have not learned from their own experience and that of the other Member States, and the hindrances to genuine change. The result is that reporting tends to be rosy when it should be frank, and incisive peer reviews are not well accepted. This would be the case – we argue – should aggregate measures of quality be selected at the beginning of the process with the aim of fostering convergence towards a single target.

One way around this problem is to encourage monitoring of the progress made by the Member States in relation to their own objectives, at their own pace of reform and using their own definitions of better regulation. We suggest Member States and the EU institutions discuss indicators as a way to reinterpret their own preferences for better regulation in the context of the EU-level strategy for competitiveness. Preferences should be articulated and reinterpreted taking into account the common EU framework in which competitiveness has to be delivered. Gradually, a common understanding of what the EU 'wants' from better regulation would emerge – and the institutionalisation of this policy would proceed.

The selection of common baseline indicators (i.e., the choice of a set of indicators drawn from system 1 discussed below) is a good opportunity for learning. To achieve that, one has reduce the emphasis on targets – perhaps even dispose of them altogether at this stage – and design a process in which the actors have incentives to re-elaborate their preferences and to redefine their priorities as their joint experience 'outpaces their initial understanding' (Sabel, 1994: 155–6). In this experimental approach to indicators and priorities for better regulation, learning and monitoring become compatible and mutually reinforcing. Each Member State should use the selection of common indicators to reveal its preferences for regulatory quality (including preferences for the key target actions in regulatory reform) and discuss openly what will be monitored, how and why.

Each year (or in the case of more complex indicators every two years) the discussion among the Member States, the Commission and the European

Parliament should not be about league tables and who is on top of regulatory quality programmes. Rather, each Member State should focus on the 'story' behind the variations in the indicators. Member States with higher degrees of institutionalisation of better regulation policy could also engage in the selection of more sophisticated indicators (provided by system 2 outlined below) and comprehensive policy evaluation (system 3).

Better regulation policies would still vary across the EU. But the framework of facilitated coordination would be indispensable to develop a common understanding. To illustrate, the policy officers in charge of better regulation could usefully discuss why they are proposing to widen or limit the range of indicators, as well as the implications of doing so for the institutionalisation of better regulation in their own countries and in the common EU-level policy. In this context, a policy conversation of what sort of convergence is being produced by open coordination could usefully take place. Note that Sabel (1994: 138) defines 'discussion' as 'the process by which parties come to reinterpret themselves and their relation to each other by elaborating a common understanding of the world'. This is our notion of policy conversation. By focusing on bottom-up convergence, rather than artificial convergence imposed from the top, the trade-off between monitoring and learning would be eased.

The discussion, selection and review of indicators should take place in an appropriate venue. This is where either the DBR or the High Level Group on Competitiveness within the Competitiveness Council can play a role. The former seems an appropriate forum for the discussion of sets of indicators. Such indicators – supported at a higher conceptual level by the Mandelkern principles – should then inform national action plans on better regulation. Directors of better regulation could report regularly on variations across time of their indicators. In this connection, the DBR could take on the role of linking Member States' indicators to national action plans and organise peer review sessions. The major obstacle in this direction is that the DBR is an informal gathering.

The open method of coordination needs a more formal body, possibly reporting to the Competitiveness Council. In this connection, the most appropriate forum might well be the High Level Group on Competitiveness within the Competitiveness Council. Clearly, it is up to the Council to designate the body in charge of open coordination. The national delegates to the Group could report on indicators, integrating the summary of national initiatives on better regulation (already available since autumn 2005). The advantage of using the High Level Group instead of the DBR is that the former is already incorporated in the formal structure of the Council formation in charge of competitiveness. All considered, it seems to us that the choice should be the Group. The DBR could still be useful as a body for technical discussion and data gathering, as suggested below.

To sum up then, commitment to the goal of measuring regulatory quality has been achieved. There is momentum for the adoption of indicators and a process (the open method of coordination) has been identified. A gradually achieved consensus on indicators would improve bottom-up convergence towards the Lisbon objectives. Interestingly, in social inclusion – a key area of the Lisbon agenda – there are different sets of indicators: two compulsory and one 'optional'. The idea is to acknowledge the diversity of Member States' approaches while at the same time making as much progress as possible in all areas where goals and policy initiatives already converge. This is not a paradoxical strategy but the logical implication of a process that is not based on harmonisation and the Community method of integration. It is the implication of a strategy for coordination that builds on diversity rather than suppressing it. In order to work, however, the strategy has to be based on shared principles and goals, and should promote the diffusion of instruments and indicators that are coherent.

The technical level

The need to balance diversity of approaches, learning and bottom-up convergence leads us to the suggestion that indicators should not be aggregated in a single composite measure. As mentioned, the most successful processes of open coordination – as adopted for employment and social inclusion – are not based on single composite indicators but on relatively large sets of them. Apart from the intellectual case for a multidimensional approach to regulatory quality (see chapter 2), there is a political case for not putting all the eggs of better regulation into the basket of one single measure. This step, in fact, would make sense only in the presence of full convergence across EU Member States. All the studies conducted over the last ten years, however, point to marked differences of better regulation programmes across Europe. The DBR (2004) report has confirmed that the pattern of convergence in RIA is limited. True, there is unanimous support for RIA. However, the samples contained in the DBR report and the evidence we collected show that RIA means quite different things in different countries.

For this reason, we do not think that the current enthusiasm in the EU for reducing the administrative burden on companies as key measure of progress has much mileage. This simple measure is unable to capture the rich information that a *set* of measures can provide (if a single measure has to be used, it should be very rich in information). There is also the fact that a reduction in administrative burden is an incomplete measure of the regulatory burdens of the firm. Moreover, the definition of administrative burden includes every administrative obligation that is mentioned in legislation. This implies that activities that would normally be carried out in the normal course of running a business (like keeping financial records) become 'administrative burdens'.

More importantly still, an agenda focused exclusively on administrative burdens would bias the overall notion of regulatory quality towards costs, ignoring that best practice in OECD countries suggests a 'net benefit principle', that is, balancing the costs with the benefits for the community. Politically, a strategy based on the costs borne by companies suffers from serious legitimacy problems. It tilts better regulation towards one single stakeholder. As such, it is not credible.

What does our evidence say about differences and convergence in Europe? One common theme in our study is 'limited convergence' – of approaches, programmes and results. Chapter 5, on the results of our questionnaire, shows that convergence is high at the level of principles and objectives of better regulation; a set of beliefs is shared. However, national policies and approaches to regulatory quality still differ. Indeed, we found clustered convergence on measuring better regulation performance. There is a cluster of Member States working on measures of regulatory quality across tools of better regulation in the context of sophisticated quality assurance processes and the pivotal role of RIA. Another cluster adopts some indicators and targets in the context of a 'lean' quality assurance process – with emphasis on administrative burdens and simplification. Finally, we found a third cluster of Member States, with no systematic experience of indicators of quality, limited investment in quality assurance and a basic approach to RIA.

If measures of burdens are inadequate, should we then look at quantification along the lines of cost–benefit analysis as the Archimedean lever of regulatory quality? We found limited diffusion of full cost–benefit analysis as the cornerstone of regulatory quality in Europe. When we probed the support network on indicators of quality arising out of a cost–benefit approach to better regulation, we found no evidence of governments consistently pursuing cost–benefit assessment of regulation as the major pathway to quality. Although quantification is considered an important element of quality, there is no evidence of systematic use of cost–benefit analysis. And in most of the twenty-five Member States, the identification of how different stakeholders may be affected by proposed regulations is more important than quantification. In consequence, our indicators will not consider quantification as an indicator of quality *per se*.

There are other reasons for that. To begin with, some important benefits[3] are often described but not quantified. Secondly, uncertainty should not be hidden or disguised behind estimates. This does not mean that ranges should substitute for estimates – wide and overlapping ranges do not provide useful information. Rather, it means that ranges should be accompanied by probabilities and different scenarios. The European Commission's (2005b) guidance goes one step further, by suggesting that thinking about scenarios should help to formulate the major trade-offs as clearly as possible. Trade-offs are open to discussion by definition, and the preference in Europe is not to suppress the discussion of trade-offs behind full cost–benefit analysis. Hence one major difference between checklists and indicators proposed by economists (see Hahn *et al.*, 2000) and our indicators is that 'quality' is not eminently a question of technical sophistication of economic analysis.

Another difference in the approaches to quality across Member States is that economists' checklists often include an indicator for RIA based on the identification of one option that is clearly justified as superior to other options. This is the case for the UK, but it is not necessarily a manifestation of quality in the Irish approach or the Commission's approach to RIA.

Ours is an approach based on quality as the impact of regulatory tools on the major actors and stakeholders (regulators, politicians, companies and citizens – see chapter 2). The idea is not to make experts think, but to make institutions think. And institutions 'think' if tools like consultation and RIA have an impact on the regulators and the stakeholders, that is, if they are taken seriously. Arguably, if uncertainty and political choices are made visible and explicit, the impact on policy-makers and stakeholders is stronger.

It is the embeddedness of better regulation tools in the regulatory process that really matters for quality. By this we mean the extent to which RIA, consultation, simplification and access are embedded in the wider regulatory policy process. In a sense, even if a RIA is impeccable in terms of economic analysis, this is not a sufficient condition for quality. The latter is achieved when better regulation tools change the way regulators think about public policy, inform ministerial decisions, affect the attitudes and behaviour of firms and organised interests, and impact on the relationship between the citizen and regulation. We operationalise this definition by designing indicators.

The implication – we hasten to add – is *not* that 'anything goes'. Reliable estimates and robust indicators provide credibility to better regulation tools. But we do not think that – at this stage at least, and considering the evidence we have presented in this volume – quality should be measured in terms approximating full cost–benefit analysis.

Having excluded the extremes of administrative burdens and full cost-benefit analysis, what, then, do we propose? Simply, we propose different sets of indicators without overall aggregation. At the same time, we insist on a high-quality, learning-oriented debate. A common approach to indicators is in itself a *sui generis* 'indicator' of major progress, although this does not mean that the set should be specified at the beginning of the process.

One fundamental element to bear in mind is that better regulation is a fully fledged policy in some Member States but not in others. By 'fully fledged policy' we mean a policy with its own aims, key issues and problems, set of solutions, and a range of actors interacting in dense networks – some actors with the key responsibility for designing and delivering policy, others with the role of stakeholders trying to shape policy formulation and implementation. Our review of the European scene (chapter 6) has revealed that better regulation is certainly an emerging *issue*, but it would be far-fetched to conclude that it is the same *policy* everywhere.

Three systems of indicators

It follows that we have not designed a single system of indicators. Neither do we suggest that the quality of better regulation policies in the EU be scored according to one single scale or overall index. In the medium term, learning in better regulation across the EU should lead to the adoption of the same systems, with national variations at the level of individual indicators. The question is, how do we get there? Politically, the open method of coordination is the best way forward. Methodologically, we cannot superimpose one set of indicators onto a still remarkably varied European scene. We cannot assume convergence at this stage and design a 'one size fits all' system of indicators, although convergence is a valuable goal.

We propose two systems and show how indicators can also contribute to a third system of external policy evaluation. Table 7.1 portrays the main characteristics of the three systems.

System 1 is a simple macro ex-ante system of indicators of quality. These indicators can be adopted by all Member States and the Commission. However, a policy conversation within a structured mode of governance is needed – to select a precise range of indicators from system 1, thus clarifying the priorities of the EU for better regulation policy.

System 2 requires the examination and ex-post measurement of the quality of RIA and other tools. It includes indicators of real-world outcome and limited use of surveys of regulators and stakeholders. The system can be used by the cluster of Member States (see chapter 5) in which consultation, simplification and the measurement of administrative burdens is already well embedded. The major obstacle to the adoption of most of the system 2 indicators across the EU is not data collection but the fact that RIA and consultation are not routinely used in policy formulation and consequently are not embedded in the law-making process. Some Member States have designed laws on RIA and simplification but apart from individual pilot projects there is no consistent effort to assess a wide range of costs and benefits in an integrated process and to consult in accordance with specific written guidance.

The third system is applicable to the Commission and to governments with sophisticated quality assurance mechanisms. It provides a bridge between measurement of regulatory quality and the systematic evaluation of better regulation programmes.

Turning to the design of the indicators, they have been devised to account for the following:

- The competitiveness agenda of the EU.
- Reference to the principles of the Mandelkern (2001) report. The Mandelkern report provides a focal point for the discussion of EU-wide principles of regulatory quality. The fact that the report was very well received in all Member States is an important step in the direction of a common language.

Table 7.1 The three systems of indicators

	System 1. *Quality of the process*	System 2. *Internal evaluation*	System 3. *External evaluation*
Scope of indicators	Preconditions for regulatory quality Ex-ante macro-analysis	Ex-post measurement of the quality of regulatory programmes Checklist and indicators of real-world outcomes	Ex-post and external evaluation of the quality of regulatory programmes External evaluation is a broad activity. It includes indicators and other methods, such as case studies and in-depth interviews Ex-post technical analysis of the performance of the indicators used in the other two systems
Design indicators	Yes	No	No
Activity indicators	Yes (impact assessment and consultation)	Yes	Yes
Output	No	Yes	Yes
Real-world outcome indicators	No	Impact of better regulation policies Survey-based indicators Indicators of economic outcome	Yes
Surveys of regulatory stakeholders	No	Yes	Yes
Who collects the indicators	Secretariat-General of the Commission Central regulatory quality units in Member States	Secretariat-General of the Commission Central regulatory quality units in Member States	External evaluators (think tanks, academics, consultancy firms)
How often	Every year	Every year	Every two years

- A preference for trend indicators instead of static indicators. The idea is to measure progress (or lack of it) over time, rather than relying on static measures.
- The balance between the main dimensions of the Lisbon process, specifically economic growth and a high level of social and environmental protection.
- The balance among actors of better regulation policies.
- The balance between different tools of better regulation policies, with the qualification that (as shown in the previous chapters) RIA is the pivotal instrument.
- A limited number of sources for data collection. As mentioned, we prefer indicators that draw on a limited number of sources to indicators that require entirely new systems of data collection.
- Clear reference to variables, activities and tools that can be changed by policy-makers and policy-officers in charge of better regulation programmes. As discussed in chapter 3, some sophisticated, complex indicators provide a considerable amount of information on the quality of regulation, but they do not enable the people in charge of specific activities or instruments to learn where and how to intervene.

Let us now look at the three systems in detail. System 1 looks at the quality of the process (see appendix 2). It is an ex-ante macro-system in that it does not go down to the level of individual RIAs or consultations. Instead, it covers the design of better regulation policy (section 1.A), the presence of a quality assurance process (section 1.B), its instruments and supporting activities, and the contents of formal guidance and strategies (sections 1.C to 1.F). We call this system 'quality of the process'. It is based on objective indicators.

The second system of indicators, the so-called 'internal evaluation', is twofold (see appendix 3). It relies on a checklist of individual tools of better regulation and some more general indicators of real-world outcome. The first part of this indicator system is based on what the tools of better regulation deliver in a given period. To illustrate, it provides simple checks on the quality of individual RIAs (section 2.A) and major consultations (section 2.B). The data for this system of indicators can be gathered via standard reporting procedures. This may seem a daunting exercise. Yet there were only twenty-three extended RIAs produced by the Commission in 2003. Should a country perform a large number of consultations and assessments, the system could be used to check on the quality of *major* regulations only (in terms of a financial threshold or scope of policy change).

The remaining two tools (simplification, section 2.C, and accessibility, section 2.D) are assessed with a focus on the overall output. Indeed, simplification and accessibility are clearly horizontal tools. One cannot speak of a single 'accessibility' action, although in some cases governments produce an annual simplification law. On balance, we think that quality control cannot be applied to a specific, individual 'product', as in the case of RIA or consultation. The most efficient assessment of simplification and accessibility programmes is to verify the factual implementation and use of the elements necessary to achieve regulatory quality. Thus, indicators look at the correspondence between strategies and empirical evidence. For example, if the strategy for simplification includes the use of RIA to assist in the process of simplification, an indicator will be whether this happens or not.

The second part of the internal system (system 2) is composed of measures that are able to capture the impact of better regulation policy. We distinguish three types of impact: direct impact on regulatory costs and net benefits (section 2.E); impacts on regulators and regulatees' perceptions of regulatory quality (section 2.F); and indirect impact on economic outcomes (section 2.G).

System 2 can be used by quality units (like the Commission's unit in the Secretariat-General or the Better Regulation Executive in the UK). It does not involve the systematic use of external evaluators. It can be implemented relatively swiftly – in fifteen to eighteen months.

In terms of data collection, on balance both the first and the second systems of indicators do not present particular problems. Most of the data for system 1 and the checklist in system 2 can be provided by a limited number of instruments, specifically:

- data that can be easily collected annually at regular DBR meetings;
- data that can be gathered by reading the official guides to better regulation and simplification – a small budget for translation is necessary, otherwise questions can be posed directly to DBR members;
- data on EU activities routinely gathered by the Secretariat-General and the DGs of the Commission when they provide guidance on better regulation tools (other data are not currently gathered but could be collected easily by the Secretariat-General and the DGs).

The second part of system 2 for 'internal evaluation' (composed of real-world outcome indicators) relies on:

- data already available via Eurostat;
- data that can be collected by the EBTP;
- data on stakeholders, which can be collected by targeting existing survey instruments, such as the single-market scorecard, Eurobarometer and Eurobarometer flash (in some cases, we do not go further than suggesting that data which were originally gathered for a single-market scorecard or Eurobarometer flash be routinely collected);
- surveys of policy-officers in charge of better regulation tools (this survey should be organised by the Secretariat-General at the EU level and by the

national administrative bodies responsible for better regulation policy at
the domestic level);
• real-world outcome indicators (on productivity, innovation, openness
  to trade, labour market, etc.) which are already collected to monitor
  progress in the context of the Lisbon agenda.

No matter how sophisticated, indicators are just a component of quality
assurance. The latter is a complex process involving strategic and operational management, specific structures and dedicated tools. One important
element of quality assurance is external evaluation.

The link between indicators and quality assurance is strong, but indicators are only a component of policy evaluation. We designed the essential
coordinates of a third system, called 'external evaluation' (see appendix 4),
which includes indicators that can be collected by professional evaluators
(certainly not by the Secretariat-General of the Commission). External
evaluation is not based exclusively on indicators. Case studies, qualitative reviews, formative appraisals and other instruments are also needed.
However, indicators can perform a useful role in the context of evaluation.
At the same time, external evaluation is the place where the indicators used
in systems 1 and 2 can be technically assessed.

Let us now discuss the use of the three systems within a possible process
of open coordination. The latter should be used to create the preconditions
for the use of the three systems across the Member States. This could be
done gradually, for example by taking the commitment to adopt a common
range of indicators from system 1. Of course, some countries may wish to
add some more 'system 1' indicators in their national plans whereas others
may not want to do so; in such circumstances, a policy conversation on
the reasons behind these different choices would be extremely useful. It
should also be acknowledged that only a minority of Member States and
the Commission are ready for the adoption of system 2 and system 3.

More importantly still, indicators should be used across time to ease the
trade-off between learning and monitoring. A Member State could thus
measure progress by looking at changes in the indicators over the years.
This is an important point: there is no objective way to draw the line at one
score or another, but progress (or lack of it) over the years will reveal how
a country is performing in terms of regulatory quality and whether some
lessons are being learned or not.

Finally, we need to clarify the relationship between external evaluation
and the open method of coordination. The former is a professional exercise.
It provides inputs to better regulation programmes by showing the results
achieved and by providing evidence of the impact of specific tools, such
as consultation and RIA. In any case, external evaluation belongs to the
technical, professional assessment of policy. By contrast, the open method of
coordination reviews national action plans, guidelines and indicators within

a political process. In turn, this process can draw on technical inputs, including professional evaluations conducted by academics, think tanks, auditing bodies and so on. Therefore, there is a link between the political and the technical assessment of indicators, but the two should not be confused.

A remark on who should do the exercise. Further to the reports by the European Policy Centre (2001; and Allio *et al.*, 2004) and the Doorn report to the European Parliament (2004), there is a lively political discussion on whether new audit bodies should be created formally to appraise ex-post the quality of better regulation tools and policies at the EU level.

From our perspective, external evaluation is more a social enterprise than an institutional matter. As documented in chapter 6, several studies have recently been completed. Think tanks, academics and organisations representing interests are the natural providers of policy appraisals. A robust network of stakeholders providing evaluations of better regulation policies arising out of different perspectives is, in our view, the best place to look for the development of our third system of indicators. In consequence, while in the case of the first two systems we envisage an open process of coordination, external evaluation should not be confined to discussions among directors of better regulation or new EU-level bodies like a possible Regulatory Audit Office (Allio *et al.*, 2004; European Policy Centre, 2001). In other words, we are not saying that the current political and intellectual discussion of the institutional design for the evaluation of EU-level better regulation policies should be abandoned. However, it should be complemented by the acknowledgement that society, establishments of higher education and private think tanks have an important role to play in pluralistic evaluation.[4]

Conclusions

In this chapter we have set out the design of our three systems of indicators of better regulation policy. One common theme throughout the chapter has been the balance between the demand and supply of knowledge. Most of the work done so far on indicators of regulatory quality has been concerned with the supply side. There has been a lively intellectual debate, both in academia and in international organisations, on the technical properties of indicators and how to aggregate them. Most of the work has been on decontextualised indicators, with the idea that they can be used to compare countries with different institutional and historical backgrounds. Decontextualised indicators are also the prime ingredients of league tables of countries. We have made an effort to address the imbalance between supply and demand by contextualising indicators. We have been quite minimalist on supply – of course, the classic properties of indicators have been discussed, but without emphasis on aggregation and complex measures. On demand, we have taken the question 'Why would governments demand indicators and in the context of what processes?' into serious consideration.

We have argued that diversity still matters in the EU, and top-down convergence is unattainable. But diversity does not mean that anything goes and that any government can pursue any notion of regulatory quality. Our systems of indicators have been designed with the aim of encouraging a more transparent discussion of better regulation policy in the EU. Serious policy conversations lead to commitments – and an open method of coordination for regulation can provide a structured process in which this can happen. Indicators should also be used to ease the trade-off between monitoring and learning. Commitments in relation to better regulation goals and discussions of variations over time of indicators can lead to more transparency, learning and convergence than league tables.

Notes

1 Quoted from the 'Presidency conclusions', point 37, Lisbon European Council, 23–24 March 2000, at http://consilium.europa.eu/ueDocs/cms_Data/docs/pressData/en/ec/00100-r1.en0.htm.
2 The Directors of Better Regulation body was originally the Directors and Experts of Better Regulation. It has therefore already evolved into a body of directors rather than directors and experts, thus showing its increasing political importance. However, it remains an informal body reporting to the ministers of public administration – a group outside Council's structures.
3 For example, those originating in the elimination of barriers to economic activity in the single market.
4 This issue was aired at the aforementioned (chapter 6) first pan-European conference promoted by DG Enterprise, 'Impact Assessment in the European Union: Innovations, Quality, and Good Regulatory Governance', 3 December 2003. The proceedings are available at http://ec.europa.eu/enterprise/regulation/better_regulation/impact_assessment/ia_conference.htm.

8

Conclusion

Conceptual innovation: quality, better regulation and indicators

Institutionalisation is a common challenge faced by emerging policies, and better regulation is no exception. In this concluding chapter, we examine different dimensions of institutionalisation and raise the question of whether better regulation in Europe represents a case of convergence merely at the level of discourse or one of convergence of decisions and actions. Institutionalisation has two dimensions: one is the creation of institutions that perform activities and deliver policy; the other – equally important– is the development of robust networks of stakeholders involved in better regulation processes. If situated in specific policy processes oriented towards knowledge utilisation, the indicators illustrated in the previous chapters can deliver in terms of institutionalisation, although the shifting priorities of the Member States open more than one scenario for the future. We conclude the chapter by relating better regulation and institutionalisation processes to visions of the regulatory state.

In this volume, we have introduced a new perspective on better regulation. Concept formation is a fundamental step in the social sciences (Brady and Collier, 2004). Conceptual analysis has covered the notion of quality, better regulation and the construction of indicators. On quality, we have chosen to problematise the concept, showing how the politician, the civil servant, the bureaucrat, the expert, the firm and the citizen use different logic, definitions of success and criteria for the assessment of better regulation tools. This approach stands in contrast to the idea that there is substantial agreement on what is good regulation and therefore policy-makers operating in different institutional contexts should share the same benchmarks. Rather, the concept of regulatory quality is prismatic. It is more complex and political than the one suggested by the literature produced by economists, governments and international organisations.

On better regulation, the conceptual innovation we put forward is simple but has important implications for the analysis and construction of indicators. Instead of looking at better regulation in terms of individual initiatives and tools, we have illustrated the reasons why it can be considered a new public policy, with its own actors, problems, processes, rules of interaction, decision processes, activities and impacts. Better regulation is a policy – we argued in chapter 5 – if the tools are integrated, rather than being seen as individual instruments. The integration of tools enhances the overall potential of the policy.

Characteristically, better regulation belongs to the stage of regulatory reform in which policy-makers are more concerned about the quality of the process of rule-making and implementation than about reforms sector by sector. As such, it is an instance of meta-regulation. Its major aim is to address regulatory failure, rather than market failure. It is an instance of regulators governing themselves and the processes through which rules are created and enforced.

Typically, meta-regulation is appraised on the basis of how effective it is in streamlining the regulatory policy process (in relation to objectives that include transparency, participation of stakeholders, accountability and evidence-based or evidence-inspired modes of decision-making) and in changing the culture of the regulators and the stakeholders. The impact on regulators and stakeholders is an important dimension of appraisal. Incidentally, this is the reason why we argue that better regulation should be appraised via a variety of instruments, including surveys of regulators and data on the changing perceptions of the stakeholders. Turning to another political impact of better regulation, one point to consider is that it has been used to increase the control of the core executive on how departments formulate legislation. Hence, from the point of view of the core executive or the prime minister, better regulation works if it reins in departmental (and agency) regulatory creep and disciplines the regulatory agendas of the other ministers.

Measures of better regulation policy have two properties. First and foremost, they appraise policy. But they also define, identify and operationalise quality. The review of the experience of Member States (chapter 4) and the findings of the questionnaire sent to the support network (chapter 5) show that this process of definition and operationalisation has not started yet. The indicators proposed in chapter 7 define quality, showing how measurement is contingent on conceptual analysis (Brady and Collier, 2004). As shown by Weiss (1999), data and indicators should not be seen as tools supporting a single decision, because very rarely are decisions taken on the basis of empirical information alone. But they have a more subtle and more profound impact when they help organisations to develop shared interpretations of complex phenomena. If indicators have to support processes of policy enlightenment (Weiss, 1999) and 'make institutions think', the context in which they are used should not be neglected. 'To make institutions think' is an ambitious aim. If taken seriously, it means that indicators should enable both policy-makers and stakeholders to appraise critically the whole regulatory process, from regulatory agendas to consultation, the analysis of different options, the choice of a regulatory technique, and compliance and enforcement. This requires both indicators that gauge the quality of different policy stages and, as mentioned, a suitable process, in which the indicators are utilised as conceptual lenses that make all the relevant actors 'see' the main critical steps. Systems of indicators, therefore, can become a control panel covering the entire policy.

International organisations have produced decontextualised indicators with the idea of comparing and 'scoring' a wide range of countries in order to provide policy recommendations. Indeed, the country score is usually associated with measures of economic growth. In contrast, in the EU the interest is not comparative – it is political. The aim is to foster progress on regulatory reform in a multi-layered political system. We have explained how the institutional context matters and have developed indicators accordingly.

The indicators discussed in chapter 7 are not 'one size fits all' measures. They respect the different degrees of institutionalisation of better regulation in the EU. More importantly still, they are intimately connected to the process in which they should be utilised. Given the variability in institutionalisation, it is important to design indicators and policy processes with political caution. It is practically and conceptually impossible to use indicators of better regulation policies for the purpose of creating targets and league tables. The diversity of better regulation policies is still too great. Indicators can instead support EU-level processes in which Member States measure their own progress, appraise the results achieved, focus on detailed reporting of what has changed between one year and the next, and balance monitoring and learning, with a preference for the latter in the early stages.

However, we are not saying that 'anything goes' and that governments should pick up the indicators as they see fit. Under those circumstances governments would choose only those measures on which their country scores well. One fundamental characteristic of the use of indicators we envisage is that they are selected within a process of facilitated coordination at the EU level. This is where an open method of coordination can situate indicators in a broader discussion of the 'hard questions'. The dual issue of indicators and processes cropped up in the discussion of the Mandelkern (2001) report – although it was considered too advanced, given the evolution of the debate at that time, and therefore was not formally included in the recommendations. Interestingly, the report insisted on a 'common method of evaluation' of the quality of regulation in the EU and the Member States.

The Mandelkern report was written at a time in which the European Commission (2001a) was preparing the white paper on governance. Indeed, some Member States (such as Denmark and Finland) made references to the reforms suggested by Mandelkern and the potential of the open method of coordination – but the link was not explicit.[1] Since the Mandelkern report, both indicators and the open method of coordination have been cited in official documents of the Competitiveness Council and in the joint statements of the EU Presidencies mentioned in the introduction to this volume.

Indicators and knowledge utilisation can thus be employed jointly to get to grips with the 'hard questions'. For us the hardest question is, what does the EU want from better regulation? Our questionnaire and desk research have revealed more than one answer. Indicators can reduce the variance around this question. Let us explain how.

The three systems of indicators refer to different degrees of institutionalisation. Facilitated coordination at the EU level should be used to make the preferences of the Member States more explicit. In a sense, the selection of indicators is a strategy to measure 'revealed preferences'. Indicators should complement an open method of coordination for better regulation which already contains several components, as shown in chapter 7. True, at the moment there is more disillusionment than enthusiasm for the open method of coordination. However, there is no alternative to a 'soft' and learning-oriented mode of governance – the Community method has nothing to say on this topic. And one should judge the open method not in the abstract but in relation to the specific policies with which it is used. As a former Belgian minister put it in an often quoted remark, 'open co-ordination is not some kind of fixed recipe that can be applied to any issue.... [It is] a cookbook that contains various recipes' (Vandenbroucke, 2002). A common criticism of the open method of coordination is that it has failed to involve civil society and to promote learning from below. For better regulation, the opportunities that should not be missed concern the principles of subsidiarity and proportionality, and the creation of a network of stakeholders, including regions and civil society.

Facilitated coordination should foster a policy conversation, with the aim of converging on the selection of a set of indicators drawn from system 1. Based on ex-ante analysis, this set of indicators covers the design of better regulation policy, the quality assurance process, the written guidance on RIA and consultation, the simplification programmes, and the strategy for regulatory transparency and access to legislation. We are not arguing for the wholesale adoption of system 1, but for a careful selection of some of the indicators contained in it.

Social inclusion is another policy arena in which the open method of coordination is being used, and here the selection of a common set of indicators is a step towards measurement – not towards targets. Discussion of system 1 indicators, leading to the adoption of a set to be used by all Member States, is a practical way to increase a common language and a common understanding of different modalities to deliver better regulation policy.

The Member States with more institutionalised policies should proceed to system 2, based on the ex-post measurement of the results actually achieved by the policy tools. More precisely, system 2 includes a checklist (relating to the monitoring of major regulations, and activity in the areas of consultation, simplification and access) and a set of real-world outcome indicators. The latter establish an important link between meta-regulation and the impact of the rules produced via meta-regulation. We suggest three classes of real-world outcome indicators: indicators of the impact of better regulation policies, survey-based indicators and indicators of economic outcome.

Finally, the process of institutionalisation should be accompanied by system 3, in which indicators become a component of the broader attempt to evaluate better regulation policy. Evaluation addresses the question of whether a policy is effective in dealing with collective problems. For reasons of credibility and quality assurance, policy evaluation can never be left in the hands of those who are evaluated. Hence, it is performed by external parties. Accordingly, while system 1 and system 2 data should be collected and operated by the central regulatory quality units in the core executives and the Commission, system 3 should involve professional evaluators. System 3 indicators are only a component of comprehensive evaluation. No system of indicators can substitute for the independent judgement of evaluators. Thus, system 3 indicators should be used in combination with case studies, semi-structured interviews, ex-post assessments of peer review performed in RIA and other common tools of policy evaluation.

What about the possibility of measuring the degree of overall progress in the EU? If better regulation policies are not compared, does this mean that, over time, some Member States will make more progress than others, and the gaps and differences will increase? Our answer is all about time and stages. At an early stage, the main effort should be about learning and under-standing what goes on in the different better regulation policies. The aim at this early stage should be to encourage institutionalisation processes, with emphasis on the construction of robust institutional designs and networks of the stakeholders in better regulation.

There is no policy without actors. So far, the experience of better regula-tion tools in some Member States has been frustrating, precisely because it has not raised the attention of actors outside the public administration. The adoption of a set of indicators drawn from system 1 is a way to start measuring progress across the EU on several dimensions (including the participation of civil society), although targets should be avoided because they would stymie learning.

Comparison becomes much more relevant as institutionalisation proceeds and more Member States move on to system 2 and to fully fledged policy evaluation. One can compare policies that exist and have at least a moderate degree of institutionalisation, not a collection of deceivingly similar bottles with different wines or even no wine at all inside. In consequence, compari-son and perhaps even common targets (should progress be so advanced as to delineate a common EU better regulation policy) will have a role to play in the medium term. But targets would only confuse the situation and hinder learning if introduced too soon.

The challenge of institutionalisation

There are structural reasons behind the current political interest in better regulation. Firstly, the cycle of deregulation, privatisation and re-regulation has not diminished the political importance of regulation. Quite the opposite: it has exposed how crucial the quality of regulation is – not only in terms of economic efficiency but also for state–society relations and the legitimacy of governments and international institutions.

The global dimension of regulation is the second structural reason we wish to discuss. An increasingly integrated world economy poses its own set of challenges to domestic rules and to the EU. Both corporate actors and civil organisations are increasingly concerned about what is regulated at the international level, by whom and with what effect. Business, environmental and social regulations at the international level represent a political interface for the domestic and EU layers of rules. The result is a dense, multi-layered regulatory web, in which pressures for more transparency and more efficiency have grown steadily. Indeed, failures (to intervene, to consider alternative policy options, to transpose, to implement and to enforce) move along the 'multi-level' ladder. Regulatory competition and pressure from civil society have increased the interdependence of domestic and international regulation (Braithwaite and Drahos, 2000).

But the global scene is important for another reason. Organisations like the OECD provide platforms for the transfer of better regulation ideas. Processes of trans-national regulatory exchange support the diffusion of best practice and models. In the global market for regulatory reforms and policy ideas, the diffusion of principles, techniques and methods to deliver high-quality regulation is more rapid than in the past – although this does not mean convergence of policies and outcomes.

The failure of some regulatory reforms and privatisation experiences, the growing awareness of what can go wrong with processes of deregulation and the demands of civil society for regulatory fairness and transparency have magnified the importance of 'getting regulation right'. They have also increased the political contestation of apparently neutral terms such as 'regulatory quality'. In this context, there has been a shift from an initial emphasis on measuring the costs and benefits of rules to the more ambitious aim of understanding the impact of institutional design on regulatory processes, stakeholders and final economic outcomes. It is in this changing scenario that better regulation has become concerned with models of governance and has moved beyond its initial focus on economic performance measures.

As a result, better regulation is firmly on the agenda of the EU. There is political momentum for a whole set of initiatives to increase the capacity to produce high-quality regulation at the EU level and in the Member States. The number of communications, action plans, statements from the EU Presidency and conclusions of the Competitiveness Council dedicated to this topic has increased dramatically since 2002. The Lisbon agenda for growth and jobs has been revised and relaunched, with the result that regulation has become even more important.

The Commission lost some precious time in the 1990s, when several projects were launched without a comprehensive master plan on better regulation. The current approach is more integrated and coherent, although the flurry of plans, technical guidelines and communications issued by the Commission may leave little time to metabolise principles and embed technical guidelines and approaches in the EU regulatory process. The ultimate success of better regulation, however, hinges on cooperation between the Commission and the other institutions of the EU, on shared commitments taken by the Member States, and on the involvement of stakeholders.

Turning to the Member States, tools such as RIA, consultation, simplification and methods to increase regulatory transparency have become popular. Beyond the tools, one can see the emerging profile of a new public policy. In turn, this policy is nested in a model of regulatory governance that has implications for the legitimacy of the state and the future of the single market. In fact, better regulation is also a response to the problems encountered by EU and domestic regulation. Its successful implementation would bring more legitimacy to regulatory governance.

In relation to better regulation, one should not consider institutionalisation a panacea for all the problems encountered by regulatory governance. One of the paradoxical implications of the success of better regulation ideas and discourse is that this solution may be applied to too many problems. But what problems exactly is better regulation supposed to fix? To begin with, there is the issue of competitiveness, mentioned in the initiatives of the EU Presidencies, the Competitiveness Council and the Commission. Better regulation can deliver on competitiveness, but there is no simple chain of causation between tools (i.e., RIA, consultation, simplification, access to regulation, etc.), good rules and economic growth. As explained in chapter 2, correlation can be spurious and causal chains interrupted at several points. The most direct impact of better regulation on competitiveness is via the changes in the regulatory culture. By changing the way in which actors think about regulation, better regulation can lead to an efficient regulatory environment for citizens and firms. This is a precondition for competitiveness.

Secondly, regulation as mode of governance (following the terminology introduced in chapter 1) is criticised for its opaque procedures, lack of transparency and limited access to diffuse interests. Accordingly, better regulation is valuable if it opens up the policy process and breaks down the intimacy of regulator–regulatees interactions in closed policy communities. This requires a drastic remodulation and continuous readjustment of the regulatory policy process. With its emphasis on open and transparent processes, disciplined consultation, fair treatment of the empirical evidence, replicability of the analysis produced by the regulators and peer review, better regulation has its role to play. Judged from this angle, institutionalisation is eminently a question of the degree of embeddedness of the tools presented in this volume in the regulatory processes. Tools generated by different governments' initiatives and programmes have started to converge towards the same principles and objectives of better regulation.

Then there is the completion of the single market. There is a clear trend towards politicisation of some key single-market issues. Even policies that were originally presented as technical complements to the design of an integrated market for capital and labour are now at the centre of heated political controversies. There is frustration on the part both of those who want to stop the excesses of liberalisation and of the 'zealots of undistorted competition' (Scharpf, 1997). Writing in the *Financial Times*, Professor Mario Monti, former Commissioner for the single market and competition policy, noted that there are still Member States, such as France and Germany, that:

> have acted to slow down the pace of energy liberalisation, to dilute the effectiveness of the takeover directive, to oppose the service directive, to try to resist the full enforcement of competition rules and to indulge in various forms of economic nationalism. (Monti, 2005: 19)

The political sensitivity of single-market regulation has become difficult to handle. The idea underpinning better regulation is to strengthen the empirical base for political decisions. However, as shown in chapter 1, empirical information has different impacts on policy decisions, depending on the level of conflict and the degree of innovation (and consequently uncertainty). High conflict and radical innovations represent the toughest conditions for the institutionalisation of tools such as RIA. At the moment, better regulation has to deliver in a politically charged environment. Should a network of stakeholders (including business, civil organisations, the regions and the media) emerge around better regulation, this would bring consensus at an early stage of the policy process and reduce conflict at a later stage. Consequently, the political role of better regulation in the single market is less about establishing the facts than about making the stakeholders aware of the major trade-offs involved in alternative options. In turn, awareness of the trade-offs, balanced and extensive consultation, and systematic analysis of alternative options are prerequisites for the legitimacy of single-market rules.

The problem is compounded by the lack of trust of the Member States in the Commission. The latter is required to consider the principles of subsidiarity and proportionality. These principles are objectively difficult to operationalise in the context of better regulation. But they can also become an asset and increase trust in the Commission. The situation is uncertain at the moment. The Commission is re-examining a large set of proposals. In 2005, it screened 183 of them and came to the conclusion that it should withdraw a third of them (sixty-eight) because they did not meet the principles of better regulation, they were inconsistent with the goals of the Lisbon agenda or they were outdated. This can be seen either as a sign that the Commission is losing confidence in the completion of the single market, or as the judicious application of subsidiarity and better regulation principles. Be that as it may, subsidiarity and proportionality have the potential to inject balanced opinion formation in the formulation of EU rules and to contribute to the legitimacy of the Commission's regulatory activity. This is an opportunity for Brussels.

The implementation and enforcement of existing rules provide their own set of political problems. In some cases, rules have become obsolete. In others, the legal framework, on the one hand, and the reality of the markets governed by the framework, on the other, still differ too much. Some years ago, John Usher, writing on the implementation of single-market rules, raised the question of the 'dichotomy between the legal framework and market performance' and concluded, pessimistically, 'is it only the tourists who fill their cars with French wine, spirits, and beer who have perceived the reality of the single market?' (Usher, 1997: 65). This explains why issues such as compliance and ex-post review of regulations have become important tools of better regulation policies.

Discourse and policy: why institutionalisation differs in the EU

The veil of optimistic and normative propositions covering the discourse on better regulation has to be lifted. Is better regulation the best way forwards, or rhetorical smoke without fire? What type of regulation and what kind of regulatory state are emerging from this agenda? The first question arises out of our scepticism about the enthusiasm shown by policy-makers for better regulation. It provides an opportunity to present and discuss other findings of our work.

We do not discuss the extent to which RIA, consultation and the other tools described in this book are central to the discourse of policy-makers, especially in the context of the 'growth and jobs' agenda for competitiveness in Europe and in OECD fora. Certainly they are. But this does not mean that better regulation has been institutionalised everywhere. The evidence we collected tells another story. Similarity at the level of discourse (on principles of regulatory governance and better regulation rhetoric) and the adoption of some commitments to some type of RIA (variously defined) of proposed regulations should not be confused with convergence at the level of use of instruments, not to mention convergence of results (achieved via the use of instruments).

Better regulation discourse can travel quite lightly. The fact that a country has a formal description of better regulation policy does not necessarily mean that ministers routinely use it in the preparation of new legislation. It does not even mean that – when they use tools such as RIA and consultation – ministers broadly follow the same steps in different countries. The timing may also be different, with some countries (or some ministers within the same country) doing RIA when the decision has practically been taken, and others using it at an early stage.

Let us look at some of the evidence discussed in detail in the previous chapters. There are different clusters of Member States in the EU. For some governments, better regulation does not go much further than some pilot projects on RIA or simplification. There is no use of indicators and measures, for the simple reason that the whole range of better regulation activities is limited. The problem is not that data and indicators are difficult to gather – the problem is that there are not much data to measure in the first place. The investment in quality assurance is minimal and the approach to consultation and RIA is basic. These governments do not have a better regulation policy. There is no relatively stable set of actors, problems, decisions and policy instruments interacting in a policy space demarcated by better regulation activities.

In another group of Member States, better regulation has been 'edited' to denote a focus on administrative burdens. Once edited down to the specificities of administrative burdens, better regulation policy has quite naturally and logically focused on the business community as the main stakeholder. Quality assurance bodies have been developed accordingly. The initial ambition of RIA – to ensure that regulation produces net benefits for the community – has been forgotten.

Finally, in a few cases there appears to be a consistent effort to assess a wide range of costs and benefits in an integrated process. The Commission has the most ambitious goal to link better regulation to an inclusive mode of governance. In this context, RIA tests the impact of new proposals along three dimensions: economic performance, sustainable development and social cohesion. Interestingly, when asked about the objectives of regulatory quality in our questionnaire (see figure 5.1), only two Member States indicated the principle of maximisation of the net benefits of regulatory measures. Four Member States highlighted the minimisation of administrative burden, six the possibility of attaining a given policy goal at the smallest possible cost and the others preferred the generic proposition of 'having effective and efficient regulations'.

So, having established that the bottle of 'better regulation discourse' is new, what type of wine do we find inside it? For the EU and the UK, we can talk of relatively new wine (the UK has been experimenting with RIA since the 1980s) in new bottles. For Belgium, the Netherlands and Denmark the wine is the old 'compliance cost assessment' and 'reduction of the administrative burden on enterprises' rebranded as better regulation. These Member States do not emphasise the assessment of benefits, especially wide societal benefits. Finally, other Member States fall in the category of 'new bottles with almost no wine inside'. As mentioned, there is political interest in the SCM (see chapter 4) and in the reduction of administrative burden across a large number of Member States. This could be instrumental in raising the profile of better regulation in the countries that have small quantities of wine inside their bottles. Put differently, the SCM can upgrade the cluster of Member States with no systematic experience of better regulation and reduce the distance from the cluster working on administrative burdens. We add some remarks on the SCM in the next section.

To sum up then, the language of better regulation has produced a community of discourse for policy-makers and has stimulated the introduction of some instruments that are labelled 'regulatory impact assessment' but in some cases exist only on paper, and in other cases disguise other practices under the same label. Diffusion at the level of 'talk' has not yielded convergence in 'actions' and 'results' – to use the classic terms suggested by Brunsson (1989) and, more recently, Pollitt (2001). Interestingly, no EU government has opposed better regulation, for example by arguing that ministers should not be constrained by economic analysis when they make law. In this sense, better regulation is a very successful discourse – everyone wants to have a bottle of this wine at home. Our conclusion is that institutionalisation and diffusion among stakeholders of better regulation policy are still limited across the EU.

The current political agenda: towards convergence on the standard cost model?

Looking at the current political priorities of the EU and the Member States, what is the prospect for institutionalisation? Most Member States are attracted by a version of better regulation policy centred on administrative burdens (see chapter 4). The SCM has gained good currency in several Member States. This may promote converge towards a common technique and more incisive commitments across the EU.

One can see the SCM as a *sui generis* accounting standard.[2] Given its focus on a narrow definition of 'regulatory cost' it can be used by Member States to account for some of the total costs and to plan for the reduction of burdens across time. This basic model allows for gradual elaboration. As shown by recent studies (SQW, 2005), the SCM can become the bedrock for the development of sophisticated measures of cumulative burdens. One crucial condition for this to happen is the integration of the SCM with other tools in an approach oriented to integrated regulatory management. The SCM can produce developments in this direction only if it is a point of departure, not a point of arrival. Another important condition for integrated regulatory management is the gradual introduction of measurement of benefits, for example by removing those regulations (and their associated costs) that produce the largest net deficit, and not just removing administrative rules *per se*.

Under these conditions, the current political interest in burdens may become the first step towards a technical dialogue between the European institutions and Member States aimed at the elaboration of regulatory budgets. Should this be the case, in the future we will see the emergence of regulatory budgets to account for the cost of regulation, with greater efficiency and transparency. These budgets require different information sources. Different methods to quantify regulatory costs should reinforce each other. Surveys of business (on regulatory costs) can validate estimates produced via engineering methodologies for the calculation of burdens. Regulatory budgets can complement the classic public finance instruments based on public expenditure and taxation. Taken together, regulatory budgets and classic 'public finance' budgets provide more capacity to control what the government does.

However, one can also raise concerns about a political agenda focused on a limited range of costs. The programmes for the reduction of administrative burdens may even contradict the philosophy of RIA if they simply erase burdens without any consideration of the benefits arising out of regulation. It is also difficult to separate out an administrative burden from other categories of costs. Thus, what looks like a simpler task (i.e., to focus on a category of cost instead of the whole set of costs) can become a much more complex exercise. Additionally, an exclusive focus on the business community and the business environment could be detrimental to the overall legitimacy of better regulation policy. However, the Belgian and the Commission's models quantify administrative burdens on citizens and the public sector – an important property in terms of potential for legitimacy.

Better regulation and images of the regulatory state

This leads us to the final question of how better regulation policy fits with images of the regulatory state or, to use the concept introduced at the beginning of this volume, regulatory governance. As shown by Moran (2003: 36), the 'dominant scholarly orthodoxy of recent years' has associated the regulatory state with new modes of governance, based on 'soft law', co-regulation, enforced self-regulation, smart post-Weberian bureaucracies, the displacement of command law and the retreat from state interventionism.

Drawing on Moran and adapting his categories to the topics discussed in this volume, we can identify the following images of regulatory governance. The first is an image of renounced command and retreat from institutional formality and hierarchy. The second is a normative variation of the first theme. It assigns a positive value to the changes described by the first image and looks at the regulatory state as 'smart' governance, governance that moves with intelligence 'between different regulatory modes according to circumstance' (Moran, 2003: 24). The third is an image of cultural and technological responses to risk, and points to the proliferation of auditing systems and intensification of system-level regulatory control, as described by Power's account of the 'audit society' (Power, 1999). The last image is

Moran's own description of the UK as a country in which the hyper-modern and hyper-innovative regulatory state has increased state interventionism in areas of social life that were previously dominated by club-like regulation.

Where does better regulation stand in relation to these images? As mentioned, one of the key arguments in the documents produced by the EU institutions in recent years (and by the OECD since the 1990s) is that better regulation makes institutions think. As such, it is consistent with the first image of regulatory governance. Better regulation arises out of the shift from the classic instruments of stabilisation and redistribution to regulation.

However, it does not necessarily produce a smart state. If, as argued by Gunningham and Grabosky (1998) and Baldwin (2005), smart regulation consists of the flexible use of different regulatory modes to suit changing circumstances, instruments such as RIA are not fit for the purpose. It is very difficult to use RIA to test mixed regulatory regimes – for example a regime that includes an enforcement pyramid (of the type suggested by Ayres and Braithwaite, 1992), with entirely self-enforced rules at the base and command law at the top. The standard approach in RIA is to test options that are neatly separated one from another. In addition, once a complex regulatory regime has been impact assessed, there is an in-built bias against flexibility, unless one is prepared to re-perform the assessments, and this may be politically and bureaucratically unwise (Baldwin, 2005).

The reason behind this lack of flexibility and the poor fit with the image of the smart state is that better regulation is essentially meta-regulation. As such, it provides more formality and, inevitably, rigidity in the regulatory process. It can be used intelligently, of course, but it is not a form of creative regulatory craft. There are advantages in terms of accountability and control in the regulation of the regulatory process, and one can be prepared to give up some flexibility and regulatory innovation in exchange for predictability and monitorability of how rules are formulated, consultation is carried out and enforcement delivered. Overall, better regulation may have a better 'fit' with the third image rather than the second, especially in relation to the embeddedness of better regulation in systems of quality assurance. In a sense, better regulation is there to increase the information needed to audit the regulatory process, and it may well be a symptom of the audit explosion described by Power.

The fourth image goes straight into the territory of politics. We cannot answer the question whether better regulation is intrusive and hyper-modernist, and we should take into account the fact that Moran has developed his own image with a particular context in mind, that is, the UK. But better regulation certainly chimes with our standard knowledge of how political principals control their agents. In effect, better regulation has been used to increase the instruments of political control of the executive over the federal executive agencies in the USA, and the power of the core executive over the other ministers in Europe. As such, better regulation is a political territory that has made the core executive, and specifically the prime minister's office, more assertive over other ministers and independent agencies. In the EU, however, the nature of the European Commission, where the Secretariat-General cannot be compared to the prime minister's office by any stretch of political imagination, is such that better regulation has more diffuse power effects. The political picture of the EU is complicated by the fact that better regulation can also be used by Member States and the European Parliament to control the Commission at the stage of policy formulation.

In conclusion, better regulation has moved from the realm of technical devices to assist bureaucracy to the much more complex territory of politics. No matter how smart or intrusive it may be, better regulation points to changes and conflicts in domestic and EU politics. Although its institutionalisation is not uniformly high in Europe, its role in regulatory politics and its impact on the legitimacy of regulatory governance is bound to increase.

Notes

1 See the comments on the white paper on governance offered by Denmark and Finland on the governance website of the European Commission, http://ec.europa.eu/governance/index_en.htm.
2 We are grateful to Ed Humpherson for this observation.

Appendix 1

Questionnaire – measuring regulatory quality

Introduction

The Lisbon agenda for competitiveness requires the EU to make a considerable effort to improve regulatory quality across sectors and levels of governance. Your responses to this questionnaire will enable us to report on the progress made in the EU and, together with the information collected via the support network and our desk research, to assess whether regulatory quality principles, tools and policies are converging. To track the progress since the Mandelkern (2001) report, we plan to make use of additional data, such as that from the OECD, the 2004 project launched by the Directors of Better Regulation Programmes, DG Market Indicators and the report produced under the aegis of the Hellenic Presidency (2003). Hence some classic questions on the quality of regulatory tools do not feature in this questionnaire. Here the main focus is on measures.

We have designed the questionnaire drawing on our framework of dimensions and tools of better regulation. The questionnaire is based on three main dimensions of regulatory quality, that is:

- design of the process
- activities and outputs
- real-world outcome

The tools used by governments to produce regulatory quality can be classified as follows:

- regulatory impact assessment (hereafter RIA)
- consultation
- simplification
- access and transparency (hereafter access)

The questionnaire serves a number of purposes:

- To illustrate how the project's analytical framework can lead to the design of indicators. We start from the definitions and principles of better regulation, look at quality assurance systems, and show the implications in terms of measures.
- To sound the support network on the meanings of quality and possible indicators. The questionnaire will enable us to detect the level of convergence in Europe around principles of better regulation, quality assurance approaches and of course

indicators. Let us know if you agree on definitions and concepts. We would like
to invite you to formulate alternative proposals or to propose other activities or
initiatives to track in the second part of the project – please send us comments in
any form.

- To invite the support network to formulate proposals for the development of
EU-level indicators.
- Finally, the questionnaire serves an educational purpose, that is, to illustrate how
indicators can be developed.

1. The objective of regulatory quality

Which of the following objectives best describes your country's approach to regulatory quality?
One answer only

☐ Maximisation of citizens' wealth
☐ Maximisation of the net benefits of regulatory measures
☐ Having effective and efficient regulations
☐ Attaining a given policy goal at the smallest possible cost to business and society
as a whole
☐ Minimisation of administrative burden
☐ Other, please specify:..
☐ No

Please attach a copy of the official document containing the objective.

2. Principles of regulatory quality

Some countries have defined the guiding principles of regulatory quality. The UK, for
example, has adopted the following regulatory quality principles: proportionality,
accountability, consistency, transparency and targeting.

Does your government set out explicit principles of regulatory quality?
☐ Yes
☐ No

If the answer is 'Yes', please tick where appropriate (multiple answers are possible):
☐ Necessity
☐ Proportionality
☐ Subsidiarity
☐ Transparency
☐ Accountability
☐ Accessibility
☐ Simplicity
☐ Other (please specify):..

Please attach a copy of official documents defining principles. This can be the same
document produced for question 1.

3. Coordination between levels of government

Does your government adopt the principle of bringing better regulation across levels of governance? If so, is there a specific process for systematic (as opposed to episodic) coordination between the national-level governmental bodies in charge of regulatory quality policy and the following levels of governance (example: a committee or a conference) in making new regulations?

European Union
☐ Yes
☐ No

Independent regulators
☐ Yes
☐ No

Regional or state (as opposed to federal) programmes
☐ Yes
☐ No

Local level (towns for example)
☐ Yes
☐ No

Comments:..

4. Tools

What are the most important tools used by your country to achieve the objective of regulatory quality? 1 indicates the lowest level of importance, 5 the highest.

Has the importance of different tools increased over the last five years?

	1	2	3	4	5	Importance increased
RIA						
Simplification						
Consultation						
Access						
Other:..............						
Other:..............						

5. Guidance

Does your government publish guidance on tools of better regulation? Guidance can take the form of handbooks, guides, checklists or minimum standards. Please insert in the last column the year of publication of the current guidance document.

	Yes	No	Year
RIA			
Simplification			
Consultation			
Access			
Other:...............			
Other:...............			

6. Quantifiable targets

Some countries have set quantifiable targets. For example, in the Netherlands the policy target is to reduce administrative burdens by at least 25 per cent as a result of RIA. This goal has to be achieved by the end of the current legislative period. In Sweden and the UK the target is full compliance with RIA requirements. In Portugal and Spain governments aim to reduce the number of days necessary to set up a business.

Does your government use quantitative targets?

☐ Yes. Please illustrate, and indicate when government started using quantifiable targets
Target(s):...

Quantifiable target(s) was first introduced in year:...

☐ No

7. Monitoring

[If you have answered *Yes* to question 6.]
How is the achievement of quantifiable regulatory targets monitored?
Multiple answers are possible.

☐ Self-reporting
☐ Reporting to the prime minister's office
☐ Reporting to parliament
☐ Monitoring via independent bodies
☐ Other (specify):...
☐ None

8. Performance measurement

Most countries now have general performance systems for the public sector (i.e., general auditing systems, budget planning).

Do performance systems make explicit reference to the achievement of the regulatory objective, principles and/or quantitative targets?

☐ Yes. Please specify how:..

☐ No

9. Financial resources

Has the budget dedicated to better regulation policies increased over the last five years?

Budget for RIA
☐ 0 (there is no dedicated budget)
☐ Yes, it has increased
☐ No, it is more or less the same or has decreased
☐ I do not know

Budget for specific training on RIA, consultation and drafting
☐ 0 (there is no dedicated budget)
☐ Yes, it has increased
☐ No, it is more or less the same or has decreased
☐ I do not know

Total budget for better regulation policy
☐ 0 (there is no dedicated budget)
☐ Yes, it has increased
☐ No, it is more or less the same or has decreased
☐ I do not know

10. Regulatory agendas and coordination of tools

(a) Does the government make use of annual regulatory agendas?
☐ Yes
☐ No

(b) Are minimum standards for consultation mandatory for the RIA process?
☐ Yes
☐ No

(c) Are the documents supporting the consultation process in the public domain?
☐ Yes
☐ No

(d) Is simplification based on economic analysis or formal RIA?
☐ Yes
☐ No

(e) Do citizens have a right to access the documents underpinning a regulatory decision?
☐ Yes
☐ No

11. Indicators of activity

(a) How many regulations were cost assessed in 2002 and 2003?
2002:..............
2003:..............

(b) How many regulations were cost–benefit assessed in 2002 and 2003?
2002:..............
2003:..............

(c) How many procedures were simplified in 2002 and 2003?
2002:..............
2003:..............

(d) What percentage of regulation in force is codified and or consolidated?..............

12. From activity to results

Does the government provide an estimate of the time and/or cost savings achieved through the use of the various tools?

☐ Yes. Please specify how:..
☐ No

13. Quantification of lives saved

Considering the data and statistics available, would you be able to establish what percentage/range of annual deaths in accidents were avoided by the new regulations issued in 2003?

☐ Yes, it would take up to a week
☐ Yes, it would take up to a month
☐ Yes, it would take up to six months
☐ Yes, it would take an undefined time
☐ No

14. Quantification of illness reduction (cancer)

Considering the data and statistics available, would you be able to establish what percentage/range of cancers related to smoking were avoided by new regulations issued in 2003?

☐ Yes, it would take up to a week
☐ Yes, it would take up to a month
☐ Yes, it would take up to six months
☐ Yes, it would take an undefined time
☐ No

15. Quantification of regulatory benefits

Considering the data and statistics available, would you be able to quantify (not necessarily in monetised form) the benefits delivered by new regulations issued in 2003?

☐ Yes, it would take up to a week
☐ Yes, it would take up to a month
☐ Yes, it would take up to six months
☐ Yes, it would take an undefined time
☐ No

16. Quantification of regulatory costs

Considering the data and statistics available, would you be able to establish what percentage of the national GDP was spent in complying with new (assessed) regulations issued in 2003?

☐ Yes, it would take up to a week
☐ Yes, it would take up to a month
☐ Yes, it would take up to six months
☐ Yes, it would take an undefined time
☐ No

Regulatory quality and the role of the European Commission

The aim of the project is to produce a set of indicators for the European Commission. As the engagement with the support network is a priority for us, we would like to sound out your opinion on the next steps.

17. What are the five key activities that the Commission should track over the next five years or so?

Maximum five answers.

☐ Regulatory impact assessment
☐ Consultation
☐ Simplification
☐ Access to regulation
☐ Codification
☐ Recasting
☐ Updating and reviewing single-market legislation
☐ Sun-setting
☐ Use of flexible market-friendly instruments
☐ Guidelines on the use of science in regulatory policy
☐ Systematic surveys of stakeholders
☐ Citizens' enquiries, deliberative polls
☐ Other instruments (please specify):..

18. Would you like to propose some indicators that the Commission should adopt to monitor progress on these activities?

....
....

Comments on the project and the analytical framework

Would you like us to expand or modify our definitions of tools and dimensions of regulatory quality? How?..

Would you like us to target our project towards initiatives that are not covered by this questionnaire?..

Would you like us to report on initiatives in your country or at the EU/OECD level that are not covered by the interim report?..

Other comments and suggestions for indicators:..

Appendix 2

System 1. Indicators for the quality of the process

This system is based on ex-ante macro-indicators. It covers six dimensions of quality, within the following sections:

A. Design of better regulation policy
B. Quality assurance process
C. Impact assessment (quality of activities and guidance)
D. Consultation (quality of activities and guidance)
E. Quality of simplification programmes
F. Strategy for access

These indicators are objective and assess the quality of the process (design, quality assurance and guidance). The tables presented in the following sections briefly present for each indicator a description of what is measured, an interpretation of the usefulness of the proposed measure and a modality for the collection of the necessary data.

1.A Design of better regulation policy

1 Is there an explicit policy (adopted by the government, cabinet or in law) promoting government-wide regulatory reform or regulatory quality improvement (i.e., a better regulation policy)?

2 Does the better regulation policy establish explicit objectives to be achieved by improving regulatory quality (e.g., reducing costs on businesses, improving compliance, etc.)?

3 Are the following principles explicitly included in the better regulation programme?
Mandelkern report's principles:
- [ ] Necessity
- [ ] Proportionality
- [ ] Subsidiarity
- [ ] Transparency
- [ ] Accountability
- [ ] Accessibility
- [ ] Simplicity

Principles of good regulatory governance across levels of governance
- ☐ Bringing the rules and principles of the World Trade Organisation (WTO) into the formulation of domestic regulations
- ☐ Local governments – regions should check the costs of their own regulations
- ☐ Independent regulators – agencies are obliged to use impact assessment

Principles governing regulatory decisions (decision-making criteria)
- ☐ Net benefit criterion (producing benefits at lower cost)
- ☐ Cost-effectiveness (choosing the lowest-cost option for an exogenously defined policy goal; for example, the lowest-cost solution to comply with the standards set by the Kyoto Protocol)
- ☐ Precautionary principle[1]
- ☐ Reducing costs on business
- ☐ Responsiveness to stakeholders
- ☐ SME-friendly

Table A.1 Purpose, interpretation and data collection of design and principles of better regulation policy indicators

Indicator	What is measured	Interpretation	Data collection
Design	Procedural and institutional steps that support the overall design of better regulation policy	Institutional design is a precondition for effective better regulation policies	
[1] Explicit policy	Definition of objectives, principles and responsibility of who does what in better regulation policy	An efficient policy programme should be clearly defined in terms of objectives, principles and responsibility	OECD questionnaires
[2] Objectives	Explicit objectives of better regulation	In order to be measured, programmes must contain clear objectives	Chapter 5 dataset and official guidance and documents provided by governments
[3] Principles	The presence or absence of principles informing better regulation policy; convergence among the EU Member States in terms of major criteria informing regulatory policy decisions	The presence of these principles shows sense of direction and political commitment. Agreement at the EU level on fundamental principles is essential to develop a consistent set of policies	Chapter 5 dataset and official guidance and documents provided by governments

Necessity	Defined by the Mandelkern report. This principle establishes that, before putting a new policy into effect, the public authorities assess whether or not it is necessary to introduce new regulations	Chapter 5 dataset
Proportionality	Defined by the Mandelkern report. According to this principle any regulation must strike a balance between the advantages that it provides and the constraints it imposes	Chapter 5 dataset
Subsidiarity	Defined by the Mandelkern report. It is a check that the objectives of the proposed action cannot be sufficiently achieved at a level closer to the citizen	Chapter 5 dataset
Transparency	Defined by the Mandelkern report. It implies broadly based and equitable access to policy formulation and the consultation process, the constituent elements of which should be made public. Participation criteria themselves should be transparent	Chapter 5 dataset
Accountability	Defined by the Mandelkern report. All parties involved in regulatory policy should be able to clearly identify the authorities that originated the policies and the regulation applying to them	Chapter 5 dataset
Accessibility	Defined by the Mandelkern report. Consistent, comprehensible regulation, which establishes who is responsible for what in the implementation of rules	Chapter 5 dataset
Simplicity	Defined by the Mandelkern report. Regulation must be simple to use and to understand	Chapter 5 dataset

WTO rules	Diffusion among Member States of a principle that requires consideration of WTO rules and principles in the formulation of domestic regulations	Reference to WTO rules in domestic policies for better regulation shows a broad international approach to regulatory quality	Chapter 5 dataset
Local governments checks	Diffusion of key principles of better regulation across levels of governance	Local governments' obligation to perform checks on the impact of their own regulations is a precondition for a better regulatory environment	Chapter 5 dataset
Independent regulators	Diffusion among Member States of RIA on regulations issued by independent regulatory agencies	Advanced policies for regulatory quality go beyond governmental regulations. They also cover independent regulators (especially economic regulators) that are obliged to justify their rules via RIA	Chapter 5 dataset
Net benefit criterion (efficiency)	Resources are allocated optimally. Given two options, preference is given to the one which produces maximum net benefits	This is the most sophisticated technical criterion for choice. It should be used for major regulations	Chapter 5 dataset
Cost-effectiveness	Minimisation of costs. Given two options, preference is given to the one that reaches the objectives at the lower cost	A technical criterion of intermediate complexity and sophistication. Instead of looking at the overall balance between benefits and costs, it focuses on costs only. It can be used for medium-range and simple regulations	Chapter 5 dataset
Precaution	A principle used to handle radical uncertainty about the future. If the consequences of an action, especially the use of technology, are unknown but are judged to have a high risk of being negative from an ethical point of view, then it is better not to carry out the action rather than risk the uncertain but possibly very negative consequences	A criterion to be used in limited cases of radical uncertainty. The WTO requires in any case the presence of empirical evidence (about risks and danger) to support regulatory choice informed by the precautionary principle	Chapter 5 dataset

Reducing costs on business	Given two options, preference is given to the one that minimises costs on business	A simple technical criterion, which can be used for regulatory programmes targeting administrative burdens, with the qualification that those are only a component of total regulatory costs faced by business	Official guidance and documents provided by governments. Chapter 5 dataset includes a question on minimisation of administrative burdens
Responsiveness	Given two options, preference is given to the one which responds to the needs of stakeholders	A political criterion, difficult to measure	Chapter 5 dataset
SME-friendly	Given two options, preference is given to the one which creates a better environment for SMEs	A general approach or policy orientation more than a criterion for choice	Official guidance and documents provided by governments. Chapter 5 dataset

1.B Quality assurance process

1 Does the better regulation programme adopt quantifiable targets or measurable benchmarks in terms of reducing costs or increasing benefits?

2 Is an individual minister responsible for ensuring progress on better regulation against measurable benchmarks?

3 Is there an administrative body (for example a central 'regulatory quality unit' in the cabinet office) responsible for ensuring progress on better regulation against measurable benchmarks?

4 Does this body monitor and report progress made on reform by individual ministers?

5 Is the performance of the central regulatory quality body monitored via quantitative performance criteria?

6 Is there a public official document explaining the government's strategy to involve the citizen and civil society in better regulation policy?

7 Have resources specifically allocated for monitoring and compliance with the better regulation policy increased, decreased or remained the same over the last five years?

8 Is progress on better regulation monitored and evaluated by:
   • an external body, that is, a body which is not reporting to the government, for example an independent audit office?
   • a body reporting to the government, for example a regulatory quality unit in the cabinet office?

Does this body monitor:
- the achievement of quantifiable regulatory targets?
- how principles of regulatory quality are implemented?
- the degree of compliance with formal guidance on better regulation?

9 Do performance management systems used in the public sector make explicit reference to the achievement of the regulatory objectives and/or quantifiable targets?

10 Does the government publish an annual progress report on regulatory reform?

Table A.2 Purpose, interpretation and data collection of quality assurance process indicators

Indicator	What is measured	Interpretation	Data collection
[1] Quantifiable targets	The existence of quantifiable targets in better regulation	Quantifiable targets facilitate the implementation, management and evaluation of better regulation	Chapter 5 dataset
[2] Minister	The existence of a clear responsibility to monitor the performance of better regulation	Having a minister accountable for delivery is a clear sign of political commitment	OECD questionnaire and the report on the progress on the implementation of the Mandelkern report
[3] Quality assurance unit	The existence of a body (typically in the cabinet office) in charge of monitoring and quality assurance	Administrative body/bodies overseeing better regulation are necessary for efficient implementation, management and evaluation	OECD questionnaire and the report on the progress on the implementation of the Mandelkern report
[4] Reporting	The existence of a commitment to produce a report on progress	Reporting enhances the accountability and transparency of better regulation. Additionally, it is useful for evaluating the policy	Chapter 5 dataset
[5] Quantitative performance of quality assurance unit	The existence of a management performance system for the administrative body	It increases the overall quality of policies by establishing quantitative criteria for success or failure of quality assurance units	Chapter 5 dataset
[6] Civil society	The existence of an official document explaining the strategy to involve citizens	A strategy to involve citizens increases the legitimacy of better regulation programmes	Official guidance and documents provided by governments

[7] Resources – trend	Trend in expenditure for better regulation	Budget provides resources	Chapter 5 dataset
[8a] Monitoring/ evaluation	The existence of a monitoring body	The establishment of an administrative body in charge of monitoring the progress and result of better regulation is evidence of a consolidated culture of monitoring and evaluation	Chapter 5 dataset plus official guidance and documents provided by governments
External body	The type of administrative body		
Body reporting to the government	The type of administrative body		
[8b] What is measured	The extent of coverage of the monitoring system	A broad coverage of topics addressed by the monitoring system is a precondition for effective evaluation	Chapter 5 dataset plus official guidance and documents provided by governments
[9] Public service performance management	The inclusion of better regulation activities in the overall performance management system used in the public sector	Evidence of the importance of better regulation. Better regulation is embedded in the overall management system used in the public sector. Individuals achieving results on better regulation are rewarded	Chapter 5 dataset plus official documents
[10] Annual report on regulatory reform	Existence of annual report	An annual report enhances the degree of accountability and transparency of the policy	A simple question to be posed at a DBR meeting

1.C Impact assessment (quality of activities and guidance)

Basic information

1 Existence of written guidance on RIA
  For EU Member States detailed sections or a stand-alone 'Guide to European Union Impact Assessment'
2 Technical guidance reviewed at least every five years
3 At least one week of training for all policy officers overseeing or supervising RIA every three years
4 At least two weeks of training for all RIA analysts every three years
5 Number of regulations that are impact assessed in a year is known
6 Overall cost of performing RIA is known to the government

Specific indicators on the quality of written guidance

Does the written guidance on RIA:

1 Contain explicit criteria to select (when applicable, on the basis of a road map) the proposals deserving RIA?[2]
2 Make reference to the maximisation of collective welfare as the main reason for RIA?
3 Require that the problem be precisely defined (for the EU RIA, at the stage of road maps) in terms of its magnitude, causes and the incentives of the various parties?
4 Identify the baseline situation and its probable change over time sufficiently clearly to compare it with proposed changes?
5 Articulate policy objectives as measurable outcomes, goals or targets?
6 Justify government/Commission action considering the option of no action or of market solutions?
7 Identify all parties that are substantially affected by the change?
8 Require estimation of the lifetime of the policy or options?[3]
9 Require that the negative impacts on all those affected be identified in each option?
10 Include a risk–risk analysis comparing the risks of the present situation with those of possible solutions?
11 Prescribe that consultation should inform the assessment of different options?
12 Contain rules on consultation with other governments and on checks on overlapping regulations (for regulations likely to impact on other levels of governance)?
13 Express uncertainty about the future in terms of scenarios or probability?
14 Contain
   • an explicit set of values
   • a framework or
   • a model
   to identify and assess the trade-offs (in terms of the Lisbon goals of growth, social cohesion and environmental protection) between alternative policy options?
15 Assess different options with reference to how they will perform in terms of enforcement and compliance levels?
16 Analyse options in terms of their impacts on market structure and competition?
17 Include pilot testing (a 'dry run') of new forms?[4]
18 Require – when relevant – a discussion of the distribution of the negative and positive impacts (among different groups of people and/or different geographical areas)?
19 Ask the regulator to explain why no review clause is proposed (the default case being that there is a review clause in proposed regulation[5])?
20 Contain procedures for monitoring and evaluating ex-post the extent to which the regulation meets its objectives?
21 Require external peer review (for the most important regulations)?
22 Ask for a contact name and website where all underlying data used in the RIA are available?

Table A.3 Purpose, interpretation and data collection of quality of guidance on RIA indicators – basic information on activities

Indicator	What is measured	Interpretation	Data collection
[1] Written guidance	The existence of written guidance	It is not possible have an effective RIA system without a written guidance. Additionally, it enhances the transparency of the regulatory process and clarifies who does what, thus increasing accountability	Chapter 5 dataset
[1a] Guide to EU RIA	Existence of written guidance on EU regulatory process and RIA	See above	A simple check on the guides produced by Member States
[2] Review of guidance	Periodical review of guidance (every five years at least)	Review of guidance shows commitment to learning from experience	Chapter 5 dataset
[3] One week of training for policy-officers	The existence of periodic training for all policy-officers supervising RIA	Training is an essential element. Periodic training diffuses best practice and skills	Member States self-assessed questionnaire
[4] Two weeks of training of RIA analysts	The existence of periodic training for all RIA analysts	See above	Member States self-assessed questionnaire
[5] Number of regulations assessed is known	Knowledge of the number of regulations that are tested via RIA	The knowledge of the RIA performed in a year provides evidence that the government has basic information on what is done and what is not done	Chapter 5 dataset
[6] Cost of performing RIA is known	Ex-post information on the cost of performing all RIA selected in a year	See above	Chapter 5 dataset

Table A.4 *Purpose, interpretation and data collection of quality of guidance on RIA indicators – quality of guidance*

Indicator	What is measured	Interpretation	Data collection
[1] Selection criteria	The existence in the guidance of clear criteria to select regulation on which RIA is performed	Clear selection criteria enhance the quality and transparency of RIA	Examination of official guides to RIA. Alternatively, this question can be posed at a DBR meeting
[2] Maximisation of welfare	The existence in the guidance of a reference to the maximisation of collective welfare as the main reason for RIA	RIA should achieve the maximisation of collective welfare	Examination of official guides to RIA. Alternatively, this question can be posed at a DBR meeting
[3] Problem definition	The existence of a requirement to have clearly defined problems	Quite often action does not address the real problem. A section of the guidance should be dedicated to methodology of problem definition	Examination of official guides to RIA. Alternatively, this question can be posed at a DBR meeting
[4] Baseline	The existence in the guidance of an explanation of the baseline situation	Baseline is a key element in the analysis. Without it, the comparison of options is flawed	Examination of official guides to RIA. Alternatively, this question can be posed at a DBR meeting
[5] Outcome, goals and targets	The existence of a guidance requirement to express policy objectives as outcomes, goals or targets of proposed regulations in measurable terms	The presence of measurable objectives or targets facilitates analysis and comparison of options. It also facilitates the ex-post evaluation of regulations	Examination of official guides to RIA. Alternatively, this question can be posed at a DBR meeting
[6] Justification of action	The existence of a requirement to justify government/ Commission action considering the option of no action or of market solutions	Justification of government action is an element of the proportionality principle and a principle of evidence-based regulatory choice	Examination of official guides to RIA. Alternatively, this question can be posed at a DBR meeting

[7] Identification of all affected parties	The existence in the guidance of a section on how to identify all the parties affected by regulation	A preliminary and essential step to qualify and/or quantify regulatory costs and/or benefits. It aids the analysis of distributive effects of proposed regulation	Examination of official guides to RIA. Alternatively, this question can be posed at a DBR meeting
[8] Lifetime policy or options	The existence in the guidance of a requirement to identify an estimate of lifetime	'[S]uch estimation allows the benefits and costs to be calculated on an annual basis and to be discounted as appropriate' (Mandelkern, 2001: 22)	Examination of official guides to RIA. Alternatively, this question can be posed at a DBR meeting
[9] Identification of negative impact	The existence in the guidance of a requirement to identify all negative impacts on all those affected	Comprehensive identification of negative impacts of a proposal is a minimum requirement of a good RIA	Examination of official guides to RIA. Alternatively, this question can be posed at a DBR meeting
[10] Risk–risk analysis	The existence in the guidance of a requirement to perform risk–risk analysis in case of regulations addressing uncertainty	Risk–risk analysis explicitly compares one risk against another and thus promotes efficient regulatory choices	Examination of official guides to RIA. Alternatively, this question can be posed at a DBR meeting
[11] Consultation and options	The existence in the guidance of a requirement that consultation should inform the assessment of different options	Consultation fills information gaps by providing essential information on alternative options. Consultation enhances the credibility and legitimacy of RIA	Examination of official guides to RIA. Alternatively, this question can be posed at a DBR meeting
[12] Consultation with local/regional governments; checks on overlapping regulations	The existence of a requirement to consult with sub-national governments and to check if the regulatory proposal is overlapping	Essential to coordinate regulation across levels of governance. It enhances the efficiency and the legitimacy of the regulatory process	Examination of official guides to RIA. Alternatively, this question can be posed at a DBR meeting
[13] Uncertainty	The existence of a recommendation in the guidance to include uncertainty in the policy analysis	Uncertainty should be always taken into account when assessing regulation because regulation is an incomplete contract. This topic should be addressed in the guidance	Examination of official guides to RIA. Alternatively, this question can be posed at a DBR meeting

[14a] Set of values for trade-offs	The existence in the guidance of a set of values to identify and assess trade-offs (in terms of the Lisbon goals of growth, social cohesion and environmental protection) between alternative policy options	The explicit identification of a set of values facilitates the assessment of trade-offs among social, economic and environmental objectives	Examination of official guides to RIA. Alternatively, this question can be posed at a DBR meeting
[14b] Framework for trade-offs	The existence in the guidance of a framework to identify and assess trade-offs (in terms of the Lisbon goals of growth, social cohesion and environmental protection) between alternative policy options	The explicit identification of a framework facilitates the assessment of trade-offs among social, economic and environmental objectives	Examination of official guides to RIA. Alternatively, this question can be posed at a DBR meeting
[14c] Model for trade-offs	The existence in the guidance of a model to identify and assess trade-offs (in terms of the Lisbon goals of growth, social cohesion and environmental protection) between alternative policy options	The explicit identification of a model provides more precision than a conceptual framework	Examination of official guides to RIA. Alternatively, this question can be posed at a DBR meeting
[15] Levels of enforcement and compliance	The existence in the guidance of a requirement that non-compliance be factored into the comparison of alternatives	The level of compliance is a key element in the quantification of regulatory costs and/or benefits and consequently in the assessment of possible options	Examination of official guides to RIA. Alternatively, this question can be posed at a DBR meeting
[16] Impact on market structure and competition	The existence in the guidance of a requirement to perform an analysis of the effects of alternatives on market functioning and on competition	Economic regulation may have relevant effects on markets and competition. Some guides include an explicit competition test	Examination of official guides to RIA. Alternatively, this question can be posed at a DBR meeting
[17] Pilot test of new forms	The existence in the guidance of a requirement to include in the RIA of a dry run of new forms	A dry run of new administrative forms provides ideas on how to improve them before they are introduced	Examination of official guides to RIA. Alternatively, this question can be posed at a DBR meeting

[18] Distribution of regulatory effects	The existence in the guidance of a requirement – when relevant – to address distributive impacts of proposed regulations (among different groups of people and/or different geographical areas)	The distributional effect of a new regulation must be considered. Policy-makers need this information when taking decisions	Examination of official guides to RIA. Alternatively, this question can be posed at a DBR meeting
[19] Review clause	The existence in the guidance of a require-ment to explain why a review is not used	Review clauses provide an automatic mechanism for updating of legislation	Examination of official guides to RIA. Alternatively, this question can be posed at a DBR meeting
[20] Procedures for ex-post evaluation	The existence in the guidance of procedures to set up monitoring and ex-post evaluation of regulations	Clearly defined proce-dures may facilitate the ex-post evaluation of regulations	Examination of official guides to RIA. Alternatively, this question can be posed at a DBR meeting
[21] External peer review	The existence in the guidance of a requirement to perform an external peer review for the major regulations	External peer review increases the credibility and legitimacy of RIA	Examination of official guides to RIA. Alternatively, this question can be posed at a DBR meeting
[22] Contact name and website	The existence in the guidance of an obligation to provide a contact name and website where all underlying data used in RIA are available	Contact name and a dedicated website increase the transparency of the regulatory process	Examination of official guides to RIA. Alternatively, this question can be posed at a DBR meeting

1.D Consultation (quality of activities and guidance)

Basic information
 1 Existence of written guidance on consultation
 2 Technical guidance reviewed at least every five years
 3 Programmes for training on consultation and specific methods
 4 Number of consultations performed in a year is known

Specific indicators on the quality of written guidance
Does written guidance on consultation establish:
 1 The timing of consultation?
 2 That the consultation timetable and planning enable those affected to comment on the final assessment?
 3 Standards on how to deal with experts' advice at the stage of policy formulation?
 4 The methodology of consultation?
 5 How innovative consultation methods are to be considered, especially when potential participants have problems in participating in traditional ways?
 6 That consultation involves affected parties in the discussion of the nature of the problem, as well as solutions?
 7 That any member of the public may choose to participate in the consultation?
 8 That consultation goes beyond a one-off event, taking place at appropriate stages during the making of regulations?
 9 That relevant supporting documents are to be provided to affected parties to explain the impact of the regulation?
10 How the input provided by consultation will be considered and responded to?
11 A mandatory report on the results of consultation?

Table A.5 Purpose, interpretation and data collection of consultation indicators – activities

Indicator	What is measured	Interpretation	Data collection
[1] Written guidance on consultation	The existence of written guidance on consultation process	High-quality consultation is based on specific steps and methods. Guidance on this process is necessary as well as a clear illustration and explanation of the methods	Chapter 5 dataset
[2] Technical guidance reviewed at least every five years	The frequency of the review of consultation guidance	Review of guidance shows commitment to learning	Chapter 5 dataset
[3] Training programmes	The presence of training programmes for consultation	Consultation is a political exercise with its own methods. Training diffuses best practice and skills. Methods require specific training. Sessions on focus groups, participatory policy analysis, etc. show that methods are taken seriously	Chapter 5 dataset
[4] Number of consultations performed is known	Knowledge of the number of consultations performed in a year	Knowledge of consultations performed in a year shows that the government knows who is doing what	Question to be posed at a DBR meeting

Table A.6 Purpose, interpretation and data collection of consultation – guidance

Indicator	What is measured	Interpretation	Data collection
[1] Consultation timing	The existence in the guidance of time standards	Standards increase the predictability and transparency of the regulatory process	Examination of consultation written guidance. Alternatively, this question can be posed at a DBR meeting
[2] Consultation timetable and planning	The existence of a consultation timetable and plans to allow affected parties to comment on the assessment of alternative options	Comments on final assessment may verify the quality of use of information gathered through consultation. Timetable and planning would enable those affected to comment on the final assessment	Examination of consultation written guidance. Alternatively, this question can be posed at a DBR meeting
[3] Standards on experts' advice	The existence in the guidance of standards about how to deal with experts' advice at the stage of policy formulation	These standards provide transparency in the use of scientific advice	Examination of consultation written guidance. Alternatively, this question can be posed at a DBR meeting
[4] Consultation methodology	The existence in the guidance of an illustration of different methodologies to use in the consultation process	Detailed consultation guidance should include a section on methods	Examination of consultation written guidance. Alternatively, this question can be posed at a DBR meeting
[5] Innovative consultation methods	Reference to innovative methods of consultation	Innovative methods facilitate the participation of affected parties that have problems with traditional methods	Examination of consultation written guidance. Alternatively, this question can be posed at a DBR meeting
[6] Affected parties involved in the discussion of the nature of the problem and solutions	The existence in the guidance of a requirement to involve affected parties in the discussion of the problem and in the identification of the possible alternative solutions	This provides fair access to the consultation process and an opportunity to comment on problem definition and alternative options	Examination of consultation written guidance. Alternatively, this question can be posed at a DBR meeting

[7] Public participation in the consultation	The existence in the guidance of a procedure enabling the general public to participate in the consultation process	This indicator measures the openness of the consultation process	Examination of consultation written guidance. Alternatively, this question can be posed at a DBR meeting
[8] Consultation goes beyond a one-off event	The existence in the guidance of the principle that consultation goes beyond a one-off event, taking place at appropriate stages during the making of a regulation	Consultation in a process and stakeholders should be given the opportunity to intervene at different stages of the process	Examination of consultation written guidance. Alternatively, this question can be posed at a DBR meeting
[9] Supporting documents	The existence in the guidance of a requirement to provide supporting documents explaining the analysis of alternative options	Supporting documents enhance the transparency and accessibility of the process	Examination of consultation written guidance. Alternatively, this question can be posed at a DBR meeting
[10] Input provided by consultation will be considered and responded to	The existence in the guidance of a requirement to show how the regulators have addressed the major issues raised by the stakeholders in the consultation process	This shows that consultation is responsive	Examination of consultation written guidance. Alternatively, this question can be posed at a DBR meeting
[11] Mandatory report	The existence in the guidance of a requirement to publish a final report on the consultation process summarising: affected parties consulted; input of consultation; explanation on how consultation has been taken into account; justification where it has not	It provides transparency and shows how consultation has been used by regulators as an opportunity to learn	Examination of consultation written guidance. Alternatively, this question can be posed at a DBR meeting

1.E Quality of simplification programmes

Basic information
1 Existence of written guidance on simplification
2 Technical guidance reviewed at least every five years
3 Number of procedures simplified is known
4 The amount of regulatory costs saved through simplification is known

Specific indicators on the quality of simplification
Does the government's or Commission's simplification programme/strategy contain the following elements:
1 Systematic, rolling and long-term programme with annual timetable for simplification and prioritised targets?
2 Quantifiable targets (for example based on the reduction of compliance or administrative costs)?
3 How to measure change and the results of simplification?
4 Provisions on the review of the simplification programme at least every three years in the light of the results achieved
5 Commitment to review and simplify existing regulation when introducing new regulation[6]
6 Commitment to use RIA for the simplification of major rules affecting business and/or citizens
7 Commitment to review proposals or existing regulations according to their consistency with the requirements of other regulatory frameworks (EU regulatory framework, the regulatory framework of major trade partners, WTO rules)
8 Requirement to introduce review or sunset clauses when new rules meet the following conditions (established by the Mandelkern report):
  8.1 Regulation was introduced at short notice
  8.2 Regulation is based on the precautionary principle
  8.3 Technology or market conditions are most likely to change
  8.4 Regulation is a pilot project
  8.5 Regulation confers rights upon the state
9 Public register of regulatory provisions accessible on-line

Table A.7 Purpose, interpretation and data collection of quality of simplification programme indicators – activities

Indicator	What is measured	Interpretation	Data collection
[1] Guidance on simplification	The existence of specific guidance on simplification	Simplification programmes should specify the methods used to assess rules. Guidance illustrates these methods as well as the objectives, time frame and steps of simplification	Chapter 5 dataset
[2] Technical guidance reviewed at least every five years	Presence or absence of reviews of simplification guidance	It shows political commitment and commitment to learning	Chapter 5 dataset
[3] Number of procedures simplified is known	Knowledge of the number of procedures simplified in a year	It shows that the government knows what has been done in a given year and thus can keep track of simplification	Chapter 5 dataset
[4] Cost savings from regulatory simplification	Ex-post knowledge of the savings from simplification	Information on cost savings from simplification programmes is an important indicator for evaluation	Chapter 5 dataset

Table A.8 Purpose, interpretation and data collection of quality of simplification programme indicators – simplification strategy

Indicator	What is measured	Interpretation	Data collection
[1] Annual timetable for simplification and prioritised targets	The existence in the simplification programme of a timetable and prioritised targets	The definition of a timetable and priorities is indispensable for the management of the simplification programme	Examination of simplification programmes. Alternatively, this question can be posed at a DBR meeting
[2] Quantifiable targets	The existence of simplification programme targets, for example based on the reduction of administrative burdens (as suggested by the Council and the EU Presidency)	Measurable targets facilitate evaluation and review of simplification programmes	Examination of simplification programmes. Alternatively, this question can be posed at a DBR meeting

[3] How to measure change	The existence of a commitment to measure change resulting from simplification	This indicator provides useful information for the evaluation of the quality of simplification programmes	Examination of simplification programmes. Alternatively, this question can be posed at a DBR meeting
[4] Review of simplification	The existence in the simplification programme of a specific provision to review	Periodic review shows commitment to learning. It keeps the simplification programme up to date	Examination of simplification programmes. Alternatively, this question can be posed at a DBR meeting
[5] Simplify existing regulation when introducing new regulation	The existence of a commitment to simplify existing and overlapping regulation when proposing new regulatory requirements	Suggested by Mandelkern report, this action connects the ex-ante and ex-post stages of regulatory quality programmes	Examination of simplification programmes. Alternatively, this question can be posed at a DBR meeting
[6] Use of RIA	Presence or absence of RIA as main tool for simplification	RIA is an efficient tool for simplification. This indicator shows coordination between two tools (simplification and RIA)	Examination of simplification programmes. Alternatively, this question can be posed at a DBR meeting
[7] Consistency with the requirements of other regulatory frameworks	The existence in the simplification strategy of a commitment to review regulation according to the consistency with other regulatory frameworks (e.g., WTO)	Coherence of regulations across levels of governance is an indicator of quality	Examination of simplification programmes. Alternatively, this question can be posed at a DBR meeting
[8] Review or sunset clauses in specific cases	The existence of a requirement to introduce review or sunset clauses when new rules meet specific conditions	It streamlines and keeps regulatory provisions up to date	Examination of simplification programmes. Alternatively, this question can be posed at a DBR meeting
[9] Public register	The existence of a public register of regulatory provisions accessible on-line	An inventory (available on-line) boosts access and transparency	Examination of simplification programmes. Alternatively, this question can be posed at a DBR meeting

1.F Strategy for access

Does the government's or Commission's strategy on access include the following elements:

1 Code of plain-language drafting
2 Annual regulatory agendas available on-line
3 Procedures to enable users to complain about the difficulties in complying with regulation
4 The citizens' right to access the documents underpinning a regulatory decision
5 A commitment to make the following documents available on-line through a single access portal:
   5.1 Documents supporting consultations
   5.2 Summary of consultation results
   5.3 Comments from interested parties
   5.4 Responses to comments
   5.5 All texts recalled in and supporting RIA

Table A.9 Purpose, interpretation and data collection of quality of access strategy indicators – access strategy

Indicator	What is measured	Interpretation	Data collection
[1] Code of plain-language drafting	The existence in the government's strategy of a code of plain-language drafting	Code of plain language in drafting regulation is a practical step to increase access to regulation and regulatory transparency	Examination of access programmes. Alternatively, this question can be posed at a DBR meeting
[2] Annual regulatory agendas available on-line	The existence in the strategy of an annual regulatory agenda available on-line	Annual regulatory agendas enhance the transparency of the regulatory process as well as its predictability, allowing business sufficient time to participate in consultation	Examination of access programmes. Alternatively, this question can be posed at a DBR meeting
[3] Complaint procedures	The existence of specific procedures that enable citizens to complain about the difficulties they have experienced in complying with regulation	It shows that the government has a commitment to enhancing access by making citizens' voice heard	Examination of access programmes. Alternatively, this question can be posed at a DBR meeting
[4] Rights to access documents	The presence of a formal right of citizens to access the documents underpinning a rule	It shows a commitment to transparency and access. Most importantly, rights can be enforced by courts	Examination of access programmes. Alternatively, this question can be posed at a DBR meeting
[5] Documents available on-line through a single access portal	The existence in the strategy of a commitment to make the documents available on-line through a single access portal	Single access portal to all documents supporting the regulatory process enhance access and the transparency of the regulatory process	Examination of access programmes. Alternatively, this question can be posed at a DBR meeting

Notes

1 Communication from the Commission on the Precautionary Principle, COM (2000)1, available at http://europa.eu.int/comm/dgs/health_consumer/library/pub/pub07_en.pdf.
2 The Mandelkern (2001: 23) report recommends the application of a 'test of significance' of the likely effects, including potential financial costs and disproportionate impact, without, however, giving any reference to the magnitude.
3 As the Mandelkern (2001: 22, see note 1) report puts it, 'such estimations allow the benefits and costs to be calculated on an annual basis and to be discounted as appropriate'.
4 This means that new forms have been tested on small samples and simulation exercises on time needed to fill them in have been carried out, panels of specific stakeholders like consumers and firms, and when necessary tested on SMEs.
5 See Mandelkern (2001: 22).
6 See Mandelkern (2001: 39).

Appendix 3

System 2. Indicators for internal evaluation

This system contains two different sets of indicators: a checklist and indicators of real-world outcome.

Checklist

The objective of the checklist is to provide accurate monitoring of major regulations and activity in the areas of consultation, simplification and access. The checklist should be compiled every year by governments and the Commission in order to show how specific issues were taken care of and to show progress over time. Essentially, it arises out of the previous set of indicators on 'quality of the process', specifically on the following set of indicators:

- RIA guidance;
- consultation guidance;
- elements of simplification strategy;
- components of the access strategy.

2.A Regulatory impact assessment

For each preliminary RIA or road map
[For governments making use of the two-stage RIA]
  1 Does the preliminary RIA define the problem in terms of its magnitude, causes and the incentives of the various parties?
  2 Does it make use of explicit criteria to select the proposals deserving extended RIA?
  3 Does it perform the subsidiarity test (whether regulation, if needed at all, is more efficient at the EU, national, or sub-national level)?
  4 Does it check the compatibility of proposed national rules with the single-market legislation and the *acquis*?

For each (final – in the case of a two-stage approach) RIA report
Does RIA:

1. Make use of criteria to select (when applicable, on the basis of preliminary RIA or road maps) the proposals deserving RIA?
2. Use the maximisation of collective welfare as the main criterion of choice?
3. Define the problem in terms of its magnitude, causes and the incentives of the various parties?
4. Identify the baseline situation and its probable change over time sufficiently clearly to compare it with proposed changes?
5. Articulate policy objectives as measurable outcomes, goals or targets?
6. Justify government or Commission action considering the option of no action or of market solutions?
7. Identify all parties that are substantially affected by the change?
8. Estimate the lifetime of the policy or options?
9. Identify the negative impacts on all those affected for each option?
10. Include a risk–risk analysis comparing the risks of the present situation with those of possible solutions?
11. Provide evidence that consultation informed the assessment of different options?
12. Contain evidence of consultation with other governments and information on checks on overlapping regulations (for regulations likely to impact on other levels of governance)?
13. Express uncertainty about the future in terms of scenarios or probability?
14. Provide evidence of:
    1. an explicit set of values
    2. a framework, or
    3. a model
    to identify and assess the trade-offs (in terms of the Lisbon goals of growth, social cohesion and environmental protection) between alternative policy options? Discuss the distribution of the positive and negative impacts?
15. Assess different options with reference to how they will perform in terms of enforcement and compliance levels?
16. Analyse options in terms of their impacts on market structure and competition?
17. Include simulation, pilots and 'dry runs' of new forms (for regulations introducing new forms for citizens and firms)?
18. Provide – when relevant – a discussion of the distribution of the negative and positive impacts (among different groups of people and/or different geographical areas)?
19. Justify why no review clause is proposed (the default case being that there is a review clause in proposed regulation[1])?
20. Contain procedures for monitoring and evaluating ex-post the extent to which the regulation meets its objectives
21. Contain evidence of external peer review (for the most important regulations)?
22. Include a contact name and website where all underlying data used in RIA are available?

2.B Consultation

For each consultation of major regulations
Do the consultation reports (or consultation sections of an RIA) contain the following?
1 Evidence of compliance with the timetable for consultation
2 A consultation timetable and planning which enabled those affected to comment on the final assessment
3 Evidence of compliance with standards on how to deal with experts' advice at the stage of policy formulation
4 Justification of the methodology chosen for consultation
5 Evidence of use of innovative consultation methods – when potential participants have difficulty in participating in traditional ways
6 Evidence in consultation or RIA documentation that affected parties were involved in the discussion of the problem and the identification of the possible alternative solutions
7 Evidence in consultation or RIA documentation of the use of a procedure allowing the general public to participate in the consultation process
8 Evidence in consultation or RIA documentation of compliance with the principle that consultation goes beyond a one-off event
9 Presence in consultation or RIA documentation of supporting documents explaining the impact of different alternatives
10 Evidence of how the input provided by consultation was considered and responded to
11 A summary of the results of consultation

2.C Simplification

Has simplification activity in a given year delivered the following?
1 Meeting the annual timetable deadlines
2 Information on how quantifiable targets were met
3 Information on how change and the results of simplification were measured
4 Review of the simplification programme (at least every three years) in the light of the results achieved
5 Evidence that the introduction of major new legislation has been accompanied by the simplification of existing regulations
6 Use RIA for the simplification of major rules affecting business and/or citizens
7 Evidence that simplification of major regulations is consistent with the single market and WTO
8 Use of review or sunset clauses when new rules meet the following conditions:
   • Regulation was introduced at short notice
   • Regulation is based on the precautionary principle
   • Technology or market conditions are most likely to change
   • Regulation is a pilot project
   • Regulation confers rights upon the state
9 Public register of regulatory provisions is accessible on-line

2.D Access

Does the government's or Commission's activity on access in a given year include the following elements:
1 Code of plain-language drafting
2 Annual regulatory agendas available on-line
3 Evidence on the systematic use of procedures to enable users to complain about the difficulties in complying with regulation
4 Evidence that the right of citizens to access the documents underpinning a rule is exploited
5 Documents available on-line through a single access portal. For example:
    • Documents supporting consultations
    • Summary of consultation results
    • Comments from interested parties
    • Responses to comments
    • All texts recalled in and supporting RIA

Real-world outcome indicators
Turning to the set of indicators of real-world outcome, their purpose is to evaluate the quality of better regulation policies by looking at their impact. We suggest three classes of real-world indicators:
    • indicators of the impact of better regulation policies (section 2.E);
    • survey-based indicators (section 2.F);
    • indicators of economic outcomes (section 2.G).

2.E Indicators of the impact of better regulation policies

These are indicators tracking down the impact of better regulation policies and tools in critical areas. One has to be careful to distinguish real-world indicators that measure the impact of regulatory policies from real-world indicators that measure the impact of better regulation policies. An indicator like 'Percentage of annual deaths in industrial accidents avoided by new regulations' measures the impact of the former. However, our study is focused on the latter dimension. The key issue is whether the cost of producing a unit of benefits is declining. Accordingly, our indicators focus on this issue.

A classic, although limited, indicator is the reduction of regulatory costs. Within regulatory costs, there is a political determination in the EU to target a specific sub-set, that is, administrative burdens. The EU has made reference to the reduction of administrative burdens as a possible indicator. We have reservations about using this as either the only or the most important measure of quality. However, in the context of a broader set of measures, this could be a valuable indicator. Moreover, the fact that there is consensus in the EU on this measure makes it an obvious reference point.

1 [Estimate of total regulatory costs delivered by regulations for which RIAs were prepared in year xxxx] *divided by* [Estimate of total regulatory benefits delivered by regulations for which RIAs were prepared in year xxxx]
2 [Net benefits delivered by regulations for which RIAs were prepared in year t] *divided by* [Net benefits delivered by regulations for which RIAs were prepared in year $t-1$]

3 Total cost reduction resulting from simplification in year xxxx
4 Annual rate of reduction in the total administrative burdens stemming from
   EU legislation (assuming a quantifiable target to reduce the total administrative
   burdens by 25 per cent in five years – an objective pursued in some countries
   such as the Netherlands and Belgium – the value of this rate is 5 per cent)
5 [Cost of administrative procedures eliminated in year t] *divided by* [Cost of
   administrative procedures eliminated in year $t-1$]

2.F Survey-based indicators

As illustrated throughout the book (chapter 2 in particular), one important set of
measures of impact should target changes in the behaviour of regulators and key
stakeholders. Although it is impossible to measure behavioural change at reason-
able cost, surveys of attitudes and perceptions show changes in thinking and culture
that inform behaviour. We discussed the limitations of surveys in chapter 3, but we
also highlighted their strengths. Consequently, we propose a limited set of survey
measures.

We propose a set of indicators which have either been already gathered *ad hoc*,
for special Eurobarometers, or which can be gathered by the EBTP.[2] These indicators
should be used in a trend perspective, that is, across time. It is more important to
measure progress (or lack of it) across time than to establish ex-ante thresholds.

1 Percentage of citizens who think that their views are taken on board in the
   development of single-market and enterprise policy in the EU.[3]
2 Percentage of firms which think that the quality of regulation in the EU (including both EU and domestic rules) has improved over the last three years, making
   it easier to do business in Europe.[4]
3 Percentage of firms which think that regulators consult the business sector appropriately before taking decisions on new regulations.
4 Percentage of firms which think that participation in EU-level consultation
   makes an impact on the final decision
5 Percentage of firms which say that they have participated at least once over the
   last five years in EU-level consultation
6 Percentage of firms which think that the EU better regulation policy has an
   impact in opening markets, in making it easier to compete and in generating
   competition in the manufacturing sector
7 Percentage of firms which think that the EU better regulation policy has an
   impact in opening markets, in making it easier to compete and in generating
   competition in the service sector
8 Percentage of firms which think that the EU better regulation policy has an
   impact in opening markets, in making it easier to compete and in generating
   competition in the professions
9 Percentage of firms which think that in last three years restrictions and obstacles
   to their business have disappeared altogether or been significantly reduced
10 Percentage of firms which think that regulatory changes at the EU level are
   predictable
11 Percentage of firms which think that access to information on the single market
   has improved over the last three years or so

Survey of regulators

There is no systematic survey of regulators at the moment. We would suggest that the Commission consider a biannual survey. We do not prescibe particular contents of a survey. However, to illustrate with an example, we tentatively suggest the following survey questions:

Percentage of regulators who think that RIA has the following impact:

1 Makes policy formulation more transparent
2 Speeds up/delays policy implementation
3 Reduces conflict at the stage of policy formulation
4 Reduces conflict at the stage of policy implementation
5 Is more likely to represent the preferences of affected citizens
6 Increases the likelihood that the final policy decision will be lower cost
7 Increases the likelihood that the final policy decision will be more likely to achieve policy goals

Percentage of regulators who think that RIA produces a policy that is:

8 more likely to generate a consensus among affected entities
9 more likely to be based on economic analysis
10 more likely to check one risk against other possible risks
11 more responsive to technological innovation
12 more likely to create open markets
13 more likely to create fewer trade controversies in transatlantic relations

2.G Indicators of economic outcomes

These are discussed in detail in chapter 3. In the context of this study, indicators of economic outcomes are very useful, but caveats should be considered. They are an important conceptual link between better regulation policies and the Lisbon goals. The critical issue is whether indicators of economic outcome are correlated with better regulation policies – controlling for spurious correlation. In our view, it is eminently a matter of long versus short causal chains. Some indicators (e.g., employment levels) can be linked to better regulation policies only via long causal chains, for example by arguing that 'better regulation' policies create the preconditions for better regulatory policies, that better rules produce a better business environment and flexible labour markets, that firms respond to the environment by investing, and that investment in the long term produces more jobs. At each step of this long causal chain one has to add *ceteris paribus*. A high number of *ceteris paribus* assumptions make the long causal chain unrealistic. In contrast, the chain between better regulation policies and the flexibility of the internal market is shorter and more realistic.

We distinguish between composite measures and simple measures. In the case of composite indicators, we specify the causal chain going from better regulation policies to the indicator. The indicators we propose should be measured across time to evaluate progress (or lack of it) and whether better regulation policies are contributing effectively to the Lisbon agenda. Hence we propose a consideration of the rate of change of the following indicators.

Composite indicators

[1] Internal market index
Causal chain: Better regulation policy produces better regulatory policies. This should be reflected in the decreasing importance of economic interventionism (state aid should decrease) and in open markets for the utilities. Consequently, the price of gas, electricity and telecommunications should decrease. Investment in an open and flexible internal market should increase. The internal market index is a composite measure of these variables.

Description: 'The Internal Market Index is intended to track the progress of the EU Internal Market towards becoming a fully functioning market' (European Commission, 2004c: 20). The index is composed of twelve 'individual indicators, which are all considered relevant to the Internal Market's development', as set out below; an indication is also given of the relative importance of each indicator (European Commission, 2004c: 20). It is presented each year on the Internal Market Scorecard, the publication edited by DG Internal Market. The individual indicators are the following (Tarantola *et al.*, 2002: 25):

1 sectoral and *ad hoc* state aid (as a percentage of GDP)
2 value of published public procurement (as a percentage of GDP)
3 telecommunications costs (in euros)
4 electricity prices (in euros)
5 gas prices (in euros)
6 relative price level of private final consumption, including indirect taxes
7 intra-EU foreign direct investment inward flows (as a percentage of GDP)
8 intra-EU trade (as a percentage of GDP)
9 active population in a Member State (aged 15–64) originally coming from another Member State (per capita)
10 value of pension fund assets (as a percentage of GDP)
11 retail lending interest rates over savings interest rates ratio
12 postal tariffs (20 g standard letter) (in euros)

The aggregation method is twofold. Firstly, there is a preliminary treatment of data in order to get the percentage year-to-year differences for each indicator. The resulting data are processed using the statistical method of principal components analysis.[5] This is a useful method 'to weigh the influence of each variable on the final score' (Joint Research Centre of the European Commission, 2002: 25).[6]

[2] Indicators of product market regulation
Causal chain: Better regulation policy delivers better regulatory policies. In consequence, the overall extent of regulation should diminish as a result of the systematic use of RIA, simplification, consultation and access. Smarter institutions can see the benefits of using market-friendly alternatives to regulation.

Description: Indicators of product market regulation have been developed by the OECD. They are discussed in chapter 3. These indicators rely on a detailed database covering both economic and administrative types of regulation and measures the extent of regulation. The database, set up in 1998, has been updated. A new dataset was released in April 2005 (see chapter 3). The index facilitates the evaluation of regulatory tools and can be applied to specific policies (different but related to better regulation policy, e.g. innovation policy).

[3] Summary innovation index (innovation scorecard)
Causal chain: Better regulation policy produces better regulatory policies. In turn, good regulation stimulates innovation.

Description: This index is produced by the Commission (DG Research).[7] It builds on the 'structural indicators' but with the aim of focusing on innovation policy. The Summary Innovation Index (SII) for a given country is equal to the number of indicators that are more than 20 per cent above the EU overall mean, minus the number of indicators that are more than 20 per cent below. The SII is adjusted for differences in the number of available indicators for each country; the index can vary between +10 (all indicators are above average) to –10 (all indicators are below average).

[4] Investment in the knowledge-based economy

[5] Performance in the knowledge-based economy
Causal chain: Better regulation policy produces better regulatory policies. In turn, good regulations stimulate gross fixed capital formation, investment in new sectors like e-commerce and overall productivity. These variables are included in these two complex measures. However, there are other variables for which the causal linkage is not strong. Specifically, the causal chain is weaker in relation to variables like spending on education or number of researchers.

Description: Both 'indicators attempt to capture the complex, multidimensional nature of the knowledge-based economy by aggregating a number of key variables, and expressing the result in the form of an overall index' (European Commission, 2003g). In other words, they measure Europe's performance in research and innovation.

DG Research and the Joint Research Centre collect both indexes.

Index [4] is composed of the following seven sub-indicators:
- domestic expenditure on research and development (per capita);
- number of PhDs (number of new science and technology PhDs per capita);
- number of researchers (number of researchers per capita);
- gross fixed capital formation (excluding buildings) (per capita),
- the share of e–government;
- educational spending;
- lifelong learning.

   'All sub-indicators are measured per capita to neutralise the effect of the size of the countries.' (Joint Research Centre of the European Commission, 2002: 27)

Index [5] is composed of five sub-indicators:
* overall productivity (GDP per hour worked);
* patents (share of EPO and USPTO patents);
* scientific publications per capita;
* e-commerce;
* schooling success rate.

The indexes are based on the same aggregation technique – a three-stage methodology. The first step is to calculate the mean and the dispersion index (standard deviation) for each indicator. The second step consists of obtaining 'country by country and year by year the original value for each indicator', which 'are converted by "centring" them on this mean and dividing them by this dispersion index'. Finally, 'the value of the composite indicator for each country and for each year is the weighted average of the values of all the indicators' (Joint Research Centre of the European Commission, 2002: 27).

Both indicators are contained in the DG Research publication *Key Figures* on science, technology and innovation.[8] Interestingly, this publication benchmarks the indexes for Europe with the USA and Japan. This is relevant in connection to the Lisbon agenda to make the EU the most competitive knowledge-based society in the world.

Thus, [4] and [5] could also be measured in the following way:

4 – *alternative measurement*. [Rate of change of: knowledge-based investment (EU)] *divided by* [knowledge-based investment (USA)]

5 – *alternative measurement*. [Rate of change of: knowledge-based performance (EU)] *divided by* [knowledge-based performance (USA)]

To sum up, [1] and [2] have a relatively robust causal chain. [3], [4] and [5] provide useful information, but the causal chain with better regulation is weaker, especially for [4] and [5]. Accordingly, they should not be seen as key indicators to gauge the success or failure of better regulation policies. Instead, [3], [4] and [5] should be considered important background indicators. They provide a direct link with the Lisbon strategy, although their value is only in minor part determined by better regulation policies.

Single measures

Single structural indicators can be used track the progress made in the Lisbon strategy. They are key measures of real-world outcome, although it is impossible to establish a clear causal relationship between each of them and better regulation policies. We suggest they are considered across time and with reference to US performance.

Annual rate of change of the following indicators:
1 Industry-level multifactor productivity growth (collected by the OECD)
2 Variation in the net growth of start-ups (new firms minus firms that have ceased activity) (collected by Eurostat)
3 Rate of investment in high-growth sectors (telecommunications and bio-technology)
4 Time needed to set up a new firm (collected by World Bank, but not every year)
5 Administrative costs to start up a new firm (collected by World Bank, but not every year)
6 Number of procedures to hire (to fire) the first (nth) employee (collected by World Bank, but not every year)
7 Time needed to hire (to fire) the first (nth) employee (collected by World Bank, but not every year)
8 Administrative costs to hire (to fire) the first (nth) employee (collected by World Bank, but not every year)

Notes

1 See Mandelkern (2001: 22).
2 See chapter 6 and http://ec.europa.eu/yourvoice/ebtp/index_en.htm.
3 This question draws and expands on previous experience with Eurobarometer. In October 2001 Eurobarometer reported on the percentage of citizens who would like to take part in a 'dialogue on Europe': 26 per cent said that they would, but 62 per cent said that they would not; 29 per cent agreed with the statement that 'my view would not be taken into account anyway' and 17 per cent agreed that 'it would be a waste of time'.
4 The reason for not making a distinction between EU rules and domestic rules is that more often than not the firm cannot distinguish between EU rules, the domestic implementation of EU rules and domestic rules.
5 This is a statistical methodology often used in the construction of complex indicators.
6 For more details on this methodology see Joint Research Centre of the European Commission (2002).
7 See http://trendchart.cordis.lu/scoreboard2003/html/inno_index.html#.
8 See ftp://ftp.cordis.europa.eu/pub/indicators/docs/ind_kf0304.pdf.

Appendix 4

System 3. Indicators for external evaluation

Evaluation refers to the judgements about the ability of the actions to solve or to cope with collective problems. Policy evaluation answers the question of whether a policy is effective in dealing with collective problems. For reasons of credibility and quality assurance, policy evaluation should never be left in the hands of those who are evaluated. Hence policy evaluation is performed by external parties, typically professionally trained evaluators and academics.

In the case of the Commission, this means that, although monitoring (the collection of data on programmes' activities) and internal evaluation (the collection of information and data on the performance of programmes) can be performed by the Secretariat-General, full-blown evaluation must involve external parties. In chapter 7 we argued for pluralistic evaluation. A plurality of evaluations performed by private sector think tanks and organisations representing specific interests (like non-governmental organisations, trade unions and employers' associations) would provide a socially robust evaluation. We contrasted this approach with the opinion of those who press for one formal EU body in charge of auditing, but added that one does not exclude the other.

Indicators are only a component of external evaluation. No system of indicators can substitute for the independent and professional judgement of an evaluator. Indeed, indicators are only one of the possible tools of an evaluation (others include case studies, in-depth interviews, surveys, etc.).

For the purpose of external evaluation, simple indicators like the presence or absence of formal review of better regulation policies (at the macro level) and peer review and replicable models in RIA are indispensable. Questions could be added in order to ascertain whether exercises like peer review actually take place or whether economic analysis is really replicable.[1]

As shown in chapter 6, on the EU initiatives, there are several evaluation studies and policy appraisals under way or recently completed on the quality of the Commission's IAs. There are also reports on the quality of RIA and consultation in countries like the USA, Sweden and the UK. They use a combination of scorecards and more sophisticated tools. In some cases, like the evaluation of the Commission's IAs performed by Lee and Kirckpatrick, a small team (two coders) prepares the responses to the questions on the checklists. In some cases coders talk to each other and reach agreement on the response to a specific question on the checklist, while in other cases they work independently.

Indicators to be used in external evaluation make use of the subjective judgement of the evaluator or complex calculations where there is a considerable degree of subjectivity in how one compiles the data. Take the examples of RIA and consultation: to answer questions about the accuracy of cost estimates and the quality of consultation with stakeholders may require complex models, ex-post analyses and interviews with the stakeholders.

Indicators for external evaluation can be derived from recent studies on the quality of RIA conducted both in North America and in the EU. These studies are reviewed elsewhere in this book. Only a professional evaluator can collect this type of indicator, possibly in teams of coders to reduce subjectivity. It is also useful to provide measures across time and not only across space (i.e., across the Member States).

External evaluation should contain an explicit appraisal of the quality of the indicators arising out of open coordination processes and make non-binding suggestions for improvement. Thus, the technical appraisal of indicators should be conducted within external policy evaluation, while the political judgement should remain in the hands of policy-makers.

Examples of indicators suitable for system 3

1 Quality of problem definition: is the problem clearly defined and explained?
2 Quality of market analysis (understanding of how a market works, role of information and signals, how prices may shift the impact of a rule from one stakeholder to another)
3 Quality of competitiveness tests applied to proposed regulations
4 Quality of economic analysis – for example, a professional evaluator can gauge whether cost–benefit analysis of options should have been used instead of cost-effectiveness analysis
5 Quality of economic data used in RIA (reliability, credibility, etc.)
6 Quality of risk models used in RIA
7 Quality of external peer review in RIA
8 Transparency of the criteria used to handle the trade-offs of the Lisbon strategy
9 Accuracy of consultation – for example, whether the views expressed in consultation are described and attributed to the appropriate stakeholders[2]
10 Appropriateness of consultation methods (focus groups, surveys, panels, etc.)
11 Quality of the response provided to the issues raised by the stakeholders during consultation

Notes

1 Obviously, this implies also the assessment of the quality of such evaluations but this problem is quite well known in the evaluators' community (see www.evalsed.info/frame_guide_part2.asp, the section 'Managing quality assurance and quality control', in particular box 2.12).
2 This question has been used in Canada in the context of an evaluation of the quality of RIAs. See Regulatory Consulting Group and Delphi Group (2000).

References

ACTAL (Dutch Advisory Board on Administrative Burdens) (2003) *Work Programme 2004*, The Hague: ACTAL, www.actal.nl.

Alesina, A. and R. Perotti (2004) 'The European Union: a politically incorrect view', *Journal of Economic Perspectives*, 18:4, 27–48.

Alesina, A., S. Ardagna, G. Nicoletti and F. Schiantarelli (2003) *Regulation and Investment*, Economic Department Working Paper No. 41, Paris: OECD.

Allio, L., B. Ballantine and D. Hudig (2004) *Achieving a New Regulatory Culture in the European Union – An Action Plan*, EPC Working Paper No. 10, Brussels: EPC, www.theepc.net.

Allison, G. T. (1971) *Essence of Decision: Explaining the Cuban Missile Crisis*, Boston: Little, Brown.

Ambler, T., F. Chittenden and M. Obodovski (2004) *Are Regulators Raising Their Game? UK Regulatory Impact Assessment in 2002/3*, London: British Chambers of Commerce, www.chamberonline.co.uk/policy/issues/red_tape/redtape2004.pdf.

Argy, S. and M. Johnson (2003) *Mechanisms for Improving the Quality of Regulations: Australia in an International Context*, Productivity Commission Staff Working Paper, Melbourne: Productivity Commission.

ASA (Agence pour la Simplification) (2004) *Fil Conducteur pour le Test Kafka*, Brussels: ASA, www.kafka.be/doc/1108545328-6345.pdf.

Atkinson, A. B., E. Marlier and B. Nolan (2004) 'Indicators and targets for social inclusion in the European Union', *Journal of Common Market Studies*, 42:1, 47–75.

Ayres, I. and J. Braithwaite (1992) *Responsive Regulation: Transcending the Deregulation Debate*, Oxford: Oxford University Press.

Baldwin, R. (2005) 'Is better regulation smarter regulation?', *Public Law*, autumn, 485–511.

Baldwin, R. and M. Cave (1999) *Understanding Regulation*, Oxford: Oxford University Press.

Baldwin, R., C. Scott and C. Hood (eds) (1998) *A Reader on Regulation*, Oxford: Oxford University Press.

Baldwin, R., C. Hood and H. Rothstein (2000) 'Assessing the Dangerous Dogs Act: when does a regulatory law fail?', *Public Law*, summer, 282–334.

Bernauer, T. and L. Caduff (2004) 'In whose interest? Pressure group politics, economic competition and regulation', *Journal of Public Policy*, 24:1, 99–126.

Better Regulation Task Force (2003) *Champions of Better Regulation – Annual Report 2001/2002*, London: Better Regulation Task Force, http://publications. brc.gov.uk/.

Better Regulation Task Force (2005) *Less Is More. Reducing Burdens, Improving Outcomes*, London: Better Regulation Task Force, http://publications.brc.gov.uk/.

Black, J. (2005) 'The emergence of risk-based regulation and the new public risk management in the United Kingdom', *Public Law*, autumn, 512–48.

Borras, S. and K. Jacobsson (2004) 'The open method of co-ordination and new governance patterns in the EU', *Journal of European Public Policy*, 11:2, 185–208.

Botero, J., S. Djankov, R. La Porta, F. Lopez-De-Silanes and A. Shleifer (2003) *The Regulation of Labor*, National Bureau of Economic Research Working Paper No. 9756, Cambridge, MA: National Bureau of Economic Research, http://papers. nber.org/papers/w9756.pdf.

Brady, H. E. and D. C. Collier (eds) (2004) *Rethinking Social Inquiry: Diverse Tools, Shared Standards*, Lanham, MD: Rowman and Littlefield.

Braithwaite, J. and P. Drahos (2000) *Global Business Regulation*, Cambridge: Cambridge University Press.

Brown, M., G. Morgan and S. Farrow (2004) 'Expert assessment of the performance of the US system for environmental regulation', *Journal of Risk Research*, 7:5, 506–21.

Brunsson, N. (1989) *The Organization of Hypocrisy. Talk, Decisions and Actions in Organizations*, Chichester: Wiley.

Buchanan, J. M. and G. Tullock (1975) 'Polluters' profits and political response: direct controls versus taxes', *American Economic Review*, 65:1, 139–47.

Bulmer, S. and S. Padgett (2005) 'Policy transfer in the European Union: an institutionalist perspective', *British Journal of Political Science*, 35:1, 103–26.

Bulmer, S. and C. M. Radaelli (2005) 'The Europeanisation of public policy?', in C. Lesquene and S. Bulmer (eds), *The Member States of the European Union*, Oxford: Oxford University Press.

Chittenden, F., S. Kauser and P. Poutziouris (2002) 'Regulatory burdens of small business: a literature review', Department of Trade and Industry Small Business Service Research Series, Manchester: Manchester Business School, www.sbs.gov. uk/SBS_Gov_files/researchandstats/Regulation-Report.pdf.

Coen, D. (2005) 'Business–regulatory relations: learning to play regulatory games in European utility markets', *Governance*, 18:3, 373–98.

Conway, P., V. Janod and G. Nicoletti (2005) *Product Market Regulation in OECD Countries: 1998 to 2003*, Economic Department Working Paper No. 419, ECO/ WKP(2005)6, Paris: OECD.

Council of the European Union (2003) 'Interinstitutional agreement on better law-making', Legislative Acts and other Instruments (2003/C321/01), *Official Journal of the European Union*, 31 December, C321/1–5, http://europa.eu.int/eur-lex/pri/ en/oj/dat/2003/c_321/c_32120031231en00010005.pdf.

Council of the European Union (2004a) 'Outcome of proceedings of the Competitiveness Council on 24 September 2004 – Council conclusions', Document 12898/04, Brussels, 30 September.

Council of the European Union (2004b) 'Note from Presidency to High Level Working Party on Competitiveness and Growth: Follow-up to the subgroup report on the competitiveness dimension of impact assessments', DS 441/04, Brussels, 18 June.

Council of the European Union (2005a) 'Integrated guidelines: Broad economic policy guidelines', Document 10667/05, Brussels, 28 June.

Council of the European Union (2005b) 'Better regulation – Pilot project on Council impact assessment', Document 6164/05, 18 February.

Council of the European Union (2006) 'Better regulation – Handling of impact assessments in Council', Document 9382/06, 15 May.

Crain, W. M. and T. D. Hopkins (2001) *The Impact of Regulatory Costs on Small Firms*, a report for the Office of Advocacy, US Small Business Administration, Washington, DC: SBA, www.sba.gov/advo/research/rs207tot.pdf.

Cropper, M. L., W. N. Evans, S. J. Berardi, M. M. Ducla-Soares and P. R. Portney (1992) 'The determinants of pesticide regulation. A statistical analysis of EPA decision-making', *Journal of Political Economy*, 100:1, 175–87.

Danish Commerce and Companies Agency (2003) *International Study: Efforts to Reduce Administrative Burdens and Improve Business Regulation*, Copenhagen: Danish Commerce and Companies Agency.

Dawson, J. W. and J. J. Seater (2004) *Regulation and the Macroeconomy*, Department of Economics, Appalachian State University Working Paper No. 05-02, Boone, NC: Department of Economics, Appalachian State University, http://papers.ssrn.com/sol3/papers.cfm?abstract_id=495682.

DBR (Directors of Better Regulation) (2004) *A Comparative Analysis of RIA in Ten EU Countries*, report presented to the DBR meeting, Dublin, May, http://www.betterregulation.ie/index.asp?docID=66.

Derthick, M. and P. Quirk (1985) *The Politics of Deregulation*, Washington, DC: Brookings Institution.

De Vil, G. and C. Kegels (2001) *Les Charges administratives en Belgique pour l'annee 2000*, rapport final, Brussels: Bureau Federal du Plan, www.plan.be/en/pub/pp/PP092/PP092fr.pdf.

Djankov, S., R. La Porta, F. Lopez de Silanes and A. Shleifer (2001) *The Regulation of Entry*, CEPR Discussion Paper No. 2953, London: Centre for Economic Policy Research, http://ssrn.com/abstract=283839.

Dudley, S. E. and M. Warren (2005) *Upward Trend in Regulation Continues: An Analysis of the U.S. Budget for Fiscal Years 2005 and 2006*, Regulators' Budget Report No. 27, Mercatus Center at George Mason University, and Weidenbaum Center on the Economy, Government, and Public Policy at Washington University in St Louis.

Eberlein, B. and E. Grande (2005) 'Beyond delegation: transnational regulatory regimes and the EU regulatory state', *Journal of European Public Policy*, 12:1, 89–112.

Egan, M. (2001) *Constructing a European Market: Standards, Regulation and Governance*, Oxford: Oxford University Press.

European Commission (2001a) *European Governance – A White Paper*, COM (2001)428 final, Brussels: EC, 25 July, http://ec.europa.eu/governance/white_paper/index_en.htm.

European Commission (2001b) *Internal Market Scoreboard No. 9*, Commission Staff Working Paper, Brussels: EC.

European Commission (2001c) *Simplifying and Improving the Regulatory Environment*, COM(2001)726 final, Brussels: EC, 5 December.

European Commission (2001d) *Access to European Commission Documents – A Citizen's Guide*, Brussels: EC, http://ec.europa.eu/transparency/citguide/docs/en.pdf.

European Commission (2002a) *Action Plan. Simplifying and Improving the Regulatory Environment*, COM(2002)278 final, Brussels: EC, 5 June.

European Commission (2002b) *Communication from the Commission on Impact Assessment*, COM(2002)276 final, Brussels: EC, 5 June, http://europa.eu/press_room/presspacks/constit/276-4en.pdf.

European Commission (2002c) *Impact Assessment in the Commission Internal Guidelines on the New Impact Assessment Procedure Developed for the Commission Service*, Brussels: EC, October.

European Commission (2002d) *Communication from the Commission on the Collection and Use of Expertise by the Commission: Principles and Guidelines – 'Improving the Knowledge Base for Better Policies'*, COM(2002)713 final, Brussels: EC, 11 November.

European Commission (2002e) *Towards a Reinforced Culture of Consultation and Dialogue – Proposal for General Principles and Minimum Standards for Consultation and Minimum Standards of Interested Parties by the Commission*, COM(2002)704 final, Brussels: EC, 11 December.

European Commission (2003a) *Benchmarking Enterprise Policy – Results from the 2003 Scoreboard. Competitiveness and Benchmarking*, Commission Staff Working Document, SEC(2002)1278 (November), Brussels: Directorate-General for Enterprise.

European Commission (2003b) *A Handbook for Impact Assessment in the Commission – How to Do an Impact Assessment*, Brussels, EC, http://ec.europa.eu/governance/impact/docs/imp_ass_how_to_en.pdf.

European Commission (2003c) *A Handbook for Impact Assessment in the Commission – How to Do an Impact Assessment – Technical Annexes*, Brussels: EC, http://ec.europa.eu/governance/impact/docs/imp_ass_tech_anx_en.pdf.

European Commission (2003d) *Better Lawmaking 2003 – 11th Report*, COM(2003)770 final, Brussels: EC, 12 December.

European Commission (2003e) *Updating and Simplifying the Community Acquis*, COM(2003)71 final, Brussels, EC, 11 February.

European Commission (2003f) *First Report on the Implementation of the Framework Action 'Updating and Simplyfing the Community Acquis'*, COM(2003) 623 final, Brussels: EC, 24 October.

European Commission (2003g) *Key Figures 2003–2004. Towards a European Research Area Science, Technology and Innovation*, Brussels: EC, Directorate-General for Research, 2003 EUR 20735 EN, ftp://ftp.cordis.europa.eu/pub/indicators/docs/ind_kf0304.pdf.

European Commission (2004a) *Who Is Doing What on Better Regulation at EU Level – Organization Charts*, Commission working document compiled by the Secretariat-General TFAU-2 (Task Force Future of Union), Brussels: EC, 1 June.

European Commission (2004b) *Impact Assessment: Next Step in Support of Competitiveness and Sustainable Development*, Commission Staff Working Paper, SEC(2004)1377, Brussels: EC, 21 October.

European Commission (2004c) *Internal Market Scorecard No. 13*, Brussels: EC, July, http://ec.europa.eu/internal_market/score/docs/score13/score13-printed_en.pdf.

European Commission (2004d) *Internal Market DG, Policy Development, Strategic Programming and Coordination – Internal Market Strategy and Competitiveness,*

Internal Market Committee Better Regulation Expert Group, Summary Report – Annex 1, Brussels: EC, 18 May.

European Commission (2005a) *Better Regulation for Growth and Jobs in the European Union*, COM(2005) 97 final, Brussels: EC, 16 March.

European Commission (2005b) *Impact Assessment Guidelines*, SEC(2005)791, Brussels: EC, 15 June.

European Commission (2005c) *Annexes to Impact Assessment Guidelines*, SEC(2005)791, Brussels: EC, 15 June.

European Commission (2005d) *Report from the Commission 'Better Lawmaking 2004' pursuant to Article 9 of the Protocol on the Application of the Principles of Subsidiarity and Proportionality (12th Report)'*, COM(2005) 98 final, Brussels: EC, 21 March.

European Parliament (2004) *Report on Assessment of the Impact of Community Legislation and the Consultation Procedures*, Rapporteur: Bert Doorn, Committee on Legal Affairs and the Internal Market, Final A5-0221/2004, Luxembourg/Brussels: European Parliament, 24 March.

European Policy Centre (2001) *Regulatory Impact Analysis: Improving the Quality of EU Regulatory Activity*, EPC Occasional Paper, Brussels: EPC, September.

European Policy Forum (2003) *NGOs, Democratisation and the Regulatory State*, London: EPF.

European Policy Forum (2005) *Governance and NGOs of the Future*, London: EPF.

Farrow, S. and C. Copeland (2003) 'Evaluating central regulatory institutions', paper presented to the OECD expert meeting on Regulatory Performance: Ex-Post Evaluation of Regulatory Policies, OECD, Paris, 22 September.

Froud, J., R. Boden, A. Ogus and P. Stubbs (1998) *Controlling the Regulators*, London: Macmillan.

GAO (General Accounting Office) (1998) *Regulatory Reform – Agencies Could Improve Development, Documentation and Clarity of Regulatory Economic Analyses*, Washington, DC: US General Accounting Office.

GAO (1999) *Regulatory Accounting – Analysis of OMB's Reports on the Costs and Benefits of Federal Regulation*, Washington, DC: US General Accounting Office.

GAO (2000) *Regulatory Reform – Procedural and Analytical Requirements in Federal Rulemaking*, Washington, DC: US General Accounting Office.

GAO (2001) *Regulatory Management – Communication About Technology-Based Innovations Can Be Improved*, Washington, DC: US General Accounting Office.

GAO (2003) *Rulemaking – OMB's Role in Reviews of Agencies' Draft Rules and the Transparency of Those Reviews*, Washington, DC: US General Accounting Office.

GAO (2004a) *Performance Budgeting – PMB's Performance Rating Tool Presents Opportunity and Challenges for Evaluating Program Performance*, Washington, DC: US General Accounting Office.

GAO (2004b) *Performance Budgeting – Observation on the Use of OMB's Program Assessment Rating Tool for the Fiscal Year 2004 Budget*, Washington, DC: US General Accounting Office.

GAO (2005) *Economic Performance: Highlights of a Workshop on Economic Performance Measures*, GAO-05-796SP, Washington, DC: US General Accounting Office.

Gatti, J. F. (1981) 'An overview of the problem of government regulation', in J. F. Gatti (ed.), *The Limits of Government Regulation*, New York: Academic Press.

Gilardi, F. (2002) 'Policy credibility and delegation to independent regulatory agencies: a comparative empirical analysis', *Journal of European Public Policy*, 9:6, 873–93.

Goff, B. (1996) *Regulation and Macroeconomic Performance*, Boston: Kluwer Academic.

Goodstein, E. (1997) 'Polluted data', *American Prospect*, 8:35.

Government of Canada (1994) *Assessing Regulatory Alternatives*, Ottawa: Regulatory Affairs and Orders in Council Secretariat, www.pco-bcp. gc.ca/raoics-srdc/docs/publications/assessing_reg_alternatives_e.pdf.

Government of Canada (2002a) *The Government of Canada Action Plan*, Ottawa: Regulatory Affairs and Orders in Council Secretariat, www.pco-bcp. gc.ca/raoics-srdc/.

Government of Canada (2002b) *Report on Law-Making and Governance*, Ottawa: Regulatory Affairs and Orders in Council Secretariat, www.pco-bcp. gc.ca/raoics-srdc/.

Grote, J. and B. Gbikpi (eds) (2002) *Participatory Governance. Political and Societal Implications*, Opladen: Leske and Budrich.

Gunningham, N. and P. Grabosky (1998) *Smart Regulation: Designing Environmental Policy*, Clarendon: Oxford.

Hahn, R. W. and M. Dudley (2004) *How Well Does the Government Do Cost–Benefit Analysis?*, Working Paper No. 04-01, Washington, DC: AEI–Brooking Joint Center for Regulatory Studies.

Hahn, R. W. and J. A. Hird (1991) 'The costs and benefits of regulation: review and synthesis', *Yale Journal on Regulation*, 8:1, 233–78.

Hahn, R. W. and R. E. Litan (2004) 'Counting regulatory benefits and costs: lessons for the US and Europe', *Journal of International Economic Law*, 8:2, 473–508.

Hahn, R. W. and C. R. Sunstein (2002) *A New Executive Order for Improving Federal Regulation? Deeper and Wider Cost–Benefit Analysis*, Working Paper No. 02-04, Washington, DC: AEI–Brooking Joint Center for Regulatory Studies.

Hahn, R. W., J. K. Burnett, Y. H. I. Chan, E. A. Mader and P. R. Moyle (2000) 'Assessing the quality of regulatory impact analyses', *Harvard Journal of Law and Public Policy*, 23:3, 859–85.

Hahn, R. W., R. P. Malik and M. Dudley (2004) *Reviewing the Government's Number on Regulation*, Working Paper No. 04-03, Washington, DC: AEI–Brooking Joint Center for Regulatory Studies, www.aei-brookings.org/admin/authorpdfs/page. php?id=321.

Hall, P. and R. Taylor (1996) 'Political science and the three new institutionalisms', *Political Studies*, 44:5, 936–57.

Harrington, W., R. D. Morgenstern and P. Nelson (2000) 'On the accuracy of regulatory cost estimates', *Journal of Policy Analysis and Management*, 19:2, 297–322.

Heinzerling, L. (1998) 'Regulatory costs of mythic proportions', *Yale Law Journal*, 107:7, 1981–2070.

Hellenic Presidency of the Council of the European Union (2003) *Report to the Ministers Responsible for Public Administration in the EU Member States on the Progress of the Implementation of the Mandelkern Report's Action Plan on Better Regulation*, Athens: Ad Hoc Group of Experts on Better Regulation.

High-Level Group on Competitiveness (2004) *Facing the Challenge – The Lisbon Strategy for Growth and Employment*, report from the Group chaired by Wim Kok, http://ec.europa.eu/growthandjobs/pdf/2004-1866-EN-complet.pdf.

HM Treasury (2005) *Reducing Administrative Burdens – Effective Inspections and Enforcement*, London: HM Treasury, www.hm-treasury.gov.uk.

Holzinger, K. and C. Knill (2005) 'Causes and conditions of cross-national policy convergence', *Journal of European Public Policy*, 12:5, 775–96.

Hood, C., C. Scott, O. James, G. Jones and T. Travers (1999) *Regulation Inside Government: Waste-Watchers, Quality Police and Sleaze-Busters*, Oxford: Oxford University Press.

House of Common (2003) *The Operation of the Regulatory Reform Act 2001: A Progress Report. First Special Report of Session 2002–03*, HC 908, London: The Stationery Office, www.publications.parliament.uk.

Hoyle, D. (2000) *ISO 9000 Quality System Development Handbook*, Oxford: Butterworth-Heinemann.

Irish, Dutch, Luxembourg and UK Presidencies of the European Union (2004) *Joint Initiative on Regulatory Reform*, 26 January, www.hm-treasury.gov.uk/media//47C54/jirf_0104.pdf.

Irish, Dutch, Luxembourg, UK, Austrian and Finnish Presidencies of the European Union (2005) *Advancing Regulatory Reform in Europe*, 7 December, www.hm-treasury.gov.uk/media/95A/52/6presidencies.pdf.

Jacobs, C. (2005) *Improving the Quality of Regulatory Impact Assessments in the UK*, Centre on Regulation and Competition, University of Manchester, Working Paper No. 102.

Jaffe, A. B., S. Peterson, P. R. Portney and R. N. Stavins (1995) 'Environmental regulation and the competitiveness of US manufacturing: what does the evidence tell us?', *Journal of Economic Literature*, 33:1, 132–63.

Janssen, N., P. de Ruijter and M. Gramberger (2002) *Scenarios and Dynamic Policy – Summary of a Study into the Scenario Methodology as an Instrument for Regulatory Impact Assessment and the Development of Dynamic Policy*, Amsterdam: De Ruijter Management, www.deruijter.net/en/articles/pdf/scenariosum.pdf.

Johnson, P. L. (2000) *ISO 9000: The Year 2000 and Beyond*, New York: McGraw-Hill.

Joint Research Centre of the European Commission (2002) *State-of-the-Art Report on Current Methodologies and Practices for Composite Indicator Development*, paper prepared by the Applied Statistics Group, June 2002, Ispra: Institute for the Protection and Security of the Citizen Technological and Economic Risk Management.

Jordana, J. and D. Levi-Faur (2004) 'The politics of regulation in the age of governance', in J. Jordana and D. Levi-Faur (eds), *The Politics of Regulation: Institutions and Regulatory Reforms for the Age of Governance*, Cheltenham: Edward Elgar.

Kaase, M. and K. Newton (1998) *Beliefs in Government*, Oxford: Oxford University Press.

Kagan, R. (2001) *Adversarial Legalism: The American Way of Law*, Cambridge, MA: Harvard University Press.

Kagan, R. A. and L. Axelrad (eds) (2000) *Regulatory Encounters: Multinational Corporations and American Adversial Legalism*, Berkeley, CA: University of California Press.

Kalt, J. P. and M. A. Zupan (1984) 'Capture and ideology in the economic theory of politics', *American Economic Review*, 74:3, 279–300.

Kaufmann, D., A. Kraay and M. Mastruzzi (2003) *Governance Matters III: Governance Indicators for 1996–2002*, World Bank Policy Research Working Paper No. 3106, Washington, DC: World Bank, www.worldbank.org/wbi/governance/pdf/govmatters3.pdf.

Kaufmann, D., A. Kraay and M. Mastruzzi (2005) *Governance Matters IV: Governance Indicators for 1996–2004*, World Bank Policy Research Working Paper No. 3630, Washington, DC: World Bank, www.worldbank.org/wbi/governance/pdf/GovMatters_IV_main.pdf.

Kelemen, D. R. and E. C. Sibbitt (2004) 'The globalization of American law', *International Organization*, 58:1, 103–36.

Kellermann, A. E., G. Ciavarini Azzi, R. Deighton-Smith, S. H. Jacobs and T. Koopmans *et al.* (eds) (1998) *Improving the Quality of Legislation*, The Hague: Kluwer Law International.

Kingdon, J. W. (1984) *Agendas, Alternatives and Public Policies*, New York: Harper Collins.

Knack, S. and M. Kugler (2002) *Constructing an Index of Objective Indicators of Good Governance*, Washington, DC: World Bank, www1.worldbank.org/publicsector/anticorrupt/FlagshipCourse2003/SecondGenerationIndicators.pdf.

Koedijk, K. and J. Kremers (1996) 'Market opening, regulation and growth in Europe', *Economic Policy*, 11:23, 443–68.

Lee, N. and C. Kirkpatrick (2004) *A Pilot Study on the Quality of European Commission Extendend Impact Assessment*, Manchester: Impact Assessment Research Centre, Institute for Development Policy and Management, University of Manchester.

Legislative Burden Department (2003) *Focus on Burden!*, The Hague: Ministry of Finance.

Levi-Faur, D. (2002) *Herding Towards a New Convention: On Herds, Shepherds, and Lost Sheep in the Liberalization of the Telecommunications and Electricity Industries*, Politics Paper No. W6-2002, Oxford: Nuffield College, University of Oxford, www.nuff.ox.ac.uk/Politics/papers/2002/w6/herding.pdf.

Levi-Faur, D. and S. Gilad (2004) 'The rise of the British regulatory state: transcending the privatization debate', *Comparative Politics*, 37:1, 105–24.

Levi-Faur, D. and J. Jordana (2005) 'The rise of regulatory capitalism: the global diffusion of a new order', *Annals of the American Academy of Political and Social Science*, 598:1, 200–17.

Levy, B. and P. T. Spiller (1994) 'The institutional foundations of regulatory commitment: a comparative analysis of telecommunications regulation', *Journal of Law, Economics, and Organization*, 10:2, 201–46.

Liberatore, A. (rapporteur) (2001) *Report of the Working Group on Democratising Expertise and Establishing Scientific Reference Systems*, Brussels: European Commission, http://europa.eu.int/comm/governance/areas/group2/report_en.pdf.

Lijphart, A. (1984) *Democracies: Patterns of Majoritarian and Consensus Government in Twenty-One Countries*, New Haven, CT: Yale University Press.

Lindblom, C. E. (1959) 'The science of muddling through', *Public Administration Review*, 19:2, 79–88.

Lindblom, C. E. (1990) *Inquiry and Change. The Troubled Attempt to Understand and Shape Society*, New Haven, CT: Yale University Press.

Lindblom, C. E. and E. J. Woodhouse (1993) *The Policy-Making Process*, 3rd edition, New York, Prentice-Hall.

Majone, G. (1989) *Evidence, Argument and Persuasion in the Policy Process*, New Haven, CT: Yale University Press.

Majone, G. (ed.) (1990) *Deregulation or Re-regulation? Regulatory Reform in Europe and the United States*, London: Pinter.

Majone, G. (1994) 'Comparing strategies of regulatory rapprochement', in OECD, *Regulatory Cooperation for an Interdependent World*, Paris: OECD.

Majone, G. (1996) *Regulating Europe*, London: Routledge.

Majone, G. (1999a) 'The regulatory state and its legitimacy problems', *West European Politics*, 22:1, 1–24.

Majone, G. (1999b) 'Regulation in comparative perspective', *Journal of Comparative Policy Analysis*, 1:3, 309–24.

Mandelkern (Group on Better Regulation) (2001) *Final Report*, Brussels, www.cabinetoffice.gov.uk/regulation/documents/europe/pdf/mandfinrep.pdf.

Mayoux, L. (2002) *What Do We Want to Know? Selecting Indicators*, Manchester: Enterprise Development Impact Assessment Information Service, Institute for Development Policy and Management (IDPM), Manchester University, and Women in Sustainable Enterprise Development Ltd (WISE Development), www.enterprise-impact.org.uk/informationresources/toolbox/selectingindicators.shtml.

McGarity, T. O. (1991) *Reinventing Rationality – The Role of Regulatory Analysis in the Federal Bureaucracy*, Cambridge: Cambridge University Press.

McGarity, T. O. and R. Ruttenberg (2002) 'Counting the cost of health, safety, and environmental regulation', *Texas Law Review*, 80:7, 2017.

McGarity, T. O. and S. A. Shapiro (1996), 'OSHA's critics and regulatory reform', *Wake Forest Law Review*, 31:3, 587–646.

Melnick, R. S. (1990) 'The politics of benefit–cost analysis', in P. Brett Hammond and R. Coppock (eds), *Valuing Health Risks, Costs, and Benefits for Environmental Decision-Making*, Washington, DC: National Academic Press.

Metcalfe, L. (2003) 'Regulatory management and governance', paper presented in the conference Impact Assessment in the European Union: Innovations, Quality and Good Regulatory Governance, Brussels: European Commission, DG Enterprise, 3 December.

Monti, M. (2005) 'What Germany and France must rediscover', *Financial Times*, 27 October, p. 19.

Moran, M. (2002) 'Review article: understanding the regulatory state', *British Journal of Political Science*, 32:2, 391–413.

Moran, M. (2003) *The British Regulatory State: High Modernism and Hyper Innovation*, Oxford: Oxford University Press.

Morgan, B. (2003) 'The economization of politics: meta-regulation as a form of nonjudicial legality', *Social and Legal Studies*, 12:4, 489–523.

Morrall, J. F. III (2003) *Saving Lives: A Review of the Record*, Washington, DC: AEI–Brooking Joint Center for Regulatory Studies, http://aei-brookings.org/admin/pdffiles/phpPc.pdf.

Mucciaroni, G. (1992) 'The garbage can model and the study of policy making: a critique', *Polity*, 24:3, 459–82.

NAO (National Audit Office) (2001) *Better Regulation: Making Good Use of*

Regulatory Impact Assessments, report by the Comptroller and Auditor General, HC 329, session 2001–02, London: The Stationery Office.

NAO (2004) *Evaluation of Regulatory Impact Assessments Compendium. Report 2003–04*, report by the Comptroller and Auditor General, HC 358, session 2003–2004, 4 March 2004, London: The Stationery Office, www.nao.org.uk/publications/nao_reports/03-04/0304358.pdf.

NAO (2005) *Evaluation of Regulatory Impact Assessments Compendium Report 2004–05*, report by the Comptroller and Auditor General, HC 341, session 2004–05, London: The Stationery Office.

Nicoletti, G. and F. L. Pryor (2001) *Subjective and Objective Measure of the Extent of Governmental Regulation*, Washington, DC: AEI–Brooking Joint Center for Regulatory Studies, www.aei-brookings.org/admin/authorpdfs/page.php?id=424.

Nicoletti, G., S. Scarpetta and O. Boylaud (2000) *Summary Indicators of Product Market Regulation with an Extension to Employment Protection Legislation*, Economics Department Working Paper No. 226, Paris: OECD.

NNR (Board of Swedish Industry and Commerce for Better Regulation) (2002) *How High is the Quality of the Swedish Central Government's Regulatory Impact Analysis (RIAs) in the Business Sector? The NNR Regulation Indicator for 2002*, Stockholm: NNR, www.nnr.se.

NNR (2003) *How High is the Quality of the Swedish Central Government's Regulatory Impact Analysis (RIAs) in the Business Sector? The NNR Regulation Indicator for 2003*, Stockholm: NNR, www.nnr.se.

Noll, R. (1999) *The Economics and Politics of Slowdown in Regulatory Reform*, Washington, DC: AEI–Brookings Joint Center for Regulatory Studies.

OECD (Organisation for Economic Co-operation and Development) (1995) *Recommendation on Improving the Quality of Government Regulation*, Paris: Council of the OECD.

OECD (1997a) *Report on Regulatory Reform – Thematic Studies*, Paris: OECD.

OECD (1997b) *Regulatory Impact Analysis: Best Practice in OECD Countries*, Paris: OECD.

OECD (1999) *Employment Outlook*, Paris: OECD.

OECD (2001) *Businesses' Views on Red Tape: Administrative and Regulatory Burdens on Small and Medium-Sized Enterprises*, Paris: OECD.

OECD (2002) *Regulatory Policies in OECD Countries: From Interventionism to Regulatory Governance*, Paris: OECD.

OECD (2004) *Regulatory Performance: Ex-Post Evaluation of Regulatory Tools and Institutions*, Working Party on Regulatory Management and Reform, 60V/PGC/Reg(2004)6, Paris: OECD.

OECD (2005) *OECD Guiding Principles for Regulatory Quality and Performance*, Paris: OECD.

Office of Small Business (2003) *Regulatory Performance Indicators – A Guide for Department and Agencies*, Canberra: Department of Industry Tourism Resources.

Office of Technology Assessment (1995) *Gauging Control Technology and Regulatory Impacts in Occupational Safety and Health – An Appraisal of OSHA's Analytic Approach*, OTA-ENV-635, Washington, DC: US Government Printing Office.

OMB (Office Management and Budget) (2000) *Report to Congress on the Costs and Benefits of Federal Regulations*, Washington, DC: White House, www.whitehouse.gov/omb/inforeg/2000fedreg-report.pdf.

OMB (2001) *Making Sense of Regulation: 2001 Report to Congress on the Cost and Benefits of Regulations and Unfunded Mandates on State, Local and Tribal Entities*, Washington, DC: White House, www.whitehouse.gov/omb/inforeg/costbenefitreport.pdf.

OMB (2002) *Program Assessment Rating Tool – Instructions for PART Worksheets, Fiscal Year 2004*, Washington, DC: OMB.

Opoku, C. and A. Jordan (2004) 'Impact assessment in the EU: a global sustainable development perspective', paper presented at the conference on the Human Dimension of Global Environmental Change, Berlin, 3–4 December.

Owens, S., T. Rayner and O. Bina (2004) 'New agendas for appraisal: reflections on theory, practice, and research', *Environment and Planning A*, 36:11, 1943–59.

Parker, C. (2002) *The Open Corporation: Effective Self-Regulation and Democracy*, Cambridge: Cambridge University Press.

Parker, R. W. (2003) 'Grading the government', *University of Chicago Law Review*, 70:3, 1345–422.

Pelkmans, J., S. Labory and G. Majone (2000) 'Better EU regulatory quality: assessing current initiatives and new proposals', in G. Galli and J. Pelkmans (eds), *Regulatory Reform and Competitiveness in Europe, Volume 1: Horizontal Issues*, Cheltenham: Edward Elgar.

Pollitt, C. (2001) 'Convergence: the useful myth?', *Public Administration*, 79:4, 933–47.

Pollitt, C., K. Bathgate, J. Caulfield, A. Smullen and C. Talbot (2000) 'Agency fever? Analysis of an international policy fashion', *Journal of Comparative Policy Analysis*, 3:3, 271–90.

Porter, M. (1990) *The Competitive Advantage of Nations*, New York: Free Press.

Posner, E. A. (2001) 'Controlling agencies with cost–benefits analysis: a positive political theory perspective', *Chicago Law Review*, 68:4, 1137.

Power, M. (1999) *The Audit Society: Rituals of Verification*, Oxford: Clarendon Press.

Pryor, F. L. (2002a) *The Future of U.S. Capitalism*, Cambridge: Cambridge University Press.

Pryor, F. L. (2002b) 'Quantitative notes on the extent of governmental regulations in various OECD nations', *International Journal of Industrial Organization*, 20:5, 693–714.

Radaelli, C. M. (1995) 'The role of knowledge in the policy process', *Journal of European Public Policy*, 2:2, 159–83.

Radaelli, C. M. (1999) 'Steering the Community regulatory system: the challenges ahead', *Public Administration*, 77:4, 855–71.

Radaelli, C. M. (2000) 'Policy transfer in the European Union: institutional isomorphism as a source of legitimacy', *Governance*, 13:1, 25–43.

Radaelli, C. M. (ed.) (2001) *L'analisi di impatto della regolazione in prospettiva comparata*, Soveria Mannelli: Rubbettino editore.

Radaelli, C. M. (2003) *The Open Method of Coordination: A New Governance Architecture for the European Union?*, Stockholm: Swedish Institute of European Policy Studies, www.sieps.se/publ/rapporter/2003/2003_1_en.html.

Radaelli, C. M. (ed.) (2004) 'The diffusion of regulatory impact analysis in OECD countries: best practice or lesson-drawing?', *European Journal of Political Research*, 43:5, 723–47.

Radaelli, C. M. (2005) 'Diffusion without convergence: how political context shapes the adoption of regulatory impact assessment', *Journal of European Public Policy*, 12:5, 924–43.

Radaelli, C. M. and B. Dente (1996) 'Evaluation strategies and analysis of the policy process', *Evaluation*, 2:1, 51–66.

Regulatory Consulting Group and Delphi Group (2000) *Assessing the Contribution of Regulatory Impact Analysis on Decision Making and the Development of Regulation*, Ottawa: Regulatory Consulting Group and Delphi Group.

Richardson, J. J. (1996) 'Actor-based models of national and EU policy-making', in H. Kassim and A. Menon (eds), *The European Union and National Industrial Policy*, Routledge: London, pp. 26–51.

Rose, R. (2002) 'When all other conditions are not equal: the context for drawing lessons', in C. Jones Finer (ed.), *Social Policy Reform in Socialist Market China: Lessons for and from Abroad*, Aldershot: Ashgate.

Sabatier, P. A. (ed.) (1999) *Theories of the Policy Process*, Boulder, CO: Westview Press.

Sabel, C. F. (1994) 'Learning by monitoring: the institutions of economic development', in N. Smelser and R. Swedberg (eds), *Handbook of Economic Sociology*, Princeton, NJ: Princeton University Press and Russell Sage Foundation, pp. 137–65.

Sandhu-Rojon, R. (2003) 'Selecting indicators for impact evaluation', paper presented at the workshop organised by France and the DAC Working Party on Aid Evaluation, Partners in Development Evaluation – Learning and Accountability, Paris, 25–26 March.

Scharpf, F. W. (1997) *Balancing Positive and Negative Integration: The Regulatory Options for Europe*, MPIfG Working Paper No. 97/8, Cologne: Max Planck Institute for the Study of Societies, www.mpi-fg-koeln.mpg.de/pu/workpap/wp97-8/wp97-8.html.

Scharpf, F. W. (1999) *Governing Europe: Effective and Democratic?*, Oxford: Oxford University Press.

Schmidt, V. A. (2002) *The Futures of European Capitalism*, Oxford: Oxford University Press.

Scott, C. (2003) 'Speaking softly without big sticks: meta-regulation and public sector audit', *Law and Policy*, 25:3, 203–19.

Seidman, H. and R. Gilmour (1986) *Politics, Position, and Power. From the Positive to the Regulatory State*, 4th edition, Oxford: Oxford University Press.

Shadish, W. R., T. D. Cook and L. D. Leviton (1991) *Foundations of Program Evaluation: Theories of Practice*, Newbury Park, CA: Sage.

Sparrow, M. K. (2000) *The Regulatory Craft*, Washington, DC: Brookings Institution.

SQW (2005) *Evaluating the Impact of Regulation: Developing a Methodology*, report for the Department of Trade and Industry, London: SQW, www.dti.gov.uk/files/file22009.pdf?pubpdfdload=05%2F1371.

Steinmo, S., K. Thelen and F. Longstreth (eds) (1992) *Structuring Politics: Historical Institutionalism in Comparative Analysis*, Cambridge: Cambridge University Press.

Tarantola, S., M. Saisana and A. Saltelli (2002) *Internal Market Index 2002: Technical Details of the Methodology*, Joint Research Centre of the European

Commission, Institute for the Protection and Security of the Citizen Technological and Economic Risk Management Unit, http://ec.europa. eu/internal_market/score/docs/score11/im-index-2002_en.pdf.

Tavistock Institute (2003) *Evaluation of Socio-Economic Development – The Guide*, London: Tavistock Institute, www.evalsed.info/frame_guide_intro.asp.

Thompson, F. and M. Weidenbaum (eds) (1998) 'Symposium on regulatory budgeting', *Policy Sciences*, 31:4, 237–384.

Treasury Board of Canada (1996) *Federal Regulatory Process Management Standards – A Self-Assessment Guide for Departmental Managers – Compliance Guide*, Ottawa: Treasury Board of Canada Secretariat, www.pco-bcp. gc.ca/raoics-srdc/docs/publications/rpms_e.pdf.

Treasury Board of Canada (1997a) *Regulatory Reform Through Regulatory Impact Analysis: The Canadian Experience*, No. 14 in Managing Better Series, Ottawa: Treasury Board of Canada Secretariat, www.tbs-sct.gc.ca.

Treasury Board of Canada (1997b) *Performance Framework for the Assessment of Regulatory Reform*, No. 16 in Managing Better Series, Ottawa: Treasury Board of Canada Secretariat, www.tbs-sct.gc.ca.

Treasury Board of Canada (2003) *Preparation Guide Departmental Performance Reports 2002–2003*, Ottawa: Treasury Board of Canada Secretariat, www.tbs-sct.gc.ca/rma/dpr/03-04/guidance/templates_e.asp.

Unger, B. and F. van Waarden (eds) (1995) *Convergence or Diversity? Internationalization and Economic Policy Response*, Aldershot: Avebury Press – Ashgate.

Union of Industrial and Employers' Confederations of Europe (UNICE) (1995) *Releasing Europe's Potential Through Targeted Regulatory Reform. The UNICE Regulatory Report*, Brussels: UNICE.

Usher, J. A. (1997) 'Implementing the rules', in D. G. Hayes (ed.), *The Evolution of the Single European Market*, Cheltenham: Edward Elgar, pp. 49–65.

Vandenbroucke, F. (2002) *The EU and Social Protection: What Should the European Convention Propose?*, MPIfG Working Paper No. 02/6, Cologne: Max Planck Institute for the Study of Societies, www.mpi-fg-koeln.mpg. de/pu/workpap/wp02-6/wp02-6.html.

Vibert, F. (2004) *The EU's New System of Regulatory Impact Assessment – A Scorecard*, London: European Policy Forum.

Vibert, F. (2005) *The Itch to Regulate: Confirmation Bias and the European Commission's New System of Impact Assessment*, London: European Policy Forum.

Viscusi, W. K., J. Vernon and J. E. Harrington (1995) *Economics of Regulation and Antitrust*, 2nd edition, Cambridge, MA: MIT Press.

Vogel, D. (1986) *National Styles of Regulation: Environmental Policy in Great Britain and the United States*, Ithaca, NY: Cornell University Press.

Vogel, D. (1995) *Trading Up. Consumer and Environmental Regulation in a Global Economy*, Cambridge, MA: Harvard University Press.

Weaver, R. K. and B. A. Rockman (eds) (1993) *Do Institutions Matter? Government Capabilities in the United States and Abroad*, Washington, DC: Brookings Institution.

Wegrich, K. (2005) 'Stereotypes of (de)regulation', *Risk and Regulation*, 9:4.

Weiss, C. H. (1979) 'The many meanings of research utilization', *Public Administration Review*, 35:5, 426–31.

Weiss, C. H. (1999) 'The interface between evaluation and public policy', *Evaluation*, 5:4, 468–86.

Whiteley, P. (2005) 'Commands don't work. Blair needs legitimacy', *The Independent*, 23 May, p. 4.

Wilkinson, D., M. Fergusson, C. Bowyer, J. Brown, A. Ladefoged, C. Monkhouse and A. Zdanowicz (2004) *Sustainable Development in the European Commission's Integrated Impact Assessment for 2003. Final Report*, London: Institute for European Environmental Policy, www.ieep.org.uk/publications/pdfs/2004/sustainabledevelopmentineucommission.pdf.

World Bank (2004a) *Doing Business in 2004 – Understanding Regulation*, Washington, DC: World Bank and Oxford University Press.

World Bank (2004b) *Doing Business in 2005 – Removing Obstacles to Growth*, Washington, DC: World Bank and Oxford University Press.

World Bank (2005) *Doing Business in 2006 – Creating Jobs*, Washington, DC: World Bank and Oxford University Press.

Zahariadis, N. (1999) 'Ambiguity, time, and multiple streams', in P. A. Sabatier (ed.), *Theories of the Policy Process*, Boulder, CO: Westview Press.

Index

EU authorised representative for GPSR:
Easy Access System Europe, Mustamäe tee 50,
10621 Tallinn, Estonia
gpsr.requests@easproject.com

www.ingramcontent.com/pod-product-compliance
Lightning Source LLC
Chambersburg PA
CBHW061721270326
41928CB00011B/2063